The Struggle of Democracy against Terrorism

THE Struggle OF Democracy

EMANUEL GROSS

AGAINST Terrorism

Lessons from the United States, the United Kingdom, and Israel

UNIVERSITY OF VIRGINIA PRESS   CHARLOTTESVILLE AND LONDON

University of Virginia Press
© 2006 by the Rector and Visitors of the University of Virginia
All rights reserved
Printed in the United States of America on acid-free paper

First published 2006

9 8 7 6 5 4 3 2 1

LIBRARY OF CONGRESS CATALOGING-IN-PUBLICATION DATA

Gross, Emanuel, 1948–
   The struggle of democracy against terrorism : lessons from the United States,
the United Kingdom, and Israel / Emanuel Gross.
      p.   cm.
   Includes bibliographical references and index.
   ISBN 0-8139-2531-2 (cloth : alk. paper)
      1. Terrorism—Israel—Prevention. 2. Terrorism—United States—Prevention.
3. Terrorism—Great Britain—Prevention. I. Title.
K5256.G76   2006
345′.02—dc22

                                                      2005028298

To my dear wife, Dina,
whose encouragement and support for
many years enabled me to write this book.

This is the destiny of a democracy—it does not see
all means as acceptable, and the ways of its enemies
are not always open before it. A democracy must
sometimes fight with one hand tied behind its back.
Even so, a democracy has the upper hand. The rule
of law and the liberty of an individual constitute
important components in its understanding of security.
At the end of the day, they strengthen its spirit and
this strength allows it to overcome its difficulties.

—Aharon Barak, Chief Justice,
  Israeli Supreme Court

Contents

Foreword

ON SEPTEMBER 11, 2001, the United States was wounded by acts of terror. Since then its outlook on terrorism and combating terrorism has altered dramatically. Many countries have subsequently been affected. Israel did not need the events of September 11, 2001, to formulate its stance on terrorism. We had terrorism on the September 10, 2001, and for many days before that, and we had terrorism on September 13 and for many days since then. Unfortunately, terrorism has been part of our daily lives. This is what makes this book so important. It can offer guidance to a state, its authorities, and its citizens in the fight against terrorism. This guidance is based on three fundamental concepts: First, the struggle against terror cannot be conducted "outside" the law. The struggle against terror must be waged "within" the law using the tools that the law makes available to a democratic state. This is what distinguishes the state from terrorists. The state operates within the boundaries of the law. Terrorists contravene the law. The struggle against terrorism is, therefore, the struggle of the law against those who rise up against it. The statement attributed to Cicero to the effect that "in times of war the laws fall silent" reflects neither reality nor what is desirable. Second, the normative framework was established on the basis that a democracy's fight against terrorism must be grounded on a delicate balance between the need to preserve the safety of the state and its citizens and the need to safeguard human dignity and liberty. This balance is based on the need to find a synthesis between conflicting values and principles. This balance must be based, in the nature of things, on appropriate restrictions both on the fighting force of the democratic state and on the freedom of the individual. An appropriate balance is not maintained when state security is fully protected as if human rights do not exist. In a democracy's fight against terrorism, not every measure is permissible. Often a democracy will fight with one hand tied behind its back. An appropriate balance is not maintained when human rights are fully protected as if terrorism does not exist. Human rights are not a platform for national destruction. Third, the courts are available to decide conflicts relating to a state's struggle against terrorism. When it is contended that human rights have been infringed, there is no room to close the doors of the court. When a law exists by virtue of which war is waged against terror, a court exists that will determine what is permissible and what prohibited.

Against the background of these three fundamental principles, Emanuel Gross—an expert of international standing in his field—analyzes the various laws that apply to a democracy's fight against terrorism. His analysis is sharp. His knowledge wide-ranging. His approach embraces law and morals, domestic law and comparative law. I do not agree with all his conclusions. He does not agree with all the judgments delivered by me and my colleagues on the court. This is both fair and appropriate. This is the important contribution of academe, which from a certain distance observes events and expresses its views of them. Some it accepts and some it rejects. But its approach too will be subject to the critical analysis of the judiciary, part to be accepted and part to be rejected. This is the fruitful dialogue between the science of law and adjudication. I am convinced that this book will have an impact on formulating the policy of the political authorities. It will certainly influence the formulation of the outlook of the judiciary. It will assist every jurist dealing with this field, whether on the academic plane or on the practical level. It is to be hoped that the book will be translated into other languages, both to assist in shaping the laws of other democracies and to make the latter more aware of the difficulties faced by the Israeli democracy in its struggle against terror and its many successes in this field. The comments made by Justice William J. Brennan—one of the great judges of the U.S. Supreme Court—during a speech given in Israel in 1987 are relevant in this context:

> Israel, and not the United States, is the hope for the construction of judicial rulings which will safeguard civil liberties against the demands of national security. . . . The nations of the world, faced with sudden threats to their own security, will look to Israel's experience in han-

dling its continuing security crisis, and may find in this experience the expertise to reject security claims which Israel has rejected as unfounded and the courage to uphold civil liberties which Israel upholds without impairing its security. . . . I would not wonder if, in the future, the general protection given to civil liberties in times of world danger will be influenced by the experiences of Israel in its struggle to concurrently preserve the freedom of its citizens and national security.[1]

I am convinced that this book by Emanuel Gross will make an important contribution not only to shaping the important balance of the legal framework of Israel's struggle against the terrorism harming it but also to transmitting Israel's message throughout the world, "for out of Zion shall go forth the law, and the word of the Lord from Jerusalem" (Isaiah 2:3).

Aharon Barak
Chief Justice, Israeli Supreme Court

Acknowledgments

I wish to take this opportunity to thank my research assistant, Adv. Tchia Shachar, whose diligence and helpful advice greatly contributed to the publication of this book. I would also like to record my special gratitude to Richard K. Holway, the history and social sciences editor at the University of Virginia Press, for the many hours he has devoted to this project and for his invaluable advice.

Introduction

THE WAR AGAINST terrorism and its perpetrators bears no resemblance to any other struggle within the scope of the international laws of war. The laws of war, formulated over many years, were designed primarily to provide solutions to problems arising out of conflicts between sovereign states, that is, to regulate the legal ways of declaring and terminating wars, the rules of conduct binding the respective armies during warfare, the relations between disputing states and other states not participating in the war, the ramifications of the war on the countries involved, and guarantees for the safety of the civilian population of the opposing parties and neutral countries.

Armed struggle between states and individuals or nonstate parties is a relatively new phenomenon for which international law is not yet prepared. This struggle differs fundamentally from traditional armed conflicts because of the terrorists' disregard for the laws of war and conduct that is diametrically opposed to any of its principles. For the terrorists, the battleground is the civilian hinterland and not the military front. Civilians and not the army are the immediate target of the hostile activities. For the terrorists, the individual rights and freedoms of the citizens against whom they fight, and to a certain extent even the rights and freedoms of their own people "for" whom they fight, are not sacrosanct values worthy of protection but rather the principal weapon in the war.

It is clear, therefore, that finding an effective course of action in dealing with terrorism which is compatible with the values of a liberal democratic state entails finding solutions to new and unprecedented dilemmas: What are the rules of law that apply to such conflicts—rules that we know in advance only one side (the state) will regard itself as bound to follow? What is a state permitted to do or prohibited from doing within the context of its fight against terrorism? How, if at all, does the morality of classical warfare differ from the morality of war against terrorism?

The task of writing this book has been especially challenging for me. For twenty-five years I served in the Israeli Defense Forces as a military attorney, military judge, and ultimately president of the Military Tribunal of Southern Command. As a military judge I frequently tried Palestinians accused of involvement in murderous terrorist activities against Israeli civilians. Now, for over a decade, I have been a professor of law, and it is for the most part owing to my military background that I have devoted substantial research to the issue of how democratic societies ought to deal with the threat of modern terrorism.

The State of Israel, unlike other democratic nations, has been forced to contend with incessant terrorist attacks since its establishment in 1948. Israel is the only democratic nation that has grown, developed, and shaped its constitutional regime in the shadow of the constant existential threat of terrorism. For this reason it might be argued that Israel's experience in providing legal answers to terrorist threats is more rich and diverse than that of other democratic countries, which only now, since September 11, 2001, have begun to fully grasp the severity of the risks terrorism poses.

Therefore, even though this book seeks to shape appropriate legal solutions on the basis of a broad comparative perspective of international law, especially of two democratic states whose legal systems are based on similar legal structures—the United States and the United Kingdom—it focuses on the Israeli legal system, with the intention of utilizing its broad and comprehensive experience to formulate appropriate standards for conducting this unusual war.

However, in this search for appropriate legal norms in the war on terrorism, as in every other legal field, there are no absolute solutions or clear-cut boundaries between what is permitted and what prohibited, because in the law, as we have come to know, context is everything.[1] The present work, relying as it does on the Israeli experience as a starting point, reflects not only the traditional theoretical-critical perspective of the academic but also my personal experience and philosophy which I have gained during my service in the military judiciary. Whether the combination of these two perspectives should weigh for or against the validity of my views is of course something for you, as readers, to judge.

"Terrorism" is a term whose defining characteristics are not immediately apparent. It is a subject of dispute between states and between legal scholars. The international community has not yet managed to reach a consensus on a unified and comprehensive legal definition of the activities that fall within its ambit. So long as no broad agreement has been reached regarding the substance of the concept, nations will find it difficult to prosecute those who perpetrate it, and even when such persons are tried and found guilty there will always be jurists who will question the justice of their conviction. At the same time, the tremendous growth in the number of acts of terrorism around the world at the beginning of the twenty-first century has forced the states of the free world to take more serious action to fight this dangerous phenomenon and to seek legal answers to the range of dilemmas produced by this war, including the preliminary formulation of a wide-ranging agreement concerning the characteristics of "terrorism."

Issues surrounding the question of how to deal with states sponsoring terrorism have also split the countries of the free world, for political, economic, and other reasons. It seems likely that, following the collapse of the communist regime in the former Soviet Union and the broadening pact in Europe under the flag of the European Union, we shall witness the creation of a new world order led by the United States as the sole superpower. Since the brutal and shocking terrorist attack against its citizens on September 11, 2001, the United States has taken upon itself the leadership of an uncompromising world campaign against terrorism and its perpetrators. This campaign may conceivably spur steps to adapt the international laws of war to deal more efficiently with this dangerous phenomenon, as well as to construct new legal tools for this purpose.

At the same time, we must take care not to destroy, in the name of a just war against terrorism, the splendid structure of human rights which we have labored so hard to build over hundreds of years. We must not yield to the temptation to regard the uncompromising radical ideological beliefs of our terrorist adversaries as justification for abandoning our liberal ideals in the belief that only by so doing will we succeed in vanquishing that terrorism. Such a perception is unwarranted objectively. Further, and perhaps principally, the destruction of our ideals would lead to the collapse of humanitarianism and the performance of abhorrent acts that would have deleterious repercussions for our morals for many years after the conclusion of hostilities. It would also prevent us from turning back into the same democratic society we were in the past, thereby granting terrorism its ultimate victory. An example of this danger can be found in the swift reaction of the United Kingdom, and of several other European countries, who soon after the murderous terrorist attacks in London subways and on a bus in July 2005 decided to more vigorously promote new antiterrorism legislation that would provide law enforcement agencies with wider counterterrorism measures.[2] The United Kingdom government, for example, rushed to promote the enactment of a new counterterrorism bill that would include the power to deport people who encourage terrorism as well as the power to revoke citizenship from British nationals engaged in extremism. The proposed bill would also create the new offenses of receiving training in terrorist techniques in the United Kingdom or abroad, committing acts preparatory to terrorism, and indirectly inciting others to commit terrorist acts.[3] However, the most unequivocal example to the very real nature of this danger is the U.S. response to the events of September 11, 2001. The Patriot Act, passed shortly after these events, sharply altered the prevailing delicate balance between fundamental human rights and public security in favor of the latter. It is true that in times of emergency, preference should be given to security needs, even, perhaps primarily, when they infringe human rights. In other words, in the tension between the need for order and security on the one hand and human rights on the other, the former should take precedence. However, the infringement of human rights in the name of security should be carried out in a proportionate manner and as a last resort for a temporary period of time. The shock of the September 11 attack and the great panic that seized the American public over the possibility of further strikes caused the majority of citizens to accept unquestioningly, at least for several months, the need for many of the new statutory provisions, in particular those concerned solely with relaxing effective judicial review and incorporating powers to fight terrorism into the general criminal law system.

The issue of the limitations on human rights in the name of the war against terrorism occupies many philosophers and jurists. Noting that the American government has in the past engaged in disproportionate violations of human rights in the name of national security, an American jurist commented shortly after the attack of the September 11, 2001: "The detention of Japanese-Americans in World War 2, and the Vietnam era's unauthorized wiretaps and FBI 'black bag jobs' should have taught all of us by now: You don't take away our constitutional liberties in order to defend us from foreign and domestic enemies who seek to do the same thing."[4]

Terrorism is first and foremost a social phenomenon. Accordingly, understanding the legal nature of the democratic state's battle against it and delineating the proper boundaries within which it is to operate require the integration of a number of conceptual areas. For example, we cannot proffer a complete solution to the problem of the measures that should be available to a state in its struggle against terror unless we first understand the nature of the "terror" to which we refer. Identifying the enemy is impossible without understanding the ideology guiding him. For instance, we cannot seek to understand why young men who were brought up in the United Kingdom committed the horrific suicide attacks in London unless we first examine what attracted them to the path of radical Islam.[5] Thus, in order to answer the basic question of which tools a state is entitled to use in its war to eradicate terrorism, we must initially identify the nature of terrorism, its characteristics, its ideology, and the entities employing it or supporting it. In order to find these essential elements, it is necessary to voyage through a variety of fields, such as Middle Eastern studies, Islamic studies, Middle Eastern history, theology, theories of national security, and more. Law is merely one discipline to be explored against the backdrop of other sciences. And indeed, this book, although it focuses primarily on providing a comprehensive legal framework as opposed to various possible social frameworks, contemplates nonlegal aspects alongside legal theories. But if the reader seeks a fuller interdisciplinary picture, he must rely on complementary literature from other fields.

Although the current discussion focuses on the Israeli experience, it is intended to be applicable, subject to certain adaptations, to every liberal democratic country facing similar situations. Nonetheless, the perpetrators and characteristics of the terrorism facing Israel are not necessarily identical to those which have struck at the United Kingdom or have threatened Europe and the United States. "Local" contexts certainly have an impact on unique legal answers. At the same time, even though terrorist acts and the terrorists themselves may take on a wide range of forms and identities, in my opinion it is possible to characterize the terrorism of the twenty-first century from a global perspective as religious terrorism possessing nationalist-socialist features. The terrorist organizations who challenge the values underlying the theory of enlightened democracy and at the same time exploit the democratic state's commitment to these values even while fighting terrorism have established their bases in destitute, embittered corners of the world and exploited the vulnerabilities and suffering of the local people in order to instill fundamentalist and extremist nationalist ideas. I am aware that this inclusive view of the phenomenon of terrorism as a "war of religions"—or perhaps as a "clash of civilizations," to borrow the well-known title of Samuel Huntington's work[6]—may cause an injustice to individuals on the microlevel; however, in my opinion it also most accurately reflects the nature of the clash between the free world and Islamic terrorism. A correct universal understanding of the character of terrorism and its perpetrators may make a significant contribution to the formulation of appropriate methods of eradicating it, not merely for the individual states facing terrorism but for the international community as a whole.

In this book I have chosen to deal with a number of issues which I consider central to the fight against Islamic terrorism and which, though they ensue principally from the Israeli situation, have great relevance for other democratic states. A number of premises guided me in researching these issues. One premise is that the fact that a democratic state is threatened by terrorists who do not see themselves as bound by the rules of morality and international laws of war does not release the state from its own commitments to norms of international law and certainly does not permit the state to adopt equivalent improper methods. Another premise, related to the first, is that a democratic state does not have to commit "suicide" in order to prove that it is indeed democratic. "Defensive democracy," and sometimes "militant democracy," are the terms that should be adopted when we seek to examine the responses of a democratic state to terrorism. A third premise is that the struggle against terrorism must be conducted within the framework of the state's domestic laws and no governmental authority is entitled to act outside the law. Axioms regarding the rule of law in times of peace do not lose their potency in times of emergency, and they determine the manner in which the fight against terrorism will be waged. A fourth premise is that the fight against terrorism requires, within the balance between individual rights and the preservation of public and state security, that a shift in emphasis be made from human rights toward security needs. Which human rights may be infringed and the scope of the permitted infringement are the types of questions to which this work seeks to offer answers. A fifth premise is that a state may be threatened by terrorism not only from abroad but also at home. Terrorists may spring from among the citizens of the state itself. In such a case the legal rules applicable to the situation must be different.

This book, the foundations of which were laid in articles published over recent years in a number of American law journals, comprises nine chapters. Out of a desire to widen the public legal debate on these issues—a process that can only be carried out if a solid conceptual and theoretical basis exists in relation to principles of democracy, law, and morality—I have chosen to revise and update these articles in a shortened format aimed at opening a window through which the reader can contemplate the nature of the anti-Western "terrorist entity" and the array of legal norms and morals which ought to guide the West in contending with that entity.[7]

The opening chapter is devoted to an examination of the question, what is "terrorism"? I examine the characteristics that distinguish the terrorist act from other criminal acts, the defects of the various legal definitions that have been proposed at both the international and the state level, and the disputes that prevent the formulation of a universal definition and the problems caused by this failure.

Chapter 2 considers the inevitable question arising when we deal with the democratic state's fight against terrorism, namely, are there positive international laws of war which regulate this fight? The laws of war were created, primarily, in consequence of wars between states. Do the restrictions imposed on combatant states continue to apply when the dispute is taking place between a state and a terrorist organization or a state sponsoring terrorism, both of which, by definition, do not respect the laws of war?

Chapter 3 was written in response to the judgment of the Israeli Supreme Court in regard to the legitimate interrogational techniques available to the General Security Service when investigating terrorist activists suspected of possessing information concerning future hostile acts against the citizens of the state. For the first time in Israel's history, and even in the history of the West, a court has given a judgment of principle in relation to this hugely important issue, which for years has been outside the purview of public debate. Through a comparative examination of the laws of the United States and the United Kingdom, I seek to analyze the degree of justification of the normative arrangement which was established by the judgment.

Chapter 4 examines the administrative powers of military commanders to fight terrorism. The State of Israel controls the areas of Judea, Samaria, and the Gaza Strip through military force. While occasionally reaching Israel from abroad, terrorist activity is generated primarily in these territories. What powers are granted by Israeli law and international law to military commanders in the fight against terrorism? What statutory oversight mechanisms exist in relation to the exercise of these powers? What restrictions have been imposed by the Israeli Supreme Court regarding the manner of exercising these powers, and do these restrictions—bearing in mind the statutory oversight provisions—grant military commanders sufficiently broad powers which are at the same time adequately restricted?

Chapter 5 is devoted to an examination of the appropriate use of one of the most drastic measures available to the state in its fight against terrorism—placing a person in administrative detention. I give special emphasis to the issue of using this power as a negotiating device.

Chapter 6 concerns the search for the proper moral and legal balance between the basic right of an individual to his or her private life and the requirements of national security, which on occasion requires an invasion into the privacy of all citizens in order to locate among them the few who exploit this right for the purpose of planning and carrying out hostile activities. As mentioned, terrorist organizations fight in order to destroy the democratic paradigm; however, at the same time they exploit the democratic state's commitment to liberal values in order to carry out their plans. Acts of terror, which are but the external culmination of a range of preparatory preliminary activities, might be foiled more easily were the state ready to invade the privacy of its residents and succeed in identifying these activities in advance. Nonetheless, by their nature, such steps would entail a violation of the privacy of multitudes of innocent people. What, then, is the proper balance between these clashing values?

Chapter 7 is devoted to a discussion of a critical moral and legal question: what are the restrictions on the use of force against terrorists who make use of civilians—both their own people and citizens of the state under attack—as human shields? When should the state be obliged to take into consideration the dangers facing civilians, and when would it be wrong to submit to such threats even if failure to do so might pose a risk to the safety of these civilians?

Chapter 8 deals with foiling terrorist acts as a preventive measure of self-defense. It considers the question whether a democratic state is entitled, in certain circumstances, to act to foil future terrorist activities by killing the leaders of terrorist organizations without first engaging in an appropriate judicial review culminating in the conviction of these terrorists and a verdict of death.

The concluding chapter surveys the major findings of the previous chapters and presents future dangers that every democratic country fighting terrorism should beware of. The discussion reveals the existence of a clear causal connection between a threat of force against a democratic regime and the infringement of human rights. The overall conclusion is that the reaction to the phenomenon of terrorism by states adhering to the same moral and legal principles is directly proportionate to the level of the threat they experience. Thus, the events of September 11, 2001, changed the traditional legal constitutional balance between security needs and human rights in more than a few Western states and caused them to react in a dramatic legal way leading to serious violations of the human rights of terrorist suspects in particular and the public in general. The judicial branch has a vital role in the preservation of human rights in times of crisis. It is only in cases where it fails to conduct an appropriate judicial review that the executive can excessively infringe the fundamental rights of the individual in the name of security interests.

It is in times of emergency that the strength of a democracy is most accurately tested—when it is required to make momentous decisions about how best to defend itself and its citizens while at the same time preserving underlying values of justice and morality. The legal answer given by a democratic state to the threat of terror is also the true test of its fortitude and the justice of its chosen path. If the state allows the cannons' roar and the sight of destruction to provide an excuse for refraining from clear-sighted self-examination of its commitment to preserve its democratic nature and the values for which it is fighting, then at the end of the war it may find that not only were its citizens killed and its symbols shattered by terrorist attacks but that the state itself was also destroyed.

The former justice of the U.S. Supreme Court William J. Brennan referred to this dilemma, and acknowledged earlier mistakes made by the United States, in a lecture delivered at the Hebrew University, Mount Scopus, in 1987:

> The ability of the United States to absorb and implement these lessons
> effectively, however, has been limited by the episodic nature of our
> security crises. The good fortune of its relatively secure position leaves
> it unhardened by the experience necessary to apply the historical
> lesson of skepticism when threats and factual issues crop up that are
> unfamiliar to a peacetime judiciary and nation. Santayana was certainly
> right when he noted, "Those who cannot remember the past are con-
> demned to repeat it." But merely remembering the past has not proved
> to be enough. Without prolonged exposure to the claimed threat, it is
> all to easy for a nation and judiciary that has grown unaccustomed to

crisis to get swept away by irrational passion, and to accept gullibly assertions that, in times of repose, would be subjected to the critical examination they deserve.[8]

It is clear from my description of the subject matter of the individual chapters that this work does not purport to collate all the issues relating to the legal treatment of terrorism. In order to complete the discussion, it is necessary to engage in further research, which will be presented in a future book. There I plan to deal with such issues as the balance between the right to vote and to be elected to government office in a democratic state and the struggle against terrorism, and whether UN institutions are capable of providing a suitable and just response to problems of world terrorism. But even without this additional material, the present book discusses numerous important issues which in my opinion must be brought into the open at this juncture in order to enable readers to deepen their understanding of this urgent problem.

This book deals with a very dynamic and timely subject. As explained above, the struggle of the Western democratic states against the phenomenon of terrorism is now only in a formative process. Therefore this book can reflect only the current normative framework, while attempting to predict its future implications.

Although for easy of writing I've used masculine pronouns in this book, all statements in it should be taken to apply equally to men and women.

ONE

What Is Terrorism?

DEFINITIONS AND CHARACTERISTICS

TERRORISM IS a phenomenon that transcends national boundaries. It is deeply rooted in the history of mankind. It is no wonder, then, that over the decades numerous sociological, theological, philosophical, psychological, and legal attempts have been made to define objectively and descriptively, in a universal, coherent, and comprehensive way, both its perpetrators and its characteristics. These attempts have shown that even though every terrorist act, by its nature, falls within the criminal sphere, it is important to distinguish between terrorism that is motivated by criminal goals and terrorism that is motivated by political ideals.[1] The former concerns individuals or criminal organizations that make systematic and extensive use of unlawful violent tactics in order to attain their narrow interests of personal gain, whereas the latter form of terrorism—on which this work focuses—concerns individuals or groups that make systematic use of unlawful violence as a strategic tool for advancing political goals of a nationalist, religious, social, or economic nature.

Public opinion condemning political terrorism is not only not milder than that directed at criminal terrorism but in fact harsher, although deep divisions remain concerning the nature of the unlawful acts encompassed by this type of activity. These divisions, expressed by the adage "one man's terrorist is another man's freedom fighter," ensue from the relativist, subjective perception of political terrorism. Put differently, all can agree that committing terrorist acts is absolutely prohibited because there are no circumstances that can justify them; however, not all would agree on a preliminary issue, namely, which circumstances, if any, would denude a particular act of its terrorist attributes.

The analytical vagueness of the concept of political terrorism has led scholars to suggest various typologies that might assist in formulating and understanding its multiple facets. Thus, for example, Thomas Thornton divides political terrorism into two types: *agitational terror*, which refers to the use or threat of systematic violence by persons seeking to replace or change the existing political order in whole or in part; and *enforcement terror*, which refers to the use or threat of systematic violence by an existing political establishment against its domestic and foreign opponents with the purpose of perpetuating the regime.[2] A similar typology is suggested by Paul Wilkinson, who distinguishes three categories of political terrorism: *revolutionary terrorism*, systematic use of violence aimed at bringing about the complete revolutionary change of the entire political system; *subrevolutionary terrorism*, systematic use of violence aimed at bringing about specific changes in an existing political structure as opposed to its complete dissolution in favor of a different system; and *repressive terrorism*, systematic use of violence by governmental bodies aimed at repressing individuals, groups, or undesirable forms of behavior.[3]

These and similar typologies have supplied an effective theoretical basis for understanding the complexity of political terrorism, yet they have not assisted in formulating an agreed universal definition of its unique characteristics. At first glance, it may be argued that the definitional issue is one of only theoretical importance,[4] since all would agree that an organization advancing its goals by kidnapping innocent civilians for use as bargaining counters or by sending its followers to blow themselves up in crowded public places is an organization that commits a criminal act, and therefore its members are answerable to the penal law. According to this approach, an act deliberately targeting the freedom, person, or property of a person is essentially a criminal act, and it is not really important whether it is formally classified as an "ordinary" criminal act or as a specifically "terrorist" criminal act. Moreover, even if we assert that "ordinary" penal law is general law and therefore incapable of providing an appropriate response to the uniquely grave nature of a terrorist act—with the ensuing need to classify particular acts as "terrorist"—why should we assert that a criminal act motivated by ideological reasons is more serious and blameworthy than the identical act motivated by greed or revenge?[5]

These arguments, which should in no way be disparaged, do not represent the dominant view or, in my opinion, an appropriate one. The terrorist act does not draw its unique gravity from the cruel and brutal way in which it is carried out or from the severe physical and mental injuries and property damage it causes its victims, since it is perfectly conceivable that ordinary criminal acts will be carried out in an equally shocking and abhorrent way. The terrorist act is distinct from other criminal acts by virtue of the unique amoral quality of its motives. The terrorist shows two faces: one to his family, friends, and neighbors, with whom he behaves like a normal citizen, and another to the entity that he perceives to be his enemy—be it the liberal democratic state whose values threaten his fundamentalist beliefs, or the enemy that controls his forefathers' land and thereby frustrates his nationalist dream, or any other enemy whose existence opposes his aspirations. In acting against this entity, the terrorist severs himself from humanity, with its moral, legal, and social customs, and devotes himself solely to his ideological beliefs. Moral values, humanitarian obligations, and basic human conventions, to the extent that they derogate from the effectiveness of his struggle, retreat before his supreme ultimate commitment. The terrorist "is a man insofar as concerns his normative life, his daily existence, and on the other hand, insofar as concerns . . . the West, he is a monster."[6] The terrorist will work to advance his cause using all the means he considers effective and will not precede this by balancing law and morality. His murderous attacks possess an apersonal aspect, in the sense that he is not interested in the identity of the concrete victim but only in the victim's affiliation with the entity against which he is fighting. His absolute perception, uncluttered by any doubts or qualifications, of the individual as a means to an end is what creates the psychological effect of fear, suspicion, and dread among the public, to a degree that bears no relation to the direct damage caused by the specific terrorist act. Every member of society is fully aware that he could have been the victim of the last attack and may become the victim of the next, that the terrorist has delivered his verdict, without trial, in accordance with the amoral normative system guiding him.[7]

It is these unique characteristics of the terrorist act, compared to ordinary criminal actions, which make it necessary to formulate a special offense of terrorism. We shall therefore consider some of the definitions suggested for this phenomenon at the international and domestic levels.

In 1994 the UN General Assembly passed a resolution concerning measures for eliminating international terrorism which held that "[c]riminal acts intended or calculated to provoke a state of terror in the general public, a group of persons or particular persons for political purposes are in any circumstance unjustifiable, whatever the considerations of a political, philosophical, ideological, racial, ethnic, religious or any other nature that may be invoked to justify them."[8] A decade later, in October 2004, following a series of grave acts of terror, including the murder of more than three hundred hostages, most of them young children, at a school in Beslan, Russia, the ruthlessly suicide attacks and beheadings in Iraq, and the simultaneous explosions at two resorts in Sinai, the UN Security Council unanimously adopted a resolution condemning terrorism, in all its forms and manifestations, as one of the most serious threats to peace, security, and global stability and prosperity. The resolution states that

> criminal acts, including against civilians, committed with the intent to cause death or serious bodily injury, or taking of hostages, with the purpose to provoke a state of terror in the general public or in a group of persons or particular persons, intimidate a population or compel a government or an international organization to do or to abstain from doing any act, which constitute offences within the scope of and as defined in the international conventions and protocols relating to terrorism, are under no circumstances justifiable by considerations of a political, philosophical, ideological, racial, ethnic, religious or other similar nature . . .[9]

In Britain, Section 14(1) of the Prevention of Terrorism (Temporary Provision) Act (1984), and Section 20 of the Prevention of Terrorism (Temporary Provision) Act (1989), defined terrorism as "the use of violence for political ends and includes any use of violence for the purpose of putting the public or any section of the public in fear." This definition was replaced by Section 1 of the Terrorism Act, 2000, which defines terrorism as:

(1) . . . the use or threat of action where—
(a) the action falls within subsection (2),
(b) the use or threat is designed to influence the government or to intimidate the public or a section of the public, and
(c) the use or threat is made for the purpose of advancing a political, religious or ideological cause.
(2) Action falls within this subsection if it—
(a) involves serious violence against a person,
(b) involves serious damage to property,
(c) endangers a person's life, other than that of the person committing the action,

(d) creates a serious risk to the health or safety of the public or a section of the public, or

(e) is designed seriously to interfere with or seriously to disrupt an electronic system.

(3) The use or threat of action falling within subsection (2) which involves the use of firearms or explosives is terrorism whether or not subsection (1)(b) is satisfied.[10]

In the United States, the Federal Bureau of Investigation defines terrorism as "the unlawful use of force or violence against persons or property to intimidate or coerce a government, the civilian population, or any segment thereof, in furtherance of political or social objectives." The binding legal definition of terrorism is that contained in Section 2331 of the Criminal Code, as amended by the Patriot Act, whereby

(1) the term "international terrorism" means activities that—

(A) involve violent acts or acts dangerous to human life that are a violation of the criminal laws of the United States or of any State, or that would be a criminal violation if committed within the jurisdiction of the United States or of any State;

(B) appear to be intended—

    (i) to intimidate or coerce a civilian population;

    (ii) to influence the policy of a government by intimidation or coercion; or

    (iii) to affect the conduct of a government by mass destruction, assassination, or kidnapping; and

(C) occur primarily outside the territorial jurisdiction of the United States, or transcend national boundaries in terms of the means by which they are accomplished, the persons they appear intended to intimidate or coerce, or the locale in which their perpetrators operate or seek asylum;

(2) . . .

(3) . . .

(4) . . .

(5) the term "domestic terrorism" means activities that—

(A) involve acts dangerous to human life that are a violation of the criminal laws of the United States or of any State;

(B) appear to be intended—

    (i) to intimidate or coerce a civilian population;

    (ii) to influence the policy of a government by intimidation or coercion; or

(iii) to affect the conduct of a government by mass destruction, assassination, or kidnapping; and
(C) occur primarily within the territorial jurisdiction of the United States.[11]

In Israel, the binding definition of terrorism is found in Section 1 of the Prevention of Terrorism Ordinance, which defines a "terrorist organization" as "a body of persons resorting in its activities to acts of violence calculated to cause death or injury to a person or to threats of such acts of violence."[12] But in 2005 the parliament enacted the Prohibition on Financing Terrorism Law, which defines a "terrorist act" as

> an act which comprises an offence, or a threat to commit an act as aforesaid, which has been committed or is planned to be committed in order to promote a political, ideological or religious cause, and where all the following apply:
> 1) it has been committed or planned to be committed with the purpose of provoking fear or panic among the public or with the purpose of coercing the government or other governmental authority, including the government of a foreign state, to perform an act or refrain from performing an act . . . ;
> 2) the act that has been committed or was planned to be committed or the threat was capable of:
> (a) harming a person's body or his freedom, or placing a person at risk of death or grievous injury;
> (b) creating a real danger to the health or safety of all or some of the public;
> (c) causing serious harm to property;
> (d) causing serious interference with essential infrastructure.[13]

A comparison of the above definitions shows that all are directed at protecting the lives, bodies, and property of individuals and public order. Some do so by classifying the terrorist act as a criminal act, some do not refer specifically to the criminal character of the act but merely to the commission (or threat of commission) of injurious acts of violence, and some refer to both its criminal and its violent character. All the definitions (apart from that in the Israeli Prevention of Terrorism Ordinance, which is exceptional in its broad and inclusive formulation) refer to the fact that the motivation for committing the act is ideological and that its nature is such as to provoke fear, suspicion, anxiety, panic, or dread among all or specific sections of the public.

Alongside these common factors, there are some singular elements:

First, some of the definitions confine themselves to acts directed against noncombatant members of the public or their property, whereas other definitions apply also to acts directed against government or military personnel or sites, so that there is no uniformity in relation to the various possible targets.

Second, none of the definitions, apart from that in the UN resolutions, clarifies whether legal or moral justifications for the ideological cause that the perpetrators seek to advance by their acts, in those cases where any justifications exist, are relevant to characterizing the acts as terrorist. While there are some who believe that the end—however just—cannot validate the use of illegal means, there are others who contend that a struggle for a just cause legally anchored in international law, such as the right of peoples to self-determination or the right of minority groups to recognition of their identity, validates the commission of acts which in other circumstances would be regarded as having a terrorist character.[14]

Third, most of the definitions are not compatible with modern times, when terrorists occasionally combine physical fighting with cyberterrorism—that is, use technological equipment to interfere with essential information systems, such as flight control systems, traffic signal systems, and computer systems used by the emergency services—although it is sometimes possible to hold the terrorist liable for the violent consequences of his acts by virtue of the presumption of intention, under which a person intends the natural consequences of his acts, or alternatively, by virtue of the principle of expectation, under which a person who foresees to a near degree of certainty the possibility of the occurrence of the harmful consequence that will naturally ensue from his act is deemed to have intended it.

Fourth, all the definitions—some more so than others—are formulated in broad, sweeping, and inclusive language, thereby creating the danger that they will encompass violent acts committed, on the one hand, by the security and police forces of the regime for the purpose of preserving public peace and security and, on the other, by legitimate protesters against the government or certain parts of it, even though such activities express constitutional values of freedom of expression; the right of association, assembly, and demonstration; the right to dignity and freedom; and the right to equality held by all persons in a democratic regime.

These differences represent the major difficulties that have prevented the formulation of an agreed international universal definition of a terrorist offense. A number of international conventions, such as the Convention for the Suppression of Terrorist Bombings (Dec. 15, 1997) and the Convention for the Suppression of the Financing of Terrorism (Dec. 9, 1999), were indeed signed with the intention of regulating the manner in which the international community would deal with specific aspects of terrorist activities. However, the provisions of these conventions have remained effective solely at the declarative level and will continue to lack any real operative effect until a consensus is reached concerning the nature of the acts of "terror" which they are intended to eradicate.

It follows that the international community is currently dealing with the phenomenon of international terrorism solely in terms of those traditional international offenses established in the past which express the international obligations imposed directly on every person. It is appropriate, therefore, to examine whether these offenses provide a sufficient answer to the international struggle against terrorism. One avenue for examining this issue is via an assessment of one of the new institutions of the international community—the International Criminal Court (ICC), which sits in The Hague. This court, which was established by the Rome Statute of the International Criminal Court with the support of 120 states, 7 states opposing (including the United States and Israel) and 21 states abstaining,[15] commenced operation in July 2002 with the declared purpose of providing a permanent judicial tribunal that would deal with crimes having international importance and thereby obviate the need to establish ad hoc special international tribunals, such as those convened in Tokyo and Nuremberg following the Second World War. The ICC is intended not only to deter serious infringements of fundamental human rights but also to act as a "sentinel," that is, as a supranational agency to enforce international legal norms in those cases where the states themselves are not interested in or incapable of implementing their own internal criminal enforcement mechanisms.

The ICC's jurisdiction embraces four types of offenses: crimes of genocide, crimes against humanity, war crimes, and crimes of aggression.[16] In accordance with the principle of constitutionality—which prevents a person from being prosecuted for an offense that is vague or uncertain in its application—Articles 6 to 8 of the ICC statute clearly elucidate the nature of the first three offenses; however, concerning the crime of aggression, which is not defined, the statute provides: "The Court shall exercise jurisdiction over the crime of aggression once a provision is adopted . . . defining the crime and setting out the conditions under which the Court shall exercise jurisdiction with respect to this crime."[17] The crime of aggression was left undefined in order to allow this category to embrace terrorist crimes. Nonetheless, the states drafting the statute proved incapable not only of formulating an agreed definition of "terrorism" but also of agreeing on the very need to include acts of international terrorism under ICC jurisdiction. The United States, for example, opposed inclusion of terrorism within the scope of the ICC, claiming that the offense of terrorism was not yet well defined, that some acts of terrorism were not sufficiently serious to warrant prosecution by an international tribunal, that prosecution by national courts was generally more efficient than by international tribunals, and primarily that inclusion of terrorism offenses could politicize the ICC, since states that support terrorism might initiate prosecutions against government officials and military personnel acting on behalf of states fighting terrorism in an attempt to sabotage efforts to defeat international terrorism.[18] Consequently, at present it is possible to prosecute terrorists in the ICC only if their offense is also falls into at least one of the other three categories.

The Crime of Genocide

Article 6 of the ICC statute, which adopted the language of Article 2 of the Convention on the Prevention and Punishment of the Crime of Genocide (1948) defines genocide as:

> . . . any of the following acts committed with *intent* to destroy, in whole or in part, a national, ethnical, racial or religious group, as such:
> (a)   members of the group;
> (b)   Causing serious bodily or mental harm to members of the group;
> (c)   Deliberately inflicting on the group conditions of life calculated to bring about its physical destruction in whole or in part;
> (d)   Imposing measures intended to prevent births within the group;
> (e)   Forcibly transferring children of the group to another group.
> [Emphasis added.]

According to this definition, the crime of genocide is not a results-oriented crime, which would depend on the perpetrator's achieving the sought-for result, but rather a behavioral crime, determined by the *mens rea* at the time of the commission of the offense, that is, on the perpetrator's intention to destroy a particular group—in whole or in part—by performing one of the five acts listed in the article. While the acts listed in subparagraphs (c) and (d) refer to acts committed against the group as a collective, the acts listed in the other subparagraphs refer to acts committed against individuals belonging to the group, and therefore the commission of even one of these acts against a single member of the group may amount to genocide if it is part of a series of similar acts performed with the intention of destroying the group to which the victim belongs.[19]

Can terrorist crimes be regarded as crimes of genocide? In my opinion, not always. True, terrorist crimes almost always meet the requirements of at least one of the five subsections listed above.[20] Nonetheless, I believe that it would be a mistake to assert that all acts of terrorism are performed with the intention of bringing about the complete or partial destruction of the group under attack. There are certainly terrorist organizations that have as their ultimate goal the destruction of the members of the group against which they are struggling. However, many terrorist organizations—despite the heinous nature of their activities—do not seek to destroy their "enemies" but rather perceive their violent struggle as a strategic means for attaining specific objectives.

Take, for example, the Palestinian Islamic Jihad, a radical Sunni Muslim organization which combines fundamentalist Islamic ideology with Palestinian nationalist ideology, and which was established in 1981 in the Gaza Strip as a splinter group of the Muslim Brotherhood. If we examine the ideological basis of this group, we see that it aspires to bring about a global Islamic Muslim nation by liberating all Islamic states from foreign rule. In order to achieve this goal, the organization seeks first to attain internal unity, which alone will prepare the ground for *jihad*—armed struggle—against all the foreign regimes, with a view to bringing them down. In this situation the infidels (i.e., the non-Muslims) would be guaranteed a life of dignity as minorities subject to the laws of Islam. The organization perceives the existence of the State of Israel within the territory of Palestine as an obstacle to achieving complete internal unity, an essential prerequisite to the establishment of the universal Muslim nation; this perception in turn ensues from the Jihad leaders' understanding of the condition of the Arab world. In their view, the lessening power of Islam and the concurrent growing influence of Western culture in the Arab world began with Napoleon's invasion of Egypt in 1798 and reached its peak in 1918 with the collapse of the Ottoman Empire, which symbolized Arab unity. From then on, the Western world's control of the Arab world accelerated. Western paradigms seeped into Arab society and led to the secularization of large sections of the community. The separation of religion from the state weakened the stand of the Arab world against Western imperialism and enabled the establishment of the State of Israel and the realization of the Zionist dream. Today, the very existence of the State of Israel perpetuates the supremacy of Western culture over the Arab world, and consequently is the main source for the spiritual malaise of Muslim society which prevents the sought-after internal Islamic unity. The first task of Muslims is therefore to wage an inflexible armed struggle to eradicate the Zionist entity. True, this struggle is incapable of bringing about the complete defeat of Israel. However, it can—and this is its objective—weaken it and thereby accelerate the unification of the Arab world under the flag of Islam and enable the establishment of the united Islamic nation, which will complete the task by jihad.[21]

This is also the ideological basis of the Palestinian National Liberation Movement (Fatah), an organization that from the end of the 1960s to the present has represented the mainstream in the Palestinian Liberation Organization (PLO). The PLO was established in June 1964 with the support of the Arab states, which intended it to operate as an institutional organ to lead and represent the Palestinian body in its struggle for national liberation. Concurrently with the establishment of other PLO institutions, militant organizations were formed which supported the use of armed struggle as the sole strategic method for liberating Palestine, and they called for the PLO to be turned into a fighting organization. Fatah, under the leadership of Yasser Arafat, was one of these organizations. Initially, Fatah was motivated by nationalist ideology calling for violent struggle to free Palestine from Israeli occupation and create a democratic secular Palestinian state in all its territory. Over the years, however, and particularly following the October 1973 war, the leadership of the organization understood that this dream was unrealistic and that at most it could achieve partial independence for the Palestinian people in certain portions of Eretz Yisrael, that is, in the West Bank and Gaza Strip, through political negotiation with Israel combined with violent struggle, which it perceived as a tool for achieving its political goals.[22]

These two terrorist organizations therefore attack Jews, not out of a desire to destroy the Jewish people—in whole or in part—as a collective, but out of a desire to weaken and undermine the determination of the State of Israel. I have described the ideological bases of these two organizations only for the purpose of explaining the assertion that the offense of genocide can provide only a *partial* answer to the prosecution of terrorists.

Crimes against Humanity

International law first defined the acts that constitute an offense against humanitarian law in Article 69(c) of the Charter of the International Military Tribunal, which was established in 1945 in order to prosecute the major war criminals of the European Axis.[23] The article defines crimes against humanity as follows: "Murder, extermination, enslavement, deportation, and other inhumane acts committed against any civilian population, before or during the war, or persecutions on political, racial or religious grounds in execution of or in connection with any crime within the jurisdiction of the Tribunal, whether or not in violation of the domestic law of the country where perpetrated."

Since then, the offense has been defined in other ways, the last definition appearing in Article 7(1) of the statute of the ICC, which provides that crimes against humanity means

> any of the following acts when committed as part of a widespread or systematic attack directed against any civilian population, with knowledge of the attack: (a) murder; (b) extermination; (c) enslavement; (d) deportation or forcible transfer of population; (e) imprisonment or other severe deprivation of physical liberty in violation of fundamental rules of international law; (f) torture; (g) rape, sexual slavery, enforced prostitution, forced pregnancy, enforced sterilization, or any other form of sexual violence of comparable gravity; (h) persecution against any identifiable group or collectivity on political, racial, national, ethnic, cultural, religious, gender as defined in paragraph 3, or other grounds that are universally recognized as impermissible under international law, in connection with any act referred to in this paragraph or any crime within the jurisdiction of the Court; (i) enforced disappearance of persons; (j) the crime of apartheid; (k) other inhumane acts of a similar character intentionally causing great suffering, or serious injury to body or to mental or physical health.

The definition in the ICC statute is indeed wider than that found in the 1945 Charter: the scope of the acts falling within the definition is broader, and it does not require that the acts have been carried out before or during the course of war. Nonetheless, statute definition still fails to provide a suitable basis for prosecuting terrorists. The offense of crimes against humanity is a results-oriented offense, in which the perpetrator must be aware of his conduct and intend to engage in it; he must also intend to cause the particular consequence or, alternatively, be aware of the near certainty that the particular consequence will occur in the ordinary course of events.[24] In practice, acts of terrorism fall within this definition, as these acts consist of systematic and repeated attacks directed at the civilian population where the perpetrators are aware of the possibility that they will cause the harmful consequence and hope for that outcome. At the same time, I am of the opinion that this is insufficient for the purpose of prosecuting terrorists, since including terrorism within this general offense strips it of its unique and discrete character and positions it as one of many acts that constitute a crime against humanity. Put differently, the terrorist is prosecuted solely by reason of his brutal attack on his victims and not because of the amoral nature of his acts, which express a sweeping rejection of agreed moral and legal principles of human society. Neither the random and arbitrary character of the terrorist's acts nor their threatening psychological impact—which is entirely disproportional to the direct damage caused—is reflected in cases where the terrorist is prosecuted for his acts by way of the application of jurisdiction for crimes against humanity.

War Crimes

Article 8 of the statute of the ICC provides a lengthy list of the types of acts that amount to war crimes, breaching the customary and conventional laws of war that regulate international and internal armed conflicts. In the following chapter I shall deal extensively with the complexities involved in applying the laws of war to acts of terrorism. Here I shall merely note that, first, as a rule, it is unclear whether the laws of war indeed apply to acts of terrorism as such, and even if the laws of war do apply, it follows from the language of Article 8 of the statute that an individual is not regarded as having committed a war crime in every case of the infringement of the laws of war but only when he has committed grave breaches or serious violations. Consequently, in the same way that the crime of genocide is selective in nature, so too may war crimes be deemed to embrace only certain types of acts of terror, which by their character, nature, and quality amount to a grave breach of the laws of war and exclude other lesser acts of terror. Second, here too one may see the difficulty to which I alluded above when considering the possibility of prosecuting terrorists for the offense of crimes against humanity—namely, by assimilating terrorist crimes into existing international offenses, their unique and discrete character is denied. Terrorism is not graver than crimes against humanity or war crimes; however, it is different from them in a number of respects which per se justify and even compel it to be regarded as a discrete and independent crime.

It follows, therefore, that current international criminal law enforcement is capable of providing only a partial help in the international community's fight against terrorism, a fight which today is playing an increasingly important role among states that in the not-too-distant past regarded themselves as immune from its effects. Even though to date states have not succeeded in reaching an agreed definition of the enemy at their gates, I believe that the growing impact of international terrorism—thanks to the weapons now being used by terrorists, the sophisticated measures employed by them, and their growing motivation—will not allow the international community to pursue this path for much longer and will compel it to set aside its disputes and reach agreement on the characteristics of this bitter and difficult opponent to contemporary world peace. It is not practicable, in my opinion, to provide the concept of terrorism with *one* strict definition, since the various aims such a definition is meant to serve—for example, the legal purposes of prosecuting terrorists, gathering intelligence regarding terrorist incidents, preventing terrorist organizations from laundering monies; the political purposes of imposing diplomatic or economic sanctions on states that provide support to terrorist organizations; the social purposes of understanding the origins and motivations of the phenomenon of terrorism—may require different definitional elements.

Nevertheless, it is certainly possible to define the *core characteristics* on which definitions for all purposes should be based. Hence, I conclude that every definition of international terrorism should properly embrace the systematic and deliberate commission (or threat of commission)—whether by violent or technological means—of injurious acts which in the circumstances of their commission provoke fear and panic among all or part of the public, where the commission of these acts is directed against innocent civilians or their property for the purpose of advancing political, social, or religious ideology. Similar acts directed against government or military targets not only constitute acts of terrorism but also amount to actual acts of war.[25] Likewise, it would be appropriate for the definition to make it plain that moral and legal justifications arising from the cause being fought for by the terrorist, in those cases where any such justifications exist, are not relevant to the determination of the terrorist character of the acts, since the motive—however just—cannot justify the use of unlawful terrorist means.

Only a clear and detailed definition of this type will succeed in coherently delineating the boundaries of the offense of terrorism and prevent it from being improperly exploited against security and police services, which by virtue of their functions must exercise proportional force in order to preserve public order and safety, or against legitimate protest activities carried out against the government by opposition groups, activities that form an inseparable part of their freedom of expression.

TWO

The Laws of War Waged between Democratic States and Terrorist Organizations

As EXPLAINED in the previous chapter, the task of devising an international legal definition of terrorism embraces not only objective normative factors but also, and perhaps primarily, subjective, relativist perceptions of morality, society, nationality, and religion. Apart from declarative condemnations of terrorism and the formulation of a number of international conventions which have proved futile in eradicating it, the international community lacks any really effective means of combating the phenomenon. Consequently, we must look at the obligations of every state—arising by virtue of its status as a state—to guarantee the proper and orderly lives of its citizens, including their personal safety and security.

This obligation is of greater force in democratic states. The democratic regime, unlike other regimes, exists because of its citizens and for them. Therefore all its activities are designed to supply its citizens with the set of conditions necessary to shape their lives as autonomous beings possessing freedoms and rights through which they can mold their individual ways of life reflecting their personalities and values, without the state opposing them through coercion, pressure, or manipulation, preventing their free, voluntary, and educated choices, save in those cases where these choices harm the freedoms of other individuals and derogate from their ability to realize their own personal autonomy.[1] Indeed,

it is the obligation of the democratic state to safeguard the civilian infrastructure, conditions which enable the citizens to realize their basic rights, within their appropriate boundaries, in accordance with the free will of each and every citizen. The central component in this civilian infrastructure is human life. The most important condition, the condition which is essential for the citizen to realize his basic rights, is the life of the citizen, as such. Everything is dependent on this condition. Without it, it is not possible to enjoy the possibility of realizing basic rights . . . it is worth recalling that this obligation of the democratic state, to afford its citizens real protection of their lives . . . is a moral obligation, as it ensues from the moral principles under-pinning the democratic state.[2]

It follows that it is not only the right but also the legal and moral duty of the democratic state to use appropriate measures, including force, to thwart the dangers posed to the security of its citizens. This brings us to the most complex question of all: which measures of force may be used by a democratic state to protect its security and the security of its citizens in times of emergency? Clearly, not every means is permitted, since both in times of calm and in times of crisis, it is the legal norms that delineate what is permitted and what is prohibited. However, even though in times of war the law is not silenced, those same laws will occasionally permit a deviation from the legal norms prevailing in times of peace, since in its time of trouble a state is not required to self-destruct on the altar of the basic rights and freedoms of its citizens and is entitled to restrict them to the extent needed to deal effectively with its enemies: "There is no choice—in a democratic society seeking freedom and security—but to create a balance between freedom and dignity on the one hand and security on the other. Human rights cannot become a pretext for denying public and state security. A balance is needed—a sensitive and difficult balance—between the freedom and dignity of the individual and State and public security."[3]

The true, and perhaps most difficult, test of the democratic state is its ability to draw an appropriate balance between these two competing values. Finding this balance is not an easy task. Accompanying the difficult legal questions are many moral dilemmas. In the following chapters I shall deal extensively with the identification of the appropriate fundamental balances when fighting the war against terror between the interests of national security and the protection of the rights and freedoms of the individual—both of the terrorist and of innocent civilians. In this chapter, however, I shall deal with the preliminary question, namely, the identification of the law that regulates the battle waged by the democratic state against the terrorist. Is this the domestic emergency law of any state regarding the use of force when defending itself against terrorist acts, or are state laws subject to general international law regarding the conduct of hostilities?

The Use of Force in Contemporary Times: In Which Circumstances?

In the nineteenth century, international law conferred a legal right upon every state to go to war at its own absolute discretion. War was the principal prerogative of the sovereign state and evidence of the existence of sovereignty.[4] This doctrine, acknowledging freedom to declare and initiate war, is no longer valid. In contemporary times, both treaty and customary international law prohibit war in interstate relations.

The international law effort to restrict the freedom to wage war commenced with the Hague peace committees of 1899 and 1907. Article 2 of the Hague Conventions of 1899 and 1907 for the Pacific Settlement of International Disputes provided that in the event of a serious conflict the contracting parties would agree, before resorting to force, to accept the mediation or good offices of a friendly state insofar as circumstances permitted.[5]

The 1928 Kellogg-Briand Pact changed this.[6] The pact renounced the right to go to war; the contracting parties condemned war as a means of resolving international disputes and agreed to settle their disputes by peaceful means alone. The general renunciation of war was not all-embracing, however. Three circumstances permitted a declaration of war: in self-defense, as a foreign policy measure, and as a measure outside the mutual relations between the contracting parties.[7]

The most important development concerning the prohibition on the use of force as a means of resolving disputes was the UN Charter, effective October 24, 1945, shortly after the end of the Second World War. This Charter founded the United Nations as an international intergovernmental organ that would replace the League of Nations, which had proved unable to fulfill its function of preserving world peace. The primary purpose of the UN is to preserve international peace and security by nurturing friendly relations between states and, where necessary, by taking diplomatic and even military action to resolve international disputes.[8] Consequently, Article 2(3) provides, "All Members shall settle their international disputes by peaceful means in such a manner that international peace and security, and justice, are not endangered." Article 2(4) provides that all "Members shall refrain in their international relations from the threat or use of force against the territorial integrity or political independence of any state, or in any other manner inconsistent with the purposes of the United Nations."

In effect, the UN Charter entrenches and adds to the basic principles that developed as a matter of customary international law subsequent to the Hague Conventions. The UN Charter prohibits the use of force for the entire international community. Thus, Article 2(4) prohibits the use of force against "any state" not only against a member state. Nor is the prohibition limited to the contracting states. Article 2(6) requires the organization to ensure that states which are not members of the United Nations act in accordance with these principles.

The principle prohibiting the use of force, which is widely regarded as an inviolable imperative rule (*jus cogens*) of general international law,[9] is subject to two exceptions: the exception of self-defense, set out in Article 51 of the Charter, and the exception, set out in Article 42, empowering the Security Council to take military enforcement measures in conformity with Chapter VII of the Charter.[10]

The Right to Self-Defense in the Modern Age

Customary law and treaty law give rise to two sets of norms that are independent and of equal value. Accordingly, the fact that the customary law doctrine concerning the right to self-defense, subject to certain amendments, is entrenched in Article 51 of the UN Charter does not derogate from the effect of the customary rule, and the two continue to prevail concurrently.[11] I shall first examine how the right to self-defense is expressed in customary international law, and then turn to an examination of its application in international treaty law.

Self-defense in Customary International Law

Custom is the most ancient normative source of international law. Its definition in Article 38(1)(b) of the Statute of the International Court of Justice "as evidence of a general practice accepted by law" has been interpreted by the court as comprising two cumulative elements.[12] The first, *an objective element*, refers to the existence of a practice. States must operate (whether by acting or by refraining from acting) consistently with the rule; in cases where a state deviates from the rule, it can only be, not because it denies the rule, but rather because it asserts that an exception exists which justifies the deviation. Other states must accept this assertion or see the deviation as a breach of the rule. The length of time needed to establish the custom is not uniform, and it is not inconceivable that, in appropriate circumstances, a practice being followed for only a short period of time will nonetheless create a custom. Likewise, the number of states needed to establish a custom is not uniform but is dependent on identifying states whose conduct is relevant to determining the existence of a custom on a particular matter. The second, *a subjective element*, refers to the existence of a practice because of a sense of legal obligation (*opinio juris*). Conduct which amounts to a practice does not necessarily express the wish of the state acting in that way to create a binding legal rule. In order for a practice to be transformed into a custom, states must engage in it while fully aware that they do so by virtue of a binding legal duty.

Self-defense in customary international law is based on the dispute between the United States and Great Britain which gave rise to the "*Caroline* Doctrine." In 1837 rebels rising against British rule in Canada enjoyed the support of the American population along the border. The rebels took control of an island on the Canadian side of the Niagara River and used the American steamer *Caroline* to smuggle people and weapons from the United States to the island. The American authorities knew of these activities but preferred to turn a blind eye to them. When British protests failed to close down this supply line to the rebel forces, a British military force captured the vessel in the middle of the night in U.S. territorial waters, set it on fire, and cast it adrift to be destroyed over Niagara Falls. Two American citizens were killed during the incident. The U.S. government protested against the violation of U.S. sovereignty, but Britain argued that it had acted in self-defense. In response, the U.S. secretary of state, Daniel Webster, presented the U.S. view of the requirements for a legitimate claim of self-defense. In his opinion, which was later accepted as an authoritative standard of customary law, a nation can argue self-defense only if it can show a need to defend itself which is "instant, overwhelming, leaving no choice of means, and no moment for deliberation."[13]

It follows from this explanation that self-defense accompanied by the use of force may be applied only in rare cases where there is an existential, or at least real and tangible, imminent threat; where the need for self-defense is immediate; where there is no possibility of employing other, less harmful measures; and where the response is essential and proportional to the threat and all peaceful means of resolving the dispute have been exhausted.

In the case of the *Caroline*, Britain had not approached the U.S. government with a request that it stop the illicit activities of the vessel. An alternative approach was available, the approach of peace, which should have been adopted before drastic measures were taken—and therefore the requirements of self-defense, as defined, had not been met.[14]

Customary law permits self-defense in every case of aggression, while treaty law, as we shall see, permits self-defense only in cases of armed attack. There is a significant difference between the two. Whereas "aggression" includes assistance to armed organizations that emerge in the territory of one state and invade the territory of another, or the refusal of a state providing cover to prevent terrorist operations notwithstanding the requests of the state being attacked—even before it is attacked—there is controversy over whether the term "armed attack" also includes these circumstances. According to customary international law, it is possible to adopt the tactic of preemptive war, "defensive war," as an act of permitted self-defense upon being threatened or subjected to declarations of future aggression, with the object of foiling the anticipated disaster.[15] After September 11, 2001, the Bush administration has formed a new doctrine of anticipatory self-defense which is based on the foundations of the *Caroline* case but expands the right of preemption against an imminent attack into a right of preventive war against potentially dangerous adversaries. By asserting that the United States must adapt the concept of imminent threat to the capabilities and objectives of today's adversaries, the doctrine maintains that while it is not justified to use force in all cases to preempt emerging threats, the United States is entitled to use forceful preventive measures against private terrorist groups that threaten the country, against states that support such terrorists within their borders, and against rogue states or tyrannical regimes that take actual steps to develop weapons of mass destruction.[16]

Self-defense in International Treaty Law

Article 51 of the UN Charter qualifies the prohibition on the use of force found in Article 2(4) as follows: "Nothing in the present Charter shall impair the inherent right of individual or collective self-defense if an armed attack occurs against a Member of the United Nations, until the Security Council has taken measures necessary to maintain international peace and security." The Charter does not create a new right to self-defense but refers to a preexisting customary international law ("the inherent right" to self-defense). Nonetheless, the right entrenched in the Charter is not identical with the customary law right.[17] This can be seen inter alia from the fact that the Charter refers to the exercise of the right to self-defense against armed attack, whereas customary international law is concerned with self-defense against acts of aggression. The term "armed attack" is not defined in the Charter, with the result that differing interpretations—a restrictive one and a broad one—have been given to it.

The *restrictive interpretation* relies on the language of the Charter and asserts that use of the term "armed attack" as opposed to "aggression" is deliberate and not an oversight, as evident by the fact that other articles in the Charter do use the term "aggression."[18] The framers of Article 51 deliberately chose to use the term "armed attack" in order to circumscribe the scope of activity available to a state when engaging in self-defense. Armed attack is a form of aggression; however, while threats and declarations alone are sufficient to establish aggression, they are insufficient to constitute an armed attack. The attack must be carried out with weapons. It must consist of the use of actual physical force against a state in order for that state to have the right to engage in self-defense. Accordingly, preemptive self-defense is not permitted under Article 51, even though it is permitted by customary international law.[19]

Self-defense is not allowed save as a response to a direct physical attack or, at the least, a high and real likelihood of such an occurrence carried out by one state within the territory of another state.

The general consensus is that the UN Security Council has consistently adhered to the restrictive interpretation. In the majority of its decisions, the Security Council has condemned actions taken in self-defense by the state "under attack."[20] However, the Security Council is a political organ. In contrast to the court, it is not bound by its previous decisions. Every decision is dependent on its own special circumstances. An example of a case where the restrictive interpretation was not adopted is the decision taken by the Security Council following the terrorist attack on the United States on September 11, 2001, where it identified a right to self-defense in connection with an act of terror. It is possible to understand from this decision that an act of terror can in fact be an armed attack.[21]

The *broad interpretation* asserts that, in light of the special language used by the Charter that "nothing . . . shall impair the inherent right of . . . self-defense," it is clear that the drafters intended to preserve the right to self-defense as acknowledged in customary international law. Indeed, Article 51 emphasizes only one form of legitimate self-defense, namely, a response to armed attack, but this does not have to be interpreted as negating other forms of self-defense that are permitted as a matter of customary international law.[22] The interpretation given to "inherent right" is the use of force for the purpose of self-defense according to the requirements established by the *Caroline* Doctrine. Moreover, the right is absolute, since the Charter declares that "nothing . . . shall impair" it.[23] Others assert that the language of the Charter does not require a direct armed attack, with the result that different forms of attack are included so long as they are armed.[24]

Some supporters of the broad interpretation contend that the view that self-defense refers only to the use of force by a state in response to a real threat to its territorial integrity or sovereignty ignores the fact that the Charter characterizes the right to self-defense as "inherent." Thus, states will defend their citizens even when the attack does not amount to a real threat to their territory or independence. Adopting the restrictive interpretation of the right to self-defense would give terrorists an enormous advantage in their war against democracy.[25] The broad interpretation would adapt the right to self-defense against an armed attack to the modern meaning of the term. In other words, today an armed attack may be carried out in a variety of ways, quite apart from invading the territory of another state in the traditional sense. These ways include terrorist acts as well as the use of chemical and biological weapons. The restrictive interpretation is not suitable in such cases and may lead states to conclude that international law in its present form does not provide an adequate answer to modern developments in armed conflicts.

It is true that one cannot allow a situation where states may react with military force against every threat to their security and the security of their citizens even when these threats do not reach the level of an armed attack. It is necessary for control and restrictions to be imposed on the exercise of military force. Accordingly, the UN must adapt the criteria for the exercise of self-defense to global developments, which show that armed attacks are no longer restricted to invasion by a state.[26] One way of doing this is by interpreting the term "armed attack"— which is not defined in the Charter—in accordance with the meaning ascribed to "aggression" by the General Assembly in 1975: "The use of armed force by a state against the sovereignty, territorial integrity or political independence of another state, or in any other manner inconsistent with the Charter of the United Nations, as set out in this definition."[27] Paragraph 2 of the resolution states that opening fire is, prima facie, an act of aggression, and Paragraph 3 states that each of the following is an act of aggression (while Article 4 clarifies that this list is not closed):

1. Invasion, an attack by armed forces, military occupation, or the forced annexation of another state

2. Bombing or use of any weapons against the territory of another state
3. Blockading the coast or ports of another state
4. Attacks by the armed forces of one state against the land, sea, or air forces of another state
5. Use of the military force of one state, located in the territory of another state under an agreement with that state, in breach of the said agreement
6. Permitting a second state to make use of the territory of the first state in order to carry out an act of aggression against a third state
7. Sending armed bands to carry out serious attacks against another state, which are in the nature of the acts listed above.

Such a definition of an armed attack will justify a state responding in self-defense to an act of terror carried out by an armed group. This assertion is based on the assumption that it can be shown that the armed group was sent by a sovereign entity. Alternatively, since the list is not closed, it may be adjusted to the circumstance where an armed attack is initiated by an armed force, such as a terrorist organization, which is not sent by one specific state against another.

The United States has interpreted Article 51 as embracing three possible cases of self-defense: in the face of the real use of force or hostile actions; as a preventive action in the face of immediate activities where it is anticipated that force will be used; in the face of a persistent threat.[28] Such an interpretation reflects a balance between the restrictive and the broad interpretations. The first alternative concerns the situation of an actual attack, which clearly falls within the narrow definition of "armed attack." The second situation expands the definition to situations where the attacks have not yet taken place but there is an expectation that they will occur. The third situation is compatible with the broader interpretation, whereby "armed attack" also embraces situations where an attack has not yet occurred but there is a persistent and continuing (as opposed to onetime) threat of the occurrence of an armed attack.

In the *Nicaragua* case (1986), it was held that

> There appears now to be general agreement on the nature of the acts
> which can be treated as constituting armed attacks. In particular, it
> may be considered to be agreed that an armed attack must be under-
> stood as including not merely action by regular armed forces across an
> international border, but also "the sending by or on behalf of a state of
> armed bands, groups, irregulars or mercenaries, which carry out acts of
> armed force against another state of such gravity as to amount to"

(*inter alia*) an actual armed attack conducted by regular forces, "or its substantial involvement therein." . . . The Court sees no reason to deny that, in customary international law, the prohibition of armed attacks may apply to the sending by a state of armed bands to the territory of another state, if such an operation, because of its scale and effects, would have been classified as an armed attack rather than as a mere frontier incident had it been carried out by regular armed forces.[29]

There is a dual difficulty in classifying terrorist acts as an armed attack within this definition. First, in many cases it is difficult to prove that private terrorist organizations are acting in the name of or on behalf of a state. Second, terrorist attacks are not an armed attack in the classic sense, since the attacks are not directed against government and military targets but at civilian targets; the attacks are not prolonged but intermittent; and there are no defined battle zones, but every civilian site is a legitimate target in the eyes of the terrorists. At the same time, in most cases the attacks are not spontaneous but are meticulously planned, sometimes after intelligence has been gathered; they have great impact and can cause serious physical harm and property damage; and the group may possess an organized armed force and a hierarchical structure with a political branch that directs the activities of the operational branch. Under these circumstances, the terrorist act, even if isolated, contains some of the principal characteristics of the traditional armed conflict. In my view, therefore, it may legitimately be argued that terrorist attacks amount to armed attacks and vest the attacked state with the right to defend itself against terrorists who make use of the territory of a state which is unable or unwilling to prevent them from operating. Following the terrorist attacks on the World Trade Center in New York, the Pentagon in Washington, and in Pennsylvania, the Security Council decided to reconfirm the right to self-defense recognized in the Charter. This implicitly confirms the thesis that terrorist attacks may be regarded as armed attacks which grant the right to self-defense.[30]

It will be recalled that it is immaterial what interpretation is adopted by the state under attack in order to justify the measures it takes as self-defense. It must immediately inform the Security Council of its actions, and the latter will take all steps to preserve international peace, including forceful means in accordance with Chapter VII of the Charter. The Security Council may decide that self-defense is indeed needed or, on the contrary, that there is no need for such action. In the latter case, the state seeking to engage in self-defense becomes a state acting in an aggressive manner, and it must immediately desist from further actions of the type in question.

The Moral Concepts Underlying State Self-defense

The legal perception of self-defense originates from the relations between men and women and has been acknowledged since the beginning of history. International law has applied this same ideological concept to the relations between states. In the same way that human beings need to survive and are therefore permitted to engage in self-defense, so too states need the device of self-defense in order to protect their national security, the safety of individuals living within their territory, and their basic rights. A democratic state is responsible for the preservation of the civilian infrastructure and of the conditions that enable civilians to enjoy their basic rights. The central component in this civilian infrastructure is human life. This is the fundamental condition "without which there is nothing" and which must exist before a person can realize his or her basic rights. Accordingly, within the framework of the state's obligation to preserve the civilian infrastructure it must defend as best it can the lives of its civilians against the dangers facing them. This is the reason why the prohibition on using force in international law is not an absolute prohibition. Use of force is permissible, and even a moral obligation of the democratic regime, where it is being employed in self-defense. However, use of force otherwise than in self-defense, for example, in revenge, is not morally justified on grounds of self-defense.

Does this moral obligation apply only to interstate relations or does it also apply when the enemy is not a sovereign state but rather an organized militant group of private individuals?

The concept of self-defense may be easily understood within the context of interpersonal relations or interstate relations. However, it is much more difficult to apply it in "mixed relations," that is, in the relations between a state and a private group.

When a state grants shelter to terrorist organizations located within its territory, and the targeted state is interested in exercising its right to self-defense against them, it is easier to understand how the concept of self-defense may be applied, since in these circumstances the act of the host state itself gives rise to the right to self-defense of the target state against that host state, if not against the terrorist organizations per se. However, when it is not possible to prove state support for the terrorist organization, or when the state in which the terrorists are located does not afford them active or passive support but is merely unable to prevent their operations, is the attacked state still vested with a right to defend itself against the organization, even though the host state cannot be assigned responsibility for the terrorists' actions?

From the moral point of view, there is no substantive distinction between the two situations. So long as the moral justification for the existence of the right to self-defense is the continuing survival and existence of the state, or the preservation of the safety and security of its citizens, it is irrelevant whether the source of the threat is a sovereign entity or a private body. In both cases, the moral duty of the state to defend itself and its citizens is identical, and therefore in both cases the state has an identical right to self-defense.[31]

But no matter how convincing it may be, the moral basis for allowing a state to defend itself against different classes of enemies (not only other states) is not by itself justification for taking self-defensive measures. It is necessary to have a statutory basis for such measures. Because self-defense is an exception to the prohibition on war in international law, it may be seen as a counterwar or defensive war. The relevant question becomes whether it is possible to exercise the right to a defensive war against a body which is not a state. The answer is found in the definition of war. The accepted legal definition is that "war is the clash between two or more states, by means of their armed forces,"[32] in other words, the comprehensive use of force in the relations between two or more states. This definition emphasizes that the warring parties consist of sovereign entities that deploy armed forces, and use of the latter is comprehensive insofar as concerns targets and measures. Such a definition may give rise to the claim that if the use of force is prohibited only in the relations between states, then the use of force is permissible and possible in the relations between states and an organization that is not a state, such as a terrorist organization. This claim must be rejected, since it contradicts the understanding of the UN Charter—namely, that the use of force even in cases where the clashing parties are not states poses a risk to international peace and security. Contemporary times have shown that war is no longer confined to states. In the trial of Sheikh Omar Abdel-Rahman and his nine accomplices for terrorist acts committed in 1993 in the World Trade Center, the U.S. attorney general opened by saying that "this is a case involving a war."[33]

We are used to thinking of war as involving hostilities between two defined states, involving an identifiable enemy with clear borders and known military forces. Victory takes place when geographical areas are conquered or the enemy concedes defeat. We also succeed in seeing war as a metaphor for social and political problems, such as the "war on poverty." But we fail to see the true meaning of the word when it comes to dealing with terrorism.[34] The war against terrorism is different from war in its traditional sense. Terror is not an enemy in the same way as a state. It has no army, but it does have militias. It has no tanks or helicopters, but it does have knives and hand grenades. The object is not to vanquish the opposing party by occupation or suppression but to weaken the spiritual strength of its population by spreading fear. The object is not to injure soldiers but to injure civilians. Accordingly, precise legal language today ascribes the term "war" to the use of force or violent conflict between organized groups of people and not only between states.[35]

Since the right to self-defense is intended to protect the citizens of the state, there are some who argue that when its citizens are in danger from a terrorist organization, the state is entitled to respond with the use of its armed forces.[36] In the same way that it is inconceivable to ask a man not to defend himself against a threat to his life, so too is it not possible to prevent a state from exercising its right, and even its obligation, to protect itself and its citizens from an anticipated attack—even when the prospective attacker cannot be called a state. When the lives of the citizens of a state are threatened by terrorist attacks and the use of force is the only means available to prevent the acts of the terrorist organizations, the state is justified, from a moral point of view, within the context of the principle of self-defense, to defend itself against those organizations. However, the state may not implement the right to self-defense as a pretext for aggression.

The construction of the security fence between Israel and the areas of Judea and Samaria illustrates this difference. In June 2002, after two years during which the Israeli-Palestinian conflict reached new heights of violence, and after carrying out various military operations that proved insufficient to stop the terror, the Israeli government decided to erect a separation obstacle that was supposed to prevent terrorist infiltrations from the Palestinian territories into Israel. The chosen route of the fence involved various limitations on the rights of the local Palestinian inhabitants. For example, private land was seized from its owners, peasants were separated from their agricultural lands and needed special permits in order to go from their homes to their fields, and access roads to urban centers were blocked off, preventing access to medical and other essential services.

A petition against the legality of the chosen route was filed with the Israeli Supreme Court sitting as the High Court of Justice.[37] The court held that while the decision to erect a separation barrier, along any possible route, cannot be motivated by the desire to create a de facto annexation of territories to the State of Israel, in this case the Israeli government was motivated only by security concerns.[38]

The International Court of Justice, which rendered an advisory opinion on the matter at the request of the UN General Assembly, failed to recognize the right of states to self-defense against private terrorist organizations and determined that Article 51 of the Charter recognizes the existence of an inherent right of self-defense only in the case of armed attack by one state against another state.[39] The court also found that the fence was not a temporary security measure whose sole purpose was to enable Israel to effectively combat terrorist attacks, but rather an attempt to draw new borders for Israel by creating facts on the grounds that would be tantamount to de facto annexation.

Yoram Dinstein is of the opinion that in cases where an armed attack is launched by an organization on its own, the targeted state still possesses a right of self-defense, since Article 51 of the Charter refers to armed attack against a state but not necessarily by a state, and just as a state is entitled to defend itself against an armed attack launched by another state, so too is it certainly entitled to defend itself against an armed attack by gangs operating from the territory of the "other" state. This is self-defense in the guise of an enforcement action, a term intended to express the idea that the government of the targeted state is operating within the territory of the host state in place of the government there and doing what that government should have done. If the "host" state is not capable or is not prepared to impose law and order in its territory, it is not entitled to object to another state—which has been injured by the terrorist actions—doing so in its place.[40]

Oscar Schachter believes that injury to civilians in a foreign state constitutes an armed attack within the meaning of Article 51 of the Charter and gives rise to the right to self-defense.[41]

Alberto Coll also contends that it would be a mistake to interpret Article 51 as absolutely prohibiting a military response to terror: "Self-defense consists essentially of measures necessary to protect the state and its people from outside armed attack in all its conventional and non-conventional forms, including terrorism."[42] From this it follows that terrorist attacks against innocent civilians justify acts of self-defense.

As noted, following the September 11 attack against the United States, Resolution 1368 of the UN Security Council identified the inherent right of every state to defend itself against acts similar to those which occurred in the United States, that is, acts of terrorism. It would seem that the Security Council has recognized the need to equate acts of terrorism in general—at least acts of terrorism of extensive force, quality, and scope—with armed attacks in the sense of Article 51 of the Charter.

The resolution refers to such acts as threatening international peace and security and permits that all necessary measures be taken to respond to the acts of terror. Even those who believe that this resolution does not amount to an express authorization to respond with armed force to terrorist attacks agree that it indicates that the Security Council accepts that a right to self-defense is born upon the occurrence of a terrorist attack.[43] This resolution is evidence of an important development in international law in relation to the interpretation given to "armed attack"—an essential development in view of the phenomenon of international terrorism.

Acknowledging the right to self-defense in the context of terror is not sufficient. The conditions for exercising the right must be regulated. As noted, the *Caroline* Doctrine and the UN Charter deal with cases of self-defense where the identity and location of the attacker (a state) are not in doubt. In contrast, the location of terrorist organizations is often unknown, and a period of time is needed to determine their location and whether they are being supported by a state. The reaction, therefore, cannot be immediate.

If the right to self-defense is only permitted against a real, concrete, and imminent threat, it is difficult to exercise the right against the activities of terrorist organizations, where the termination of one terrorist act will not end the threat of further terrorist activities on some uncertain future date. It would seem that as long as the threshold for exercising the right to self-defense continues to be so high, it will not be possible to exercise the right against international terror.

But if it is understood that the traditional doctrines in international law developed in a completely different atmosphere—that in earlier times there was no danger and no prospect of danger from terrorist organizations operating throughout the world, obtaining financing from a variety of sources, holding biological and chemical weapons and capable of mass destruction—the use of armed force to cope with the terrorist threat per se need not be a breach of international law.

Against this backdrop there are those who argue that since the phenomenon of terror is not a phenomenon foreseen by the drafters of the Charter—whose only experience was with states posing existential threats—a state must be allowed to defend itself against the terrorist threat in accordance with a new construction. That construction is as follows: a state threatened by a terrorist organization is entitled to act against the organization as such; a measure taken by the state will not be deemed to be a breach of Article 2(4) of the Charter, since it will amount to the use of limited and temporary force directed solely at removing the terrorist threat. So long as the activity is not directed against the civilians or property of the state in which the terrorists are located, and it is not intended to conquer territory or achieve political gains, the use of force will not constitute a violation of territorial integrity or sovereignty and therefore will not be contrary to Article 2(4) of the Charter. Such an interpretation eliminates the need for justification of the use of force under Article 51 of the Charter.[44] Others argue that since terrorism is a new phenomenon, a limited incursion into the territory of the state in which the terrorists are located will be recognized as a new independent exception standing alongside self-defense as an exception to the general international law prohibiting the use of force by one state against another.[45] Terrorism presents a different threat from what states are accustomed to face. Political or economic sanctions that influence states do not influence terrorists. Today it is feared that terrorists will use unconventional weapons. Accordingly, a limited and transitory incursion into a host state that refuses or is unable to take measures against the terrorists in its territory is necessary in response to terrorism in the modern age.

It should be pointed out that it is not clear that the exercise of force—however transitory, limited, and focused for the purpose of removing a terrorist threat—in the territory of another state does not violate that state's sovereignty. There are many who believe that "most uses of force, no matter how brief, limited, or transitory, do violate a state's territorial integrity."[46] Nonetheless, the theory that a state has a right to violate in a limited manner the sovereignty of another state that cannot act against terrorists located within it, where these terrorists pose a serious threat to the first state, is a theory that is acceptable to most nations.

The use of armed force in order to attack terrorist organizations located in other countries must be made compatible with Article 2(4) of the UN Charter. First, the state that plans to use force must ensure that the objectives being targeted for attack pose a terrorist threat, that the threat is presumed to occur, and that the state where the terrorists are located is unable or unwilling to deal with them. The level of proof needed is not beyond any reasonable doubt. However, at the least, clear and convincing evidence must be presented,[47] in view of the possibility that innocent people will be killed and the immorality of taking such a large risk without being certain that the planned target is appropriate and that the threat is real and serious.

This view is also compatible with the minimal evidentiary requirements—emerging from the decision of the International Court of Justice in the *Nicaragua* case—that must be met before a military response may be launched against a terrorist organization. First, the state must carefully examine the evidence available to it in order to guarantee a high level of certainty as to the identity of those responsible for the terrorist attack against it and the imminence of further attacks.[48] Second, the use of power must be limited to one purpose only—removal of the terrorist threat. So long as the host state does not support the organization, no action may be taken against its own facilities and military camps. Third, the use of force must be restrained and proportional to the size of the threat. Fourth, while the threat need not be imminent in accordance with the requirement in Article 51 of the UN Charter, it must be likely that the threat will indeed be realized.[49] Fifth, force may not be used unless all nonviolent means have been exhausted, or it is clear that the threat is about to be realized before the conclusion of efforts to resolve the dispute by peaceful means.[50]

The latter requirement—exhausting peaceful measures—is the most important and problematic of the requirements where the enemy is a terrorist organization.

We have seen that self-defense is an exception to the theory whereby disputes are resolved by the normative structures of the rule of law: either within the state, by the authorities responsible for the enforcement of the law between states; or on the international level, in accordance with the UN Charter. The latter offers a mechanism for resolving disputes peacefully with the help of the Security Council, unless there is an imminent existential threat requiring immediate defensive action, and even in such a case notification of the action must be given to the Security Council, which will examine whether it is indeed indispensable.

In other words, the requirement that disputes that provide grounds for war must first be resolved by means of negotiations is compatible with the Charter and international law. The State of Israel, for example, acted in this way with the Palestinian Authority before engaging in military actions required to defend its citizens. Likewise, the UN Security Council acted in this way with the Taliban government in Afghanistan, which was sheltering terrorist organizations under the leadership of Osama bin Laden.

In Resolution 1333 the Security Council condemned the Taliban government and demanded that it respond to the demands already made on it in the prior Resolution 1267 (1999) to extradite Osama bin Laden, close the training camps of the terrorists, and take all necessary measures to ensure that the territory under its control not be used by terrorist organizations for their needs.[51] The Security Council indicated that it saw the refusal of the Taliban government to respond to these demands as a threat to international peace and security.

The Taliban government's response was given on September 11, 2001, with the brutal attacks against American citizens inside the United States. This response focuses our attention on the central problem—that terrorist organizations do not see themselves as bound by the provisions of the UN Charter or as subject to the resolutions of the Security Council. In fact, the council, which is responsible for bringing disputes to peaceful resolution and preventing armed struggles, does not have the tools to fight terrorist organizations. Moreover, it is not competent to act against them, since these organizations have no institutional or contractual connection with the UN. This is the reason why they are not subject to its authority, and it is also the reason why there is no logical basis for asking a state threatened by a terrorist organization to turn first to the Security Council for the latter to attempt to deal with the threat within the framework of its normative structures.

Nonetheless, it should be pointed out that the United States did act in accordance with the requirements described above before taking military action. After the September 11 attack, the president of the United States demanded that the Taliban government close the terrorist training camps and extradite the terrorist leaders to the United States. The United States turned to military action only upon the Taliban's failure to meet these demands; the United States also went to great lengths to emphasize that it was not attacking Afghan civilians but was confining itself to Taliban military targets and terrorist organizations being sheltered by the Taliban regime.

We have stressed the importance of the requirement that disputes be resolved by negotiation, and we have seen that this requirement is ineffective when the clash is with terrorist organizations. The inevitable conclusion is that when states, seeking to defend themselves against a terrorist threat, are dissatisfied with one alternative, they must seek another that stands on its own and directly addresses ways of coping with international terror. The solution, in my opinion, may be found in a modern development of the second type of self-defense dealt with by Article 51 of the Charter.

Article 51 does not deal only with individual self-defense exercised by a single state. The article also refers to collective self-defense. Collective self-defense is in essence team action taken by a number of states in response to an armed attack. Two situations are contemplated. First, self-defense by a number of states that have simultaneously fallen victim to an armed attack by a single enemy and all act together in a coordinated counterattack. The second situation is where a single state has fallen victim to an armed attack by a single enemy, and a second state decides to join the defensive war.

We considered the narrow interpretation given to a defensive war under which only the injured state may react to an armed attack. Such an interpretation makes the second category of collective self-defense meaningless.

Under the threat of international terrorism, which is spreading swiftly and dangerously throughout the world, the narrow interpretation of self-defense would turn Article 51 of the Charter into a suicidal provision. There is no question that this was not the intention of its drafters. On the contrary, when one understands the theory underlying the Charter—the lessons learned from the Second World War—collective self-defense may be seen to be the only insurance policy in the international community against armed attack.[52]

When the Charter was formulated, the prevailing fear was of an armed attack by a great military power against a number of other countries. Today, the fear is of a different type of power, a power that is not embodied by a defined and recognized state. Rather it is the terrorist power of fundamentalist Islam, whose tentacles reach out throughout the world, threatening international peace and security by carrying out destructive armed attacks of a terrorist nature. This complex situation is likely to lead every state that believes itself subject to future attack, a belief supported by evidence that an existential threat is indeed hovering over it, to the conclusion that it must launch a counterattack on the basis of the right to individual self-defense. The ramifications of such a situation are likely to be calamitous and irreversible. If every state decides to fight terrorism on its own, to fight an enemy which is not identified and which is not located solely in one country, the outcome is likely to be a third world war. Such a result would be a victory for international terrorism.

The inescapable conclusion is that recognition must be given to collective self-defense in order to fight terrorism. The rule of proportionality of self-defense requires that the response conform to the degree of the threat. Since the threat is not directed at a single state and the danger is international, the reaction must also be international. An international body must be set up that will have the competence and power to launch a war against terrorist organizations.

The source of power for establishing such a body may be found, in my opinion, in the UN Charter itself.

Article 39 of the Charter enables the Security Council to exercise collective security in every case of a threat to peace, breach of the peace, or act of aggression. Collective security means institutionalization of the legal use of force by the international community. Collective security is exercised by virtue of a legally binding resolution of a central organ of the international community. The central organ according, to Chapter VII of the Charter, is the Security Council.

It should be recalled that whereas Article 51 enables a state to respond only to an armed attack, Article 39 enables the Security Council to respond, within the framework of collective security, to an attack that does not amount to an armed attack. Thus, for example, the Security Council is entitled to decide on a preventive war in response to a threat to the peace. Article 40 enables the Security Council to engage in provisional measures, before making the final decisions in accordance with Article 39, in order to prevent the situation from being aggravated. According to Article 42, if the council considers that the measures referred to above would be inadequate or have proved to be inadequate, it may take such action by air, sea, or land forces as may be necessary to maintain or restore international peace and security. In other words, it may decide to launch a war against the aggressor state.

As noted, the UN Charter speaks of states. A breach of international peace and security may, according to the Charter, issue solely from sovereign entities—states—and therefore measures of collective security may be directed only against states and not at international terrorist organizations which are not states.

In light of the above, two alternatives exist. First, the Charter may be interpreted in the same way as a constitution, in the spirit of the times, and therefore as including the possibility of self-defense against a terrorist organization. Second, one may learn the lessons of the recent terrorist attacks against the United States, to the effect that the provisions of the Charter fail to provide a satisfactory answer to the terrorist threat. In such a case, action must be taken to unite all the states of the free world in an international convention that will establish cooperative measures of a legal, political, and strategic nature in the fight against international terrorism. The convention may adopt the UN Charter as a basis for counterterrorism structures, but it will focus on this issue only and will establish an international body, in the nature of a permanent international force, whose soldiers have only one objective—to fight terror.

Limitations on the Use of Force in a War between a Sovereign State and a Terrorist Organization

Besides the *jus ad bellum* described above (i.e., the laws that regulate the declaration and termination of war), even when a state is legally entitled to resort to force, it does not have unlimited freedom of choice in relation to the nature of the armed force it may exercise.

The *jus in bello* (i.e., the laws regulating the manner in which a war may lawfully be conducted, which are primarily found in the Hague Conventions of 1899 and 1907, the Geneva Conventions of 1949, and the Additional Protocols to the Geneva Conventions of 1977, and which in part have now become customary laws) restricts the parties from making free use of all the effective means at their disposal. First, a distinction is drawn between combatants and noncombatants: the war is to be conducted solely between the combatants, who are required to refrain, insofar as possible, from harming the civilian population and civilian objects, and protect insofar as possible the rights of the civilian population that finds itself in the hands of the enemy during the course of the fighting.

Second, the laws of war provide that, even though combatants voluntarily expose themselves to the risks inherent in war, not all forms of conduct are permitted. The combatants of one side are prohibited from causing the combatants of the other superfluous injury or harm greater than that unavoidable to achieve legitimate military objectives. Consequently, there is a prohibition on the use of types of weapons which may cause such harm, for example, there is a prohibition on the use of expanding bullets or bullets that flatten easily inside the human body, a prohibition on the use of poison or poisoned weapons, a prohibition on the use of asphyxiating or poisonous gases or any other analogous lethal chemical material or bacteriological or biological warfare techniques, a prohibition on the use of military environmental modification techniques having widespread, long-lasting, or severe effect, and the like. Once the combatants have willingly (after having yielded) or by force (because of injury, illness, or stranding at sea) departed the battle zone and fallen into the hands of the enemy, they become entitled to the status of prisoners of war. This status confers advantages in terms of humanitarian treatment—the duty of the captors to safeguard the prisoners' lives, health, and dignity—and immunity from prosecution and punishment for acts committed during the course of the fighting. In contrast, illegal combatants are not regarded as prisoners of war, and therefore they may be prosecuted and punished severely for crimes committed as a result of unlawful warfare.

Earlier I referred to the problems involved in classifying a terrorist attack as an armed attack within the meaning of Article 51 of the UN Charter, although I concluded that the special character of the terrorist act allows and even makes it desirable to regard it as amounting to an armed attack and consequently as vesting the attacked state with the right to defend itself by making use of force within the context of the exception of self-defense. Accordingly, it is necessary to turn now to the ancillary issue of the choice of law that regulates the manner in which the state will use this force, that is, whether implementing the right to self-defense is subject to the restrictions of international law regarding the manner of conducting hostilities or whether, when the right to self-defense against a terrorist organization is implemented, the provisions of *jus in bello* do not apply and the armed force is governed solely by the domestic law of the defending state.

The answer to this question requires us first to consider the status accorded to terrorists in international law.

The Status of Terrorists in International Law

International law distinguishes between those who take an active part in the fighting and those who do not. A person who takes an active part in the fighting and is a member of the armed forces of the state is a combatant.[53]

Civilians are protected in a state of war. The participating states must refrain from any step likely to cause harm or suffering to the civilian population.[54] The Geneva Conventions provide protection to combatants who are captured by the enemy in times of war. This protection is provided to lawful combatants only.

Apart from the distinction between civilians and combatants, there is a distinction between lawful and unlawful combatants.[55] Only lawful combatants are entitled to the status of prisoners of war upon falling into the hands of the enemy, and this status prevents the captor from prosecuting them for acts amounting to crimes committed during the course of the fighting. This protective umbrella does not apply to unlawful combatants, who may be prosecuted for offenses committed while engaged in hostilities. The U.S. government, for example, does not render captured Al Qaeda fighters held at the Guantánamo Bay Naval Base the status of prisoners of war, on the grounds that they do not fight on behalf of a state and consequently are not party to the Geneva Conventions. Taliban fighters who belonged to the regular forces of the government are also being denied the status of prisoners of war, on the grounds that they do not meet the necessary preconditions for being granted this status, such as the requirement to clearly separate themselves from the civilian population.[56]

The distinction between lawful and unlawful combatants is designed to preserve the distinction between combatants and civilians. If combatants were able to disappear within the civilian population, every civilian would be suspected of being a hidden combatant and would suffer the inevitable consequences. In order to remove civilians from the battle arena, sanctions must be imposed on those attempting to exploit the distinction and thereby endanger it. A person is not entitled to claim two identities at once—one civilian and one engaged in military activities. Such a person is not a civilian and also not a soldier; he is an unlawful combatant who does not enjoy the privileges of a prisoner of war and is subject to ordinary criminal sanctions.[57]

Article 43 of the Protocol I Additional to the Geneva Conventions expands the protection afforded by international conventions to combatants and offers it also to freedom fighters, fighters who are not part of the official armed forces of the state but are still considered lawful combatants. The recognition accorded this new class of combatants is intended to give them the protection of prisoners of war. Article 43(1) of Protocol I makes entitlement to this protection contingent on the fighters acknowledging themselves to be bound by the rules applicable to combatants in international law.

This condition is compatible with Article 4(2)(d) of the Third Geneva Convention, which provides that one of the conditions that must be satisfied before persons can be recognized as being prisoners of war is "that of conducting their operations in accordance with the laws and customs of war." In addition, a party including within its armed forces others who assist it must notify the other parties to the conflict of the same. This is a necessary precondition for these persons to be recognized as combatants within the framework of the Geneva Conventions and thereby entitled to the protection available to prisoners of war.[58]

It should be pointed out that Rule 1 of the Hague Rules recognized that the rights and obligations of war did not apply solely to armies but also to militia and volunteer corps which did not form part of the army.[59] However, in order for these "fighters" to be entitled to rights, they had to meet all the following cumulative conditions: to be commanded by a person responsible for his subordinates; to wear a fixed distinctive emblem recognizable at a distance; to carry arms openly; and to conduct their operations in accordance with the laws and customs of war.

The Geneva Conventions reiterated these conditions and added the condition of organization and affiliation with a combatant party. This recognition of freedom fighters preserves the principle of reciprocity which underlies the rules restraining the parties in time of war. An essential condition that has to be met in order to obtain the status of a freedom fighter is compliance with the rules of international law. Notwithstanding that the opposing parties are not two states but rather a state and an organization of people—freedom fighters—the principle of reciprocity is maintained. Both sides are subject to the rules of international law and comply with them. Alongside this development and the recognition accorded to freedom fighters, a new development has seen terrorist groups begin organizing for the purpose of creating a new world order. Are these terrorists freedom fighters?

The answer to this question is an unequivocal no. To fight for freedom means to fight against oppression, to fight against the violation of human rights. Clearly, terrorists who themselves violate human rights, and in particular the right to life, can never be freedom fighters.

Protocol I Additional to the Geneva Conventions, like the Hague Rules, establishes a number of requirements that must be met before civilians can be recognized as freedom fighters, such as the requirement that these freedom fighters refrain from intermingling with the civilian population, that they wear uniforms or other recognizable means of identification, and that they carry their weapons openly. Underlying these requirements is the need to distinguish fighters from the protected civilian population, to ensure that the parties to the conflict know against whom they are fighting and that civilians who are not combatants will not be endangered. One of the most destructive consequences of terror is the way it obfuscates the distinction between combatants and civilians. Terrorists carry out their attacks from the heart of population centers, which serve as shelters for them, in the knowledge that the state fighting them will not target these population centers. Terrorists infringe the rules of international law, they do not act openly, and their primary purpose is to deliberately attack innocent civilians.

The greatest danger is that the humanist principles that underlie the rules of international law in relation to the protection of the innocent will be tainted by the conferral of protection on terrorists. Article 44(3) of the protocol recognizes an exception to the requirement that combatants distinguish themselves from civilians and thereby enables terrorists not to comply with the laws of war and still retain their status as lawful combatants. That kind of norm makes a mockery of the international law. Israel, the United States, and Britain have all refused to sign Protocol I on the grounds that the article under discussion would enable terrorist organizations to be recognized as combatants and thereby allow them to be granted the rights of prisoners of war.

Some writers assert, and I agree with this view, that terrorists do not meet any of the requirements of combatants in international law nor do they meet the requirements of freedom fighters: "Lawful combatants must be organized under a responsible command, must be subject to an internal disciplinary system to enforce compliance with international law applicable in armed conflict (such as the rules protecting civilians from indiscriminate attacks) and must bear arms openly during military deployment and engagement. A casually attired driver of a van carrying a concealed bomb does not fit anyone's definition of a lawful combatant."[60]

Currently, terrorists are principally people who do not regard themselves as subject to legal constraints. They do not balk at any measures that they believe will further their cause, namely, achieving a new world order primarily on the basis of an extreme Islamic militant ideology which seeks to revive the glory of Islam and dominate the world. For this purpose, terrorists are willing to risk their lives and injure their opponents by reason of the latter's status per se: "Their anger is directed not only against a political system, but against social and cultural ones as well. Their protest is general, and so are the targets of their attacks. In the past, terrorists' targets were often political or military, and civilian victims were merely caught in the cross fire. Today, however, indiscriminate killing appears to be the goal rather than the by-product of terrorism. Everyone is a potential target. Moreover, terrorists have no scruples as to how many people they kill or maim."[61] Is it conceivable that the law will protect this class of "combatants" and type of warfare? So long as these people do not respect the restraining rules imposed by international law in times of war, there is no reason for international law to respect them, protect them, and acknowledge them as lawful combatants.

Are terrorists entitled to the status of civilians? The definition of the term "civilians" or "civilian population" appears in Article 50 of Protocol I Additional to the Geneva Conventions. Since this article is formulated in the negative, one may think that if certain persons do not fall within the category of combatants, they must be civilians. However, in my opinion it would not be right to interpret the article in this way, since the drafters of the convention did not intend to grant terrorists the status of civilians. In addition, the defenses granted to civilians are broader than the defenses granted to combatants. Thus, for example, it is forbidden to attack civilian populations. It follows that if it is not proper to regard terrorists as combatants and thereby grant them the protection due to combatants, a fortiori it is improper to regard them as civilians who are not combatants and thus grant them even more extensive rights.[62]

But although the laws of war do not positively regulate the status of terrorists, there is no legal vacuum, because the existing situation should be interpreted as a negative arrangement. Under international law, terrorists are unlawful combatants—that is, armed fighters who conduct their warfare outside the legal framework by committing acts that constitute a violation of the laws of war. In the matter of *Ex parte Quirin*, the U.S. Supreme Court held that unlawful belligerency negates the legal protection given to lawful belligerents and thus exposes the unlawful combatants to the domestic criminal sanctions of the state that was the victim of the acts that rendered their belligerency unlawful.[63]

It should be stressed that certain acts of terror might be considered as declarations of war or rather, in modern terms, as a state of armed conflict and therefore might also be defined as war crimes, provided that owing to their character, nature, and quality they amount to grave breaches or serious violations of the laws of war. Hence, the state that is the victim of these acts, and other neutral states as well, have universal jurisdiction in prosecuting their perpetrators as war criminals.[64] However, the state which prosecutes the terrorists must act in accordance with the minimal humanitarian norms, which shall be discussed below.

The Type of Armed Conflicts Governed by International Law

Following the occurrence of a terrorist attack it is necessary to identify its perpetrators: were they soldiers sent from a sovereign state to attack civilian targets within the territory of another state; or were they a group of armed men not belonging to the regular armed forces but nonetheless acting in the name of and on behalf of a state and sent by that sovereign state; or were they members of a private terrorist organization not supported by a state but operating from its territory or even from the territory of the state that was attacked?

In the first case there is no doubt that the fighting is regulated by supranational law, since Article 2 common to the four Geneva Conventions of 1949 provides that the normative restrictions contained in the conventions are intended to apply to international armed conflicts (i.e., to disputes between two or more entities possessing an international legal personality), whether or not all the parties concerned officially recognize and declare the existence of a state of war between them. Article 1(4) of Protocol I Additional to the Geneva Conventions expands the definition of an armed conflict to include situations in which peoples fight against a colonial regime, foreign occupation, or racist regime within the framework of their struggle for self-determination.

The second case is more problematic, since international law provides that it is possible to attribute the activities of nonstate actors to a state supporting their actions only when that state has effective control over them,[65] or as the International Law Commission proposed, in the same spirit: "The conduct of a person or group of persons shall be considered an act of a state under international law if the person or group of persons is in fact acting on the instructions of, or under the direction or control of, that state in carrying out the conduct."[66] An absurd situation arises in these circumstances. On the one hand, the great majority of terrorist organizations are indeed supported by sovereign states which ensure their continued existence; on the other hand, it is extremely difficult to find sufficient evidence that those states are indeed providing shelter in their territory to terrorists or are assisting their cause by providing them with weapons, logistical help, or financing, since these activities are carried out stealthily and with a great deal of care to cover up all suspicious tracks. Accordingly, only in a few situations will it be possible to apply the doctrine of effective control and assign liability to the supporting state for the terrorist acts perpetrated in the territory of another state. In the remaining situations, the laws governing the battle between a state and a terrorist organization are the former's domestic laws, save in circumstances where the armed conflicts are not of an international character, that is, they are internal disputes taking place within the territory of a certain state between the state itself and nonstate armed groups. In the latter situation, Article 3 common to all the Geneva Conventions applies and provides for minimal humanitarian norms that bind all the parties to the dispute.

It follows that the central question is whether Article 3 applies to the third case, that is, terrorist attacks on sovereign states carried out by terrorist organizations that are not supported by a state or where such support cannot be proved. Article 3 does not expressly refer to terrorist acts but sets out two cumulative conditions for its application: first, that an armed conflict exists, and second, that the conflict is not of an international character. In order to meet the first requirement, proof must be adduced that the terrorist attacks are not solely domestic riots but amount to a real armed conflict. Even though international law has not yet agreed on a definition of the term "armed conflict," it is clear that terrorist acts, by their nature and character, are not armed conflicts in the traditional sense; nonetheless, as mentioned, these acts possess some of the basic characteristics of the classic armed dispute.

All these characteristics should properly be assessed after a balance is drawn between the humanitarian objectives of the Geneva Conventions, on the one hand, and respect for the sovereignty of states within their own territory and the need to refrain from international intervention in internal tensions, on the other.[67] It follows that even if it is not possible to clearly delineate the boundaries of application of the term "armed conflict," it is still possible to assert that it applies to hostilities that constitute or threaten to constitute grave breaches of international humanitarian law. It also follows that while not every terrorist attack will amount to an armed conflict, in those cases where the perpetrators are organized groups that systematically carry out planned and coordinated attacks against civilians which cause serious harm, it would be appropriate to regard those attacks as amounting to an armed conflict.

The second condition for the application of Article 3 is that the conflict is not of an international character. The vagueness of this formulation has led to it being interpreted as applying to three different situations:[68] first, to every armed conflict which is not governed by Article 2, that is, a conflict in which only one of the parties is a sovereign state and the other party is a private body; second, only to civil wars; and third, only to armed conflicts between a state and domestic (but not foreign) terrorist organizations. The purpose of Article 3, and its adaptation to global events (which show that terrorism is spreading rapidly without the international community being able to formulate a suitable plan for eradicating it), require that the first construction be preferred. Because of the difficulty in defining the nature of the acts that constitute terrorism, international law does not provide expressly for the application of humanitarian law in cases where the state realizes its right to self-defense against a terrorist organization. The significance of this is that unless it is possible to bring terrorist acts within one of the constructions described above, the state's battle against it will be governed by its domestic laws, subject to international human rights laws. Even though there is nothing necessarily wrong with handling disputes in accordance with domestic laws—these laws may circumscribe the state's activities even more than international humanitarian law—I am still of the opinion that it is essential to apply international humanitarian law, which, since it attracts broad support from the nations of the world, provides a stable normative framework for handling disputes.[69]

The international laws of war are based on the principle of mutuality under which both parties are obliged to comply with the restraints on the use of force, whereas in a war against a terrorist organization only the state accepts such restraints. Nonetheless, this too cannot affect the foregoing conclusion, since the democratic state per se possesses an *absolute duty* to protect itself and its citizens within the framework of the law, and in no circumstances can it assert "exceptional circumstances," such as the fact that its enemies see themselves as unconstrained by these restrictions, as a factor easing its moral and legal burden. Subjecting the war to international humanitarian law is therefore significant not only on an operative level but also on an equally important declarative level. Thus, for example, even though the Israeli Supreme Court concluded that the government had decided to construct the separation fence as a result of valid security needs, as opposed to political considerations, it nevertheless determined that some parts of the fence's route were illegal because they injured the local inhabitants to the extent that there was no proper proportion between this injury and the security benefit of the fence. Consequently, the court held that although alternative routes would have a smaller security advantage than the route originally chosen by the government, they would cause significantly less damage to the humanitarian needs of the local inhabitants than the original route.[70]

Victory in the War between a Democratic State and a Terrorist Organization

"War" in its traditional sense is a term that deals with a struggle between two states. The term "victory in war" was coined to apply to the parties to that war—states.

Therefore, victory has a dual aspect: an objective one, achievement of the political goals for which the war was launched, and a subjective one, society's sense that the price paid to engage in military action to achieve the goals of the war was reasonable. Assessing the cost of a military action is inherently dependent on the importance attributed to the political objectives of the war.[71]

When the war is being waged between states, it is easier to define the nature of the victory. A war may end with a single victor when the enemy is forced from the battle zone; the enemy may capitulate upon recognizing that he has been defeated, putting a halt to the fighting and enabling the other party to achieve his political goals; or the enemy may acknowledge his inferiority if caused sufficient death and destruction.

A genuine victory in war is a situation in which one of the parties succeeds in achieving the goals formulated by decision makers before and during the military campaign. In this type of victory there may be more than a single victor; alternatively, the victory may be partial and achieve only some of the objectives identified.

What is victory over terror?

Following the September 11 attack, the president of the United States, George W. Bush, declared in his speech before Congress that "our war on terror begins with Al Qaeda, but it does not end there. It will not end until every terrorist group of global reach has been found, stopped and defeated."[72]

The ultimate objective, therefore, is the total eradication of terrorist organizations. Accordingly, partially attaining this goal would not be in the nature of a victory. According to one analyst: "One must wonder whether such a war can even be won. Radical Islamist leaders, such as Osama Bin Laden and Sheik Abdel-Rahman have a widespread following and potentially huge reserves of willing martyrs at their disposal, so that for every one captured or killed, there are ten to take his place. When faced with such a dedicated adversary, the most likely outcome is a war of attrition rather than a decisive victory in the conventional military sense."[73] The war on terror is not a war against an identifiable enemy. Identifying the location of a single terrorist organization, attacking and eliminating it, is a victory in only one battle. Victory in the war is a much lengthier and more complex process.

The primary motivation for the global terrorist network is anti-Western hostility. The goal is to drive the West back and, in its place, impose an extreme and fundamentalist version of Islam as the dominant world power. The terrorists, who have complete faith in the justice of this ideology, adhere to it and are willing to sacrifice their lives for it, in the belief of a heavenly reward. The success of a single terrorist action strengthens the resolve of terrorists dispersed over the entire world and causes others who believe in the same ideology to join their ranks. "The goals of terrorism, as shown on the 11th September in the United States, are completely different from most of the successful terrorism of the 20th century. We are talking of fundamentalist Islamic elements, which see the perpetrators as part of a 'Jihad,' 'holy war'—perceived by the faithful to be a religious, global and unlimited obligation, which will continue until the entire world accepts the Muslim faith or is placed under Muslim control."[74] Such a situation raises the question whether a genuine victory over terrorism—one that will cause the phenomenon of terrorism to disappear absolutely and forever—is feasible.

Since the phenomenon of terrorism is based on faith and ideology, we can never be certain that a person, living according to his beliefs, will not decide to put his beliefs into practice by whatever means necessary to achieve that result. And while a state can take measures that will undermine the terrorists' capabilities, this can only bring about a halt in the fighting for a period; it will not be a victory in the sense of eradicating the threat of terrorism forever.

The classic way to end a war between two states is by a peace treaty, which not only puts an end to the armed dispute but also concludes the conflict as a whole and regulates the peaceful relations between the parties. A peace treaty ensures to a standard of near certainty that the objective victory in the war—defeat of the enemy—is attained. Nothing is allowed to undermine this achievement, not even the vanquished state, which has entered into the treaty and acknowledged defeat.

In a war between states and terrorist organizations, this ideal manner of ending the war, a peace treaty, is not applicable. First, in the eyes of the terrorist organization, peace is a "death blow" that will lead to its disbanding, and therefore no circumstances can exist that will cause the organization to enter into a peace treaty with its "democratic enemy" and cease fighting it. Second, a state organ that signs a peace treaty with a terrorist organization will be according recognition to that terrorist organization, an outcome that is inconceivable.

Upon the defeat of a state, there are bodies, such as the UN Security Council, which have the function of ensuring that the military forces of the other party can no longer pose a threat. Overseeing a state with geographical boundaries, whose military activities are open to view, is much easier than overseeing a terrorist organization. In addition to the geographical difficulty and the problem of multiple branches throughout the world, which are inherent to the phenomenon of terrorism, there are many other problems. The leadership of the organization is not always known, and its ability to reestablish itself, or at least to sow the seeds for future terrorist organizations, is greater than our ability to ensure that it will not do so. Our capabilities in this regard are limited and substantially different from our supervisory capacity in relation to states. The nature of a terrorist organization and the ideology on which it is built are not matters that are tangible and subject to supervision or, indeed, our intervention. Accordingly, victory over a terrorist organization does not necessarily have the meaning attributable to victory over a state organization.

In his work *Misperceiving the Terrorist Threat*, Jeffrey D. Simon refers to the phenomenon of terrorism as war and explains that it is not a war in which a victory is possible: "A U.S. war on terrorism would be a long conflict; it would also be unwinnable in the military sense, given the multitude of terrorist groups that operate throughout the world.... Terrorists can reverse any counterterrorist 'progress' or claims of 'victory' with one well-placed symbolic bomb. This is what separates a war on terrorism from all other types of conflict. The problem can then become one of an alienated American public blaming the military for 'losing' a war that never could have been won."[75] President Bush, aware of this problem yet determined to win the war against terrorism, has explained: "Americans are asking: How will we fight and win this war? We will direct every resource at our command—every means of diplomacy, every tool of intelligence, every instrument of law enforcement, every financial influence, and every necessary weapon of war—to the disruption and to the defeat of the global terror network."[76]

Victory in such a war requires a fight on numerous fronts. Besides necessary military action against the terrorists themselves, stringent diplomatic, economic, and military sanctions must be imposed on states sponsoring terrorism. Imposing and enforcing such sanctions requires exceptional cooperation between the nations of the free world. The cooperation must be based on unequivocal and unreserved agreement; the policy toward terrorism must be uncompromising and involve the termination of all governmental support and collaboration with terrorism.

International terrorism of the twenty-first century, as seen in the terrorist attacks of September 11, and the dangers entailed by biological, chemical, and atomic weapons, require the international community to cooperate at least insofar as relates to the extradition of terrorists and the enforcement of the criminal law against them. As Cherif Bassiouni writes,

> The new terrorist threats to contemporary society's wide-ranging vulnerabilities necessitate a more determined will on behalf of the international community to effectively cooperate in detecting, preventing, and deterring potential perpetrators and prosecuting and punishing those who commit such crimes. Specifically, enhanced international cooperation is needed in the areas of extradition, mutual legal assistance, transfer of criminal proceedings, transfer of prisoners, seizure and forfeiture of assets, and recognition of foreign penal judgments.[77]

Today there are a number of international conventions dealing with terrorism; the most recent is the Convention for the Suppression of

Financing of Terrorism adopted in 1999.[78] Bassiouni argues that it is necessary to consolidate all the conventions and criminal regulations concerning terrorism in a single international code:

> Multilateralism should replace the archaic, inefficient and politicized bilateralism, and all modalities of inter-state penal cooperation should be integrated. Thus, multilateral treaties and national legislation should integrate the following modalities: extradition, legal assistance, transfer of criminal proceedings, transfer of prisoners, transfer of sentences, recognition of foreign penal judgments, tracing, freezing and seizing of assets derived from criminal activity, and law-enforcement and prosecutorial cooperation.[79]

Unquestionably, it is impossible to talk of victory over terrorism without eliciting strong and genuine cooperation against the terrorist organizations, articulated in a convention of the type described and, most important, enforced in practice. Enforcing the conventions on the international plane is the only way to deny terrorists the capacity to plan their operations, gather intelligence, collect weapons, and so on. Terrorists will be precluded from implementing their beliefs, leaving the rest of the world to practice theirs, and perhaps allowing the U.S. president's promise that "we will win the war on terrorism" to be fulfilled.

Conclusion

The terrorist attack on the United States on September 11 and the declaration of war on international terrorism which followed in its wake raise many questions in relation to the lawfulness and rules of this war. In this chapter I have tried to examine whether the prevailing laws of war in international law may be interpreted in a manner that accords with modern reality, in which war is no longer confined to sovereign entities but is waged between democratic states and terrorist organizations.

In view of the special nature of the enemy—terrorists who, by definition, do not see themselves as subject to the rules of war—it is difficult to conclude that the rules as they exist today, and in particular the concept of self-defense under Article 51 of the UN Charter, provide an adequate solution to the terrorist threat. Even if we accept the interpretation of self-defense which permits a democratic state to defend itself against the terrorist threat by way of military action, numerous questions arise in relation to the rules of engagement. How will a democratic state conduct a war against an undefined enemy that is dispersed among the civilian population? Should the democratic state remain subject to the rules of war and avoid causing harm to population centers and thereby also avoid causing harm to the terrorists themselves? Or does the goal of eradicating terrorism justify all means, including collateral injury to innocent civilians, merely because the terrorists have found shelter among them?

Is it conceivable that in time of war the law falls silent? This is precisely the time when we most need the legal norms to set the boundaries for what is permissible and what is prohibited, as the president of the Supreme Court of Israel, Justice Aharon Barak, has asserted: "When the cannons roar the muses fall silent. However, even when the cannons roar, it is necessary to preserve the rule of law. A society's ability to withstand its enemies is based on its recognition that it is fighting for values worthy of protection. The rule of law is one of these values."[80] Terrorism has directed its efforts at demolishing what democratic societies have sought to build. The rule of law is a central and basic component of democratic society. Therefore, if we were to allow a democratic state in its war against terror to breach the laws of war on the grounds that the other side also breaches them, we would not thereby be helping the state to defeat its enemy; we would be helping the enemy defeat us. We would undermine the rule of law and the stability of civilized society. We would cause democratic states to lose their character. We must avoid this result at all costs.

Terrorism is an international problem that feeds on the unusual cooperation between those dealing with terrorism throughout the world. The solution too must be international, and it too must be nourished by a unique cooperation between the elements of the free world facing a terrorist threat.

As noted, the laws of war must be modified. We must formulate new laws for the war waged between democratic states and terrorist organizations. These laws will not relate to war in its traditional sense of aircraft, tank, and infantry attacks. The term "war" will be given a different meaning. The laws will have one common denominator: cooperation. The first step is to take action against those sponsoring terrorism. The laws of the new war must be shaped in such a way as to exert intense international pressure on states sponsoring terrorism to persuade them to desist.

Beyond this, we must establish a new normative framework whose purpose is to create a new world order based on justice. Innocent civilians must no longer fall victim to horrific terrorist acts while the guilty parties walk free.

A new convention should unite the nations of the free world in order to fight for the future of humanity. However, this fight cannot take the form of a military operation targeting single organizations. One or two operations cannot eradicate the phenomenon of terrorism. The fight is much more complex: it is a hybrid comprising passive and active defense measures to ward off terrorist groups. The combination of the two should have sufficient deterrent effect to eliminate the terrorist threat hanging over democratic states.

Accordingly, the new convention should reflect the combination of diverse measures available to democratic states in their fight against terrorism, and should especially include an unequivocal authorization to use defensive force in order to obstruct future attacks, cooperation between the state parties in imposing multilateral economic sanctions on every state sponsoring terrorism, and intelligence and law enforcement cooperation among the contracting parties which will lead to freezing the bank accounts of terrorist organizations and to the arrest and extradition of terrorists to the appropriate state for trial.

The United States has undertaken to lead the "war" against terror. In order to succeed in this difficult task, it is essential not only to unite the world on the ways and means of achieving this goal but also to understand the roots and rationale of this human phenomenon. Only an informed understanding of the ideological roots of terrorism and its reasons together with a united international front can lead to a change in the current situation.

THREE

Interrogation of Terrorists

THE BOUNDARIES BETWEEN PERMITTED
INTERROGATION AND FORBIDDEN TORTURE

EACH COUNTRY bears a moral and legal obligation to protect its citizens from domestic and foreign terrorist acts intended to provoke dread and fear among members of the public.

The security services fighting terrorism generally carry out their operations covertly, without unnecessarily exposing their work methods—for one reason, in order to prevent the terrorist organizations from circumventing them. However, the secrecy and dissimulation practiced by the security services also create the potential for these services to improperly exploit the powers at their disposal.

In recent decades, more and more states have suffered the heavy hand of terrorism on their own soil. Yet the many terrorist attacks that have actually been carried out are only a drop in the ocean compared to the attempted attacks and subversive operations that have been prevented by the various states in their struggle against terrorism. It is principally these states' security services that pursue the struggle against terrorism. Their function is not merely to capture the terrorists responsible for carrying out past attacks but, more important, to capture those currently involved in planning and executing attacks. One of the main tools used by these services is the interrogation of suspects with the aim of extracting information that may help frustrate future hostile activities.

Naturally, no offender is eager to impart information to his interrogators which might incriminate him. The terrorist, however, unlike an ordinary criminal, is not worried primarily about self-incrimination; his principal reason for refusing to cooperate with his interrogators is his desire not to let his capture detract from his friends' chances of carrying out their terrorist ambitions. Accordingly, conventional interrogational techniques and positive or negative incentives that might lead an ordinary offender to reveal information are not effective with regard to terrorists.

In addition, clearly one cannot attribute the same degree of importance to the interrogation of a person who is suspected will be involved in a future criminal act because of motives of greed or vengeance and the interrogation of a person who is suspected will be involved in future criminal acts for ideological reasons. A failure in the first case could result in the failure to thwart a future criminal act, whereas a failure in the second could result in failure to thwart a future terrorist attack. As explained in chapter 1, even though it is feasible that both acts—criminal and nationalist—will be equally grave (or even that the criminal act will be more grave than the nationalist), in regards the manner in which they are carried out and the harm they cause, the terrorist act will inevitably be much more serious, since the gravity of the act is measured not merely by the concrete and immediate injury to the victim but primarily by the objective it seeks to achieve and its unique characteristics.

It follows that preventing the terrorist act is more important than preventing an ordinary criminal act, so that while it is possible in the case of suspects in future crimes to accept unquestionably the absolute prohibition on interrogation techniques that entail elements of torture, there is a dispute whether this should also be the position when the suspects being interrogated are terrorists who possess information that may allow future terrorist acts to be frustrated. Whereas on one side of the balance are basic human rights and freedoms owed to the terrorist by virtue of his being a human being—rights which express the democratic state's commitment to values it holds dear and in the name of which it fights terrorism—on the other side are the peace and safety of the citizens of the state as well as the exceptional importance of preventing terrorist acts. The result is a hugely difficult moral and legal question in the fight against terrorism: What are the limits of the physical and psychological pressure that the interrogators of the security forces may exert against persons suspected of holding information regarding future hostile activities? Is there an absolute prohibition on using interrogational techniques involving torture, or can circumstances exist in which such techniques are permitted? This morally and legally complex question is the subject of the present chapter.

What Is Torture?

Before turning to an examination of permitted means of interrogation, it is necessary to consider what is meant by torture. There is no clear and unequivocal definition of this term.

An examination of the international conventions dealing with this issue reveals that there is a distinction between acts that amount to torture and acts that are in the nature of cruel, inhuman, or degrading treatment. However, there are no criteria that clarify the distinctions between these categories.[1] The UN Convention against Torture and Other Cruel, Inhuman or Degrading Treatment or Punishment, which was adopted in 1984 and entered into force in 1987, defines torture as

> any act by which severe pain or suffering, whether physical or mental, is intentionally inflicted on a person for such purposes as obtaining from him or a third person information or a confession, punishing him for an act he or a third person has committed or is suspected of having committed, or intimidating or coercing him or a third person, or for any reason based on discrimination of any kind, when such pain or suffering is inflicted by or at the instigation of or with the consent or acquiescence of a public official or other person acting in an official capacity. It does not include pain or suffering arising only from, inherent in or incidental to lawful sanctions.[2]

Torture can therefore be either physical or psychological. While physical torture consists of causing deliberate and direct physical pain, psychological or mental torture injures the soul of a person.[3]

The majority opinion in the case of *The Republic of Ireland v. The United Kingdom*, in the European Court of Human Rights, held that the difference between torture and cruel, inhuman, or degrading treatment lay in the intensity of the suffering caused.[4] Torture is the deliberate use of inhumane treatment which causes severe and cruel pain and suffering.[5] In contrast, Judge Franz Matscher, in the minority, was of the opinion that the difference between the two does not ensue from the intensity of the suffering. In his opinion, "[T]orture is in no wise inhuman treatment raised to a greater degree. On the contrary, one can think of brutality causing much more painful bodily suffering but which does not thereby necessarily fall within the concept of torture."[6] He held that the distinction between the two categories lies in the fact that torture is calculated, routine, and deliberate and causes physical or mental suffering, all for the purpose of breaking the spirit of the suspect in order either to coerce him into performing an act or to cause him pain for another reason, such as sadism per se. The judge did not reject the existence of a certain threshold, but in his opinion that was not the determinative test.[7]

A number of judges in the same case viewed the definition of torture in a different manner. Judge Zekia was of the opinion that it is necessary to examine whether torture is being practiced in particular circumstances using also a subjective and not just an objective test. Thus, in his opinion the definition of torture should take into account a number of additional criteria, such as the nature of the inhumane treatment; the means and practices entailed by it; the duration and repetitiveness of that treatment; the age, sex, and state of health of the person undergoing the treatment; and the likelihood that the treatment will cause psychological, mental, or physical pain to that person.[8] He explained his opinion with the example of "the case of an elderly sick man who is exposed to a harsh treatment—after being given several blows and beaten to the floor, is dragged and kicked on the floor for several hours. I would say without hesitation that the poor man has been tortured. If such treatment is applied to a wrestler or even a young athlete, I would hesitate a lot to describe it as an inhuman treatment and I might regard it as a mere rough handling."[9] Judge Sir Gerald Fitzmaurice in the same case held that the reason Article 3 of the European Convention would not be accorded a broad and precise interpretation was the desire to enable each case to be considered individually, on its merits, and to allow a decision to be made whether particular circumstances amounted to torture. Thus, the interpretation of this term had to be subjective. The judge pointed out that, nonetheless, there were a number of circumstances that, from an objective point of view, would always be regarded as torture, even though not all suffering was torture.[10]

The very application of the term "torture" to a particular case signifies the adoption of a negative moral stance in relation to it; in other words, it is an assertion that the particular act is prohibited. Accordingly, not every infliction of severe pain is torture; it may merely be the prohibited infliction of pain.[11]

From the foregoing it follows that the definition of the term "torture" is not unequivocal. Even those who proposed an objective test did not put forward a definitive definition. Determination was apparently left to discretion and common sense. Thus, the examples given in the judgment to illustrate the difference between "torture" and "pain and suffering" also turned to existing intuitions and did not assert clear boundaries.

Notwithstanding the lack of a clear definition, current theoretical research distinguishes among four different objectives of torture: torture for the purpose of extracting information or admissions from the suspect (interrogational torture); torture for the purpose of frightening the person, or indeed all the members of the group with which he is affiliated (known as "terrorist torture") in order to cause them to conduct themselves differently or to desist from performing a particular action; torture in order to punish a person for an act committed in the past; and torture in order to prevent a person from performing a future act.

There seems to be a general consensus on the absolute prohibition of torture for the purpose of provoking fright or as punishment, but views are divided on the question whether there may be circumstances that would permit torture for interrogational or preventive purposes.[12] The type of torture relevant to our discussion is, in practice, a combination of the last two, its purpose being to cause the suspect serious physical or mental pain in order to extract information from him which might help the security forces thwart future acts of terror.

The Defense of Necessity versus the Defense of Justification

As noted, there are a number of degrees of suffering which do not fall within the boundaries of torture, but rather within the boundaries of suffering or inhumane treatment. But in those cases where the suffering caused the suspect indeed amounts to torture, the question arises whether there are circumstances in which it may nonetheless be permitted, from both moral and legal points of view. If so, will those interrogators who have employed unacceptable interrogation techniques have a defense? What defenses?

When is Torture Morally Justified?

The very fact that the conventions referred to above do not contain any exceptions to the definition of torture—that is, that the moral obligation not to torture is absolute—does not mean that no situations exist in which one can find a balance between this obligation and another moral obligation equal to it in rank. However, if we start to qualify the absolute prohibition and draw a balance between conflicting obligations, we will detract from the significance of the absolute nature of the moral obligation.[13] But in contrast to the approach contending that moral obligations in general, and the obligation not to torture in particular, are absolute in nature, there is an approach that asserts that one should not make haste to attach the label "absolute" to moral obligations. Thus, although Kant was of the opinion that the duty to tell the truth is absolute even if a lie could save human life, Daniel Statman argues that one should not declare a moral obligation to be absolute. As he states, "It seems that with regard to the majority of the moral duties, if not all of them, we have a strong intuition that, in extreme cases, certainly where the existence of the whole world depends on this, the duties may be overridden. Lying, treason, killing innocent people—are all prohibited and abhorrent acts but in respect of each one of them it is possible to think of an imaginary case where breach of the duty is essential for such an important purpose that it amounts to a duty."[14] One situation where it may be morally possible to justify torture is the classic case of the "ticking bomb."

The "Ticking Bomb" Situation

The phrase "ticking bomb" refers to a situation where there is no other choice, in the limited period of time available and in order to prevent damage which is anticipated, for example, as a result of a bomb which has been activated, but to interrogate a suspect using torture. The premise is that the suspect is thought to know, directly or indirectly, details that may assist in preventing the damage or at least minimizing it. There are those who see justification for the use of torture in the case of a "ticking bomb" as obviously necessary.[15] This term is not unique to the nationalist criminal context but refers to all criminal situations, including, for example, the interrogation of a person who knows the hiding place of a criminal who has kidnapped someone and intends to torture and murder the victim. However, in this chapter I shall refer only to the "ticking bomb" situation in the criminal-terrorist context.

There is a problem with the definition of the term, in that it is not clear when a particular situation will qualify as a "ticking bomb." Generally there is only information about an abstract intention to lay a bomb, and it is not known whether this intention is serious or immediate. The duration of the "ticking" may theoretically be very long, and on occasion only an empty threat has been voiced. The investigators dealing with the suspect do not know for certain how much time they have to extract relevant information from him. Further, they do not know for certain what the particular suspect knows.

The necessary details generally become known only post facto; at the time of the investigation, the interrogators can only make conjectures and assumptions about the case at hand, and use their discretion to decide whether it indeed requires the adoption of measures generally prohibited from a moral point of view. Following the Oklahoma City bombing in 1995, some Americans perceive all terrorist militias, indiscriminately, as ticking time bombs.[16] Thus, there is a danger that in times of emergency or security alert, any person suspected of being a terrorist will be regarded as a "ticking bomb," without objective support. Accordingly, it is necessary to exercise caution and establish clearly and decisively the nature of the "ticking bomb" situation, as well as set clear limits to the duration of the "ticking" that would justify torture. It seems likely that a situation where a bomb may be set off after a year would not fall within this definition; however, a situation where a bomb will certainly be set off within twenty-four hours would almost certainly fall within it. It is possible to provide that, in cases of doubt, the determination whether it is permissible, in the absence of any other choice, to use torture will be subject to the review of higher-ranking authorities or the judicial system, which will make an immediate decision on the matter.[17]

A different problem relates to the rarity of "ticking bomb" situations. It is hardly ever known with great certainty whether the particular suspect being interrogated indeed possesses information that may frustrate the planned attack, or whether the attack against numerous people will indeed take place if the vital information is not extracted from the suspect. But despite the rarity of these circumstances, the appellation "ticking bomb" is attached to numerous situations that do not fall within the definition, in order to justify a particular style of interrogation.[18] By widening the terminology to situations where the danger is not certain or where there is no information that it can indeed be prevented, without any real possibility of supervising those situations where it is contended that a "ticking bomb" exists (since most of the details relating to those situations and suspects are not published and are shrouded in secrecy), there is the risk of creating a slippery slope, as well as the risk that the extraordinary situation will be divested of meaning, since all circumstances will fall within the boundaries of that definition.

An additional danger is that of falling into the trap of fixed ideas, that is, the situation in which interrogators are so convinced that the suspect holds the information they need that they lose the ability to assess contradicting indicators in an unprejudiced manner.[19] In other words, the moment the investigators decide that they are dealing with a man who possesses information that can prevent serious damage and that they have no choice but to torture him, nothing will prevent them from continuing to torture him until they are convinced that he has surrendered all the information they require. Even if he swears that he knows nothing, and this is the truth, they are not likely to believe him, and therefore they will continue to torture him fruitlessly until they are satisfied by a particular answer given to them.

Further, in order to enable justification of the torture from a moral point of view, the means of interrogation must be proportional to the situation the interrogators are trying to prevent. Thus, if there is information about the existence of a bomb that may kill many people, it may be possible morally to justify the torture of a suspect, even to the point of death, in order to prevent the deaths of those people. However, if it is known that the explosion has been laid in a derelict place where it is unreasonable to assume that any loss of life will occur, it will not be possible to justify interrogations involving torture to the point of death.

Justification for torturing the suspect will also increase the greater and more direct the suspect's responsibility for the crime that is about to be committed. If, for example, the suspect only incidentally heard details of the crime and was threatened with death if he disclosed those details, there is little justification for interrogating him using torture. Another aspect of that justification is that it is solely up to the suspect himself to end the torture applied during his interrogation. If he delivers up the information he had hoped to conceal, there is an assumption that his torture will be terminated.[20]

According to the utilitarian moral approach, in order to preserve the maximum general good of society, the interrogator will on occasion also have to breach values that he regards as right. Michael S. Moore, who believes that it is forbidden to torture or harm innocents, even if the result of that activity is the saving of other lives,[21] points out that the proponents of the theory of utilitarianism will never be consistent in preserving a rule such as "never torture an innocent child." This moral tenet, in his view, has a place in academic debate but not as a rule of life, because of the drawbacks of this approach in certain circumstances:

> If the rightness of action is ultimately a function of achieving the maximally good consequences available to the agent in that situation— which is what *any* consequentialist believes—then sometimes an agent ought to violate what he himself admits is the right rule. Suppose, for example, a GSS [the Israeli General Security Service] interrogator was certain about the immediately relevant facts . . . —he knows there is a bomb, that it will kill innocents unless found and dismantled, that the only way to find it is to torture the child of the terrorist who planted it. Suppose further he is already in possession of this information, and the costs of calculating utility are thus already "sunk"; suppose further that he himself is about to die and that he can keep his action secret, so that the long-term bad consequences stemming from his own or other's corruption of character will be minimal. In such a case, adhering to the best rule will not be best, on consequentialist ground.[22]

Moore poses the example of the torture of a family member of the terrorist, in particular torture of his child, in order to break the terrorist and cause him to disclose information in relation to the terrorist activity thereby preventing harm to many others. He indicates that if one continues with the line of thought of the pure theory of utilitarianism, then in such a situation, according to that theory, one is not entitled but actually obliged to torture the child. However, in Moore's view, it is wrong to justify the torture of an innocent child, even if that torture would lead to favorable results, such as the saving of other innocent lives.[23]

Necessity or Justification?

On May 31, 1987, the government of Israel decided, in consequence of two cases, to establish a commission of inquiry to examine the methods used by the GSS at times of terrorist activity. The first case concerned Izat Nafsu, a lieutenant in the Israeli Defense Forces who was accused of treason and espionage and was convicted on the basis of his confession, obtained by GSS investigators. Following his conviction, he contended that his confession had been coerced through torture. The second case related to the incident known as the Bus 300 affair. In that incident a bus was hijacked by terrorists. GSS agents gained control of the bus and were seen to capture two terrorists alive. Some time later it was announced that these terrorists had been killed. How did these terrorists die, if they were captured alive?

Because this was an issue of such great public importance, a commission of inquiry was established under the chairmanship of a former president of the Supreme Court, Justice Moshe Landau, charged with examining the investigative procedures of the GSS in cases of terrorist activities, and the related matter of giving false testimony in court about these investigations. The commission held forty-three hearings during which it examined forty-two witnesses, including prime ministers; GSS personnel, from the heads of the service to field officers; members of the legal, civilian, and military services; and other public servants. Similarly, experts in different fields were examined, as were persons who had been investigated by GSS interrogators. The commission also visited GSS interrogation centers.[24] One of the conclusions of the commission was that even if the interrogation methods of the GSS interrogators entailed torture, those interrogators could avail themselves of the criminal law defense of necessity.[25] This determination has been the subject of extensive criticism.

The Defense of Necessity

During the process of enacting any law, and in particular a criminal law, it is not possible to predict all the situations in which a breach of the law might be justified, since every punitive norm represents the typical abstract situation it is intended to prevent. As a result, the law contains a number of defenses, such as the defense of necessity, which allow a person to be discharged from criminal liability in cases where he has committed an offense but there are strong moral and social justifications for performing the act.

The uniqueness of the defense of necessity ensues from its amorphousness and broadness in relation to the question of when it will be justified to breach the law, thus making the defense compatible with the concept underlying it—taking the best possible step in the circumstances of the case.[26] The defense of necessity is applicable when a situation is forced on a person whereby, in order to prevent a real danger, his only recourse is to impair the protected interest of another—subject to the condition that there is no other way of preventing that danger and that the preventative measure causes less damage than the act prevented. This is the concept underlying the defense: enabling the prevention of a great wrong by performing a lesser wrong.

With regard to the level of difference required between the wrong preferred and the wrong to be prevented, there are two basic approaches. One requires a *clear* difference. The logic behind this demand is to reduce mistakes in the choice. In other words, since the defense relates to emergency situations that have not been foreseen or are unclear, it is desirable to prevent the possibility of an error being made when balancing the alternatives (i.e., the act to be prevented vis-à-vis the act to be performed). The second approach demands a *great* difference. The rationale behind this demand relates to the typical situation giving rise to the defense. If there is a great discrepancy between the act to be prevented (e.g., the killing of a large number of people) compared to the prohibited act (e.g., damage to property), it is clear that we would want to apply the defense. However, if the rationale behind the defense is the prevention of mistakes, we would also want the defense to apply in a situation where the discrepancy is clear but is not necessarily great.[27]

In the past there was no requirement that the emergency situation be imminent for a defense of necessity. The commission's final report (the Landau report), too, stated that there was no need whatsoever for the requirement of imminence in terms of the defense of necessity, a statement that has given rise to extensive criticism. To illustrate its contention, the commission put forward an example given by Paul H. Robinson in his monograph on criminal law defenses. The example involves a ship with a small hole in its hull. The ship is still safely anchored at harbor when the small hole is discovered. Accordingly, the commission contended, the situation is not one of imminent danger; moreover, the hole is a small one. Imminent danger will arise only in the open sea, but then it will be too late to take action and the ship will sink. Therefore, the preventative step must be taken while the vessel is still at port, when the danger is not yet imminent.[28] S. Z. Feller disputes the commission's determination, stating: "Every drop of water that enters the ship's hull at the beginning forms part of the flood that will capsize her in the end; the water's 'attack' begins with the very first drop. . . . Every advance out to sea takes time and retreat to shore will require at least equal time, if not more. . . . There is no better example than this to demonstrate and define the 'immediacy' condition inherent to 'necessity.'"[29]

In the case of the "ticking bomb" as well, there is an element of imminence, and the interrogator may have available to him the defense of necessity, whether the timer is set for an hour later or a day later. So long as the interrogator does not know with certainty how much time he has at his disposal to neutralize the bomb, he must act as if the danger will come to pass at any moment. Today, the requirement of imminence has been incorporated into the law itself.

The Defense of Justification

In contrast to the defense of necessity, which applies to situations that cannot be anticipated in advance, the defense of justification is available when a person acts in a manner contrary to the provisions of the penal code, but he does so for some justified reason given to him before the commission of the offense. Such justification can be, for example, a statutory provision, or a provision in a statutory regulation.[30] The rationale behind this defense is to enable people to act in accordance with the provisions of various laws, the implementation of which they oversee, or, in certain cases which may be anticipated, without fear that they will be put on trial for such activity. Thus, a predetermined defense is given to a certain act that is deemed to be worthwhile and beneficial to society, since it is considered desirable for people not to fear to perform it. In the case of justification, certain advance authorization is given to take a particular action in particular circumstances; in contrast, in the case of necessity, the situation is not anticipated in advance, and it is only possible retroactively to authorize the action taken. The defense of justification will apply if other conditions of the law have been met, whereas the defense of necessity will apply if the conditions of the defense itself have been met. The defense of justification ensues from the provisions of existing law, whereas the defense of necessity ensues from given facts, which are not preestablished.

Which is More Appropriate, Necessity or Justification?

Following a finding that torture had been employed during GSS interrogations, the Landau report recognized the defense of necessity as an appropriate defense for GSS interrogators. However, is it actually the defense of necessity that is appropriate in this situation? The answer seems to be—not inevitably.

The commission itself called for the enactment of legislation that would authorize and justify the activities of the GSS in general, and the form of interrogations by the GSS in particular. Reference here is to recurrent and foreseeable situations. Accordingly, in practice, the most appropriate defense in these cases is not the defense of necessity, as was asserted, but rather the defense of justification. Since it is possible to foresee a broad range of possible situations that may arise during the course of interrogations, it is possible to reduce them to writing and subject them to a particular standard, which will determine when the defense will arise. In contrast, necessity is not given to standardization, as the situations falling within this category cannot be foreseen.[31]

A criminal defense that is available to every citizen, including public servants, cannot also provide a source of authorization for certain activities. Thus, only when a person is subject to the pressure of the moment, without prior preparation for the situation he has encountered, is he likely to act out of necessity otherwise than in accordance with the law—in order, for example, to save a number of people. The position is different if the same person attempts to act in a situation that could have been foreseen, relying on authorization available to him by virtue of the defense of necessity. The defense of necessity was not created for these situations. The defense of necessity is tested in the light of a particular situation, whereas an empowering statute confers authorization to act in advance and not retroactively. In addition, the power is granted for a general and not a particular situation. An additional danger inherent in the defense of necessity ensues from the lack of clarity as to when a situation is in the nature of a "necessity." Every interrogator will interpret "necessity" in a different manner, and this lack of uniformity is also problematic. In a democratic state where the rule of law prevails, and within the principle of legality, it is necessary to specify clearly in statute the boundaries of individual rights that the government should not infringe.

If it is desired to enable certain exceptions that would make possible the infringement of individual rights, then these too must be prescribed by statute, as must be the identity of those entitled to infringe them.[32]

The contentions raised against statutory regulation of the activities of the GSS, in order that the defense of justification become available to the interrogators, include, inter alia, the contention that in order to preserve the effectiveness of the interrogation it is necessary to maintain the element of uncertainty. Among the factors influencing the suspect being interrogated is his lack of knowledge of the boundaries of the interrogation and what he may expect as it proceeds. But if these matters become entrenched in a public law or even in privileged internal guidelines, it will not be difficult for terrorist organizations to identify the limits of the interrogational pressure to which their members would be exposed upon capture (one way would be by debriefing persons interrogated and subsequently released). This would allow them to prepare and anticipate future actions and would lead the element of fear and uncertainty to disappear. If the suspect does not know whether the next stage of the interrogation will be more painful, it is likely that he will break earlier. In contrast, if no predetermined definition exists as to what is deemed to amount to moderate physical pressure, the danger of the slippery slope again arises. Interrogators are likely to regard every interrogatory measure as a measure falling within this definition.

In choosing one of these two possibilities, Feller has commented:

> The necessary conclusion is that we must choose between two alternatives: either to *prohibit any pressure,* as moderate pressure confined to present limits cannot be effective, or to *permit, by law, the use of unlimited pressure to an extent not formally predetermined* as shall be necessary to break the suspect and cause him to divulge the information sought; the only limit being that beyond which no suspect remains, physically or psychologically, to be interrogated. Only pressure thus limited, or more precisely, only pressure not formally limited can be effective.
> In our opinion . . . the first is absolutely preferable.[33]

To present the full picture, it should be pointed out that, countering the contention that interrogations are not foreseeable, it is possible to document them to some extent. Today, many interrogation practices are known, whether because they are documented in the case law itself or because they are attested to by persons who were subjected to interrogations. Further, persons who have been interrogated once are likely to be interrogated again, so that they will know more or less what is in store for them, and will know how to prepare mentally for the interrogation. Accordingly, the contention that it is necessary to preserve the secrecy of interrogation practices so that the suspects will not know where they stand and what they may expect is partially weakened.

An additional ground for asserting that there is no room for statutory regulation of interrogation practices is that whereas possibly, from a moral point of view, there are circumstances in which use can be made of extreme measures against a person, it is not customary for a democratic state to proclaim the same in a statute. The legal scholar Sanford H. Kadish has pointed out, "While it is morally permissible to use cruel measures against a person if the gains in moral goods are great enough, it is not acceptable for the state to proclaim this in its law."[34] In his view, it is wrong to declare in a law that a state is permitted to make use of cruel measures under certain conditions. A single interrogator, on the other hand, may decide, as an individual, to make use of these measures, a decision that may later be held to be justified from a moral point of view.[35]

In addition, even if there is a statutory provision prohibiting the use of cruel measures under any conditions, the interrogator will still retain discretion, according to the approach of utilitarian morality, whether or not to use them.[36] Thus, a statute that prohibits the use of these measures will in practice raise a greater obstacle against which each situation will be tested, but it will not completely prohibit the use of these measures. In contrast, a statute that permits the use of these measures in particular circumstances will fail to educate people to follow a desirable morally conscientious line, and the hoped-for result will not be achieved. Legislation that permits the adoption of these tactics and regulates the answers to such questions as, in which situations is it permitted to make use of these measures? for how long is it possible to deprive a person of sleep? will only lead to a worsening of the existing situation, such as occurred in the Middle Ages, when torture was regulated by law.[37]

The state cannot justify the activities of the GSS and enable a person to be injured in order to achieve social good. Such an outcome is not consistent with the respect that a state accords human rights. In opposition, the view has been voiced that the power to authorize this form of conduct in interrogations should not be left in the hands of individual interrogators, but rather these decisions should be directed to and addressed by an authorized body—a body such as a security committee.

Further, following the Landau report, which authorized the use of moderate physical pressure on suspects, criticism was raised that this determination turned the suspect into a mere object containing information. A suspect subject to interrogation before the report was issued was subject to physical pressure and was powerless and defenseless in the face of the force exerted by his interrogators. From the moment this situation was given normative backing by the commission, the suspect would feel even more powerless, since the law, which generally safeguarded and granted strong protection to the rights of the individual, would no longer be available to him. Thus, the commission unknowingly created a form of "law" authorizing torture, contrary to its primary intention—the prevention of torture. There is another possible danger ensuing from the authorization of moderate physical pressure. Psychologically, lowering the threshold slightly may lead to its complete disappearance—the danger of the slippery slope. Moreover, a situation may arise in which the development of sophisticated investigative methods will be brushed aside, to the extent that the use of force becomes a legitimate and acceptable work practice. This criticism will become even more valid if legislation is enacted that permits this GSS activity.

Until the enactment of a possible law, which will only see the light after public debates in which diverse views can be exchanged, interrogators must receive separate authorization for each activity from those overseeing them. In this way, in practice the defense of justification will be available to them, whether through an order of their superiors or as a matter of statutory authorization. Currently, no express written provision exists that permits the torture of a suspect under certain conditions. In contrast, the defense of necessity is not available in interrogations that have been conducted in routine situations where a suspect refuses to cooperate in an amicable manner.[38] These factors are contrary to the situation where the defense of necessity arises, as explained above.

Recently, this issue was discussed in the GSS interrogation case, where it was stated:

> General directives governing the use of physical means during interrogations must be rooted in an authorization prescribed by law and not in defenses to criminal liability. The principle of "necessity" cannot serve as a basis of authority. . . . If the state wishes to enable GSS investigators to utilize physical means in interrogations, it must enact legislation for this purpose. This authorization would also free the investigator applying the physical means from criminal liability. *This release would not flow from the "necessity defense," but rather from the "justification" defense.* . . . The "necessity" defense cannot constitute the

basis for rules regarding an interrogation. It cannot constitute a source of authority which the individual investigator can rely on for the purpose of applying physical means in an investigation.[39]

One of the judges in this case, Justice Yaakov Kedmi, proposed that the effectiveness of the judgment be deferred for a year, in order to enable the state to adapt to the new state of affairs established by the court, and out of a desire to ensure that in a genuine case of a "ticking bomb" the state would be able to cope. During the course of the proposed year, GSS interrogators would be prohibited from utilizing extraordinary interrogation methods except in rare cases of suspects defined as "ticking bombs," and even then it would be necessary to obtain the express consent of the attorney general.[40]

The Process of Interrogation: Permitted and Prohibited Practices

Israel

An investigation, by its very nature, places the suspect in a strenuous position. Every investigation is a "battle of wits" in which the investigator attempts to uncover the greatest number of details about the suspect. Not all measures are legitimate in this battle. It is necessary to determine which investigative procedures are permitted and which prohibited. In crystallizing the rules of investigation, a balance must be drawn between two interests. On one side lies the public interest in uncovering the truth by exposing offenses and preventing them; on the other is the wish to protect the dignity and liberty of the suspect. Indeed, a "democratic, freedom-loving society does not accept that investigators may use any means for the purpose of uncovering the truth. . . . To the same extent, however, a democratic society, desirous of liberty, seeks to fight crime and, to that end, is prepared to accept that an interrogation may infringe upon the human dignity and liberty of a suspect provided that it is done for a proper purpose and that the harm does not exceed that which is necessary."[41]

In addition to the conditions of imprisonment and detention, which themselves have an enormous impact on the mental state of the suspect, during the course of interrogation of a person suspected of terrorist activities, the GSS on occasion uses of interrogation methods that have recently been held by the High Court of Justice to be prohibited.[42] These methods of interrogation include a number of techniques.[43] The first is the practice known as "Shabach," described as follows:

"Shabach" is a combination of means of sense deprivation, pain and sleep deprivation, which are conducted over a long period of time. "Regular Shabach" includes tightly cuffing the hands and legs of the suspect while he is seated on a small and low chair, whose seat is tilted forward, towards the ground, so that the suspect's seat is not stable. The suspect's head is covered by a sack, which is generally opaque, and powerful loud music is played ceaselessly, through loudspeakers. The suspect is not allowed to sleep throughout the course of the "Shabach." The sleep deprivation is carried out through the above measures, as well as in an active manner, with the guards shaking all who try to doze.[44]

There are variations of the "Shabach" position. In one, known as the "freezer," an air conditioner blows cold air directly on to the suspect, generally while he is in the interrogation room. Another variation is "standing Shabach," in which the suspect stands with his hands cuffed to a pipe attached to the wall behind him; the pipe is either on the same level as his hands or his hands are pulled upward and his body inclined forward.

The second method is essentially psychological. During the interrogation the interrogators curse and threaten the suspect. The threats include threats of murder, with the ability to kill illustrated by references to persons who were killed while in detention or under interrogation; threats are also directed at members of the suspect's family.

The third method, known as "Kasa'at a-tawlah," uses a table and direct pressure to painfully stretch the suspect's body:

> The measure, which combines a painful posture and application of direct violence by the interrogator, is practiced during the interrogation itself. The interrogator forces the suspect to crouch or to sit (on the floor or on the "Shabach" chair) in front of a table, with the back of the suspect to the table. The interrogator places the arms of the suspect, cuffed and stretched backwards, on the table . . . part of the time, the interrogator sits on the table, trampling with his feet on the shoulders of the suspect and pushing him forwards, so that his arms are stretched even further backwards, or he pulls the legs of the suspect, and thereby achieves the same effect.[45]

Another method is the "frog crouch." The suspect is forced to crouch on tiptoe, with his hands tied behind his back. If he falls or tries to sit, he is forced to resume his crouching position.

A fifth method applied during interrogations takes the form of violent shaking. The interrogator holds the suspect, either seated or standing, by the edges of his clothes and shakes him violently, his fists striking the suspect's chest. The suspect's head is thrown backward and forward. This direct violence may lead to death.

A sixth interrogational method involves the use of various violent practices, including slapping, hitting, kicking, and ratcheting up handcuffs. These methods are generally accompanied by measures, not directly physical, which are intended primarily to increase the impact of the violent techniques. These include depriving the suspect of sleep, washing, and food and drink for long periods of time, or locking him up in a small cell in which he cannot lie down or stand, in full darkness, without ventilation. From time to time, the above methods are renewed and changed.

The state attempted to contend that some of the practices described above were necessary in the circumstances and were not designed to torture or cause suffering to the suspect. The "Shabach" position, it asserted, was an integral part of the interrogation itself and was carried out in order to ensure the safety of the interrogation facility, and to prevent the suspect from attacking the interrogators, as had happened in the past. The sealed sack was intended to prevent him from making eye contact with his interrogators or with other people in the interrogation facility, including other detainees, for fear that identification would impair the interrogations and cause other security damage. Shackling with handcuffs was for the security of the interrogators. Isolating the suspects and playing loud music was not done out of a desire to ill-treat the suspect but to prevent any possibility of communication between various suspects, which could endanger the success of the interrogation. Sleep deprivation was required, according to the state, because of the need for intensive interrogation and for no other reason.[46]

Until the judgment in the GSS interrogation case in September 1999, the court had refrained from making decisions of principle on such issues. Rather, it had judged each case on its merits, leaving the decisions of principle to be decided at a later stage. The rule in the GSS judgment, however, prohibited torture or degrading treatment during interrogations. In addition, the court held that, for the purpose of conducting investigations, GSS interrogators possessed the same powers as police officers and enjoyed no additional special powers:

> [A] reasonable investigation is necessarily one free of torture, free of cruel, inhuman treatment, and free of any degrading conduct whatsoever. There is a prohibition on the use of "brutal or inhuman means"

in the course of an investigation. . . . Human dignity also includes the dignity of the suspect being interrogated. . . . This conclusion is in accord with international treaties to which Israel is a signatory, which prohibit the use of torture, "cruel, inhuman treatment" and "degrading treatment." . . . These prohibitions are "absolute." There are no "exceptions" to them and there is no room for balancing.[47]

The court was willing to partially accept the explanations proffered by the state for the rationale underlying these methods of interrogation, but not the explanations in their entirety.[48] Thus, sitting is indeed an integral part of interrogation, but not sitting in the "Shabach" position on a low chair inclined forward for long hours. Merely sitting on a low chair could perhaps have been seen as a legitimate part of the power play involved in interrogation, that is, the imposition of legitimate psychological pressure on the suspect. However, inclining the chair was an unfair and unreasonable interrogation method. This measure injured the bodily integrity, rights, and dignity of the suspect beyond what was necessary. The contention that blindfolding was required for security reasons, to prevent eye contact, could have been accepted had it been a matter of blindfolding only, and not a long sack down to the suspect's shoulders, which made breathing difficult. Such a measure, even if a better ventilated sack is used, is not an integral part of the interrogation. Similarly, handcuffing for protection is acceptable, but not handcuffing to cause additional pain and suffering to the suspect by excessive tightening. Playing loud music with the intention of causing the isolation of the suspect is not legitimate, since very loud music for long periods of time also causes undue suffering. Depriving the suspect of sleep is within the power of the interrogators. A person undergoing investigation cannot sleep in the same manner as a person not being investigated. However, sleep deprivation with the intention of breaking the suspect's spirit is not a fair and reasonable use of this measure; it impairs the dignity and rights of the suspect beyond what is necessary. Accordingly, use of all the measures referred to above was prohibited so long as the intention was to break the suspect by degrading him or infringing his rights.

The GSS refrains from fully documenting its interrogations. The interrogators maintain a "memo book" in which they record the course of the interrogation. These writings only contain general information relating to the conditions in which the suspect is held. There, one may learn of interrogation schedules, eating schedules, and so on, but the memo books do not document the means employed against the suspect during the course of the interrogation itself and during the waiting period. Thus, an attempt to reconstruct the course of the interrogation itself is difficult and complex, and it is necessary to rely on "subjective evidence," namely, a the suspect's description of the situation versus that of the interrogator.

Those asserting that GSS methods must be permitted contend that the only way to safeguard the security of the state is to extract essential information from suspects. Only in this way is it possible to prevent the various types of terrorist attacks and activities. The extraction of this essential information is only possible through the use of these techniques entailing the use of physical pressure. Similarly, following the High Court of Justice case that held that these investigation methods were prohibited, security officials stated that this decision would prevent them from conducting their work efficiently, since they had been left without efficient investigative methods for preventing future terrorist attacks. In the opposing camp, there are those who contend that until this decision was delivered, the GSS had focused on the impact of interrogation measures and not on applying clever and sophisticated tactics. There were numerous legal ways of achieving the information that the GSS was accustomed to obtaining by causing suffering to suspects, and the judgment did not prevent the efficient handling of terrorist threats but only compelled the interrogators to act in legal ways, which might be more complicated to implement but which were certainly more consistent with the activities of a democratic regime that aspired to protect human rights.

The United Kingdom

Investigations conducted by the security services in the United Kingdom are not very different from those carried out in Israel. In consequence of the increase in the number of terrorist attacks committed by the Irish Republican Army (IRA) in the beginning of the 1970s, which caused the death of hundreds and the injury of thousands more, persons suspected of involvement in the activities of the organization were interrogated with the help of extraordinary investigative measures. As a result, a complaint was filed against the United Kingdom in the European Court of Human Rights.

The ensuing judgment dealt with five investigative measures, which were termed "the five techniques." A description of these methods appears in the judgment of the European Court:

(a) *wall-standing*: forcing the detainee to remain for periods of hours in a "stress position," described by those who underwent it as being "spread-eagled against the wall, with their fingers put high above the head against the wall, the legs spread apart and the feet back, causing them to stand on their toes with the weight of the body mainly on the fingers";

(b) *hooding:* putting a black or navy colored bag over the detainees' heads and, at least initially, keeping it there all the time except during interrogation;

(c) *subjection to noise:* pending their interrogations, holding the detainees in a room where there was a continuous loud and hissing noise;

(d) *deprivation of sleep:* pending their interrogations, depriving the detainees of sleep;

(e) *deprivation of food and drink:* subjecting the detainees to reduced diet during their stay at the centre and pending interrogations.[49]

The investigators of the Royal Ulster Constabulary (RUC) were taught these interrogation methods as part of their training in a seminar conducted in 1971. In a commission chaired by Sir Edmond Compton, appointed in 1971, it was found that these techniques entailed an improper use of investigative powers but that they were not brutal. This conclusion drew sharp criticism, and it was decided to set up a new commission, chaired by Lord Parker of Waddington. This second commission issued its report in 1972. The majority opinion found that it was not necessary to "rule out" the implementation of these techniques on moral grounds. However, Lord Gardiner, who represented the minority opinion, asserted that, from a moral point of view, even in "emergency terrorist situations" these interrogation methods were not justified. Both majority and minority views held that the techniques were illegal in terms of domestic law prevailing at the time. Concurrently with the publication of the report, the former prime minister declared in Parliament that no further use would be made of these techniques in security service interrogations.[50]

The interrogators who applied these interrogation techniques were not subjected to disciplinary trials or criminal proceedings, and indeed no steps were taken against them whatsoever. Special guidelines setting out appropriate measures for use by RUC interrogators were not available until 1972, when the Parker commission report was issued. Initially, ordinary directives provided that humane treatment had to be meted out and that violence should not be used. In consequence of the Parker commission report, the five techniques were specifically prohibited, and the security service was required to maintain medical files for the suspects and immediately report complaints of ill-treatment. In April 1972 army instructions in the form of RUC Force Order 64/72 were issued prohibiting the use of massive force in all circumstances. The instructions clearly prohibited inhumane conduct, violence, use of the five techniques, threats, and insults. The crown prosecutor also took care to clarify that anyone infringing the prohibition in the order would be subject to prosecution. In 1973 new regulations in relation to detention by the army emphasized the need for appropriate conduct.[51]

By majority opinion the European Court held that while the majority of the articles of the European Convention for the Protection of Human Rights and Fundamental Freedoms of 1950 are not absolute and exceptions exist, Article 3 of the convention, which prohibits torture and inhuman and degrading treatment, leaves no room for exceptions even in cases of emergency where there is a danger to the security of the state. With regard to the inhuman treatment referred to in Article 3, it was held that there is a certain minimum level of conduct which must not be passed, and beyond which the conduct will fall within the definition of inhuman treatment. This minimum level is relative and is determined by the length of time involved, circumstances of the case, physical and mental repercussions, and on occasion even the gender of the suspect, age, state of health, and the like. The court held that whereas the five techniques detailed above are regarded as inhuman treatment included in Article 3 of the 1950 convention, they are not in the nature of torture, in light of the distinction between the term "torture" and the term "inhuman treatment."[52]

Opposing this view, the minority judge Sir Gerald Fitzmaurice held that the five techniques did not even fall within the definition of "inhuman treatment":

> To many people, several of the techniques would not cause "suffering" properly so called at all, and certainly not "intense" suffering. Even the wall-standing would give rise to something more in the nature of strain, aches, and pains. . . . The sort of epithets that would in my view be justified to describe the treatment involved . . . would be "unpleasant," "harsh," "tough," "severe" and others of that order, but to call it "barbarous," "savage," "brutal" or "cruel," which is the least that is necessary if the notion of the inhuman is to be attained . . . should be kept for much worse things.[53]

A fortiori, in his view, the techniques could not be classified as torture. If the five techniques were to be classified as torture, he noted, he would not know how to classify such acts as extracting nails or propelling a stick into the suspect's rectum. Would they be classified only as torture, equivalent to the five techniques, or as more serious torture than the latter?[54]

In contrast, the minority judge Evrigenis was of the opinion that the five techniques were not in the nature of inhuman acts but amounted to torture proper. In his view, if the court failed to hold these acts to be torture, it would miss the purpose and language of the article and deprive the 1950 convention of meaning.[55]

In conclusion, sixteen judges against one reached the conclusion that the five techniques reached the degree of inhuman or degrading treatment. Thirteen judges to four held that these five techniques did not amount to torture.[56] Unanimously, it was decided that it was not within the jurisdiction of the European Court of Human Rights to order the United Kingdom to institute criminal or disciplinary proceedings against security service investigators who infringed the provisions of Article 3 of the convention.[57]

Members of the security services can indeed justify their activities, as mentioned above, by relying on one of the criminal law defenses; however, the very fact that a person is suspected of being connected to terrorist activities does not by itself confer the right to use deadly force against him.

There are a number of common denominators between the situations prevailing in the United Kingdom and in Israel, although there are also a number of distinctions. The British methods of interrogation, insofar as they are known by virtue of the judgment of the European Court of Human Rights, did not include direct physical violence such as violent shaking or unnecessary tightening of handcuffs. Another difference is the length and persistence of the use of unusual interrogation methods. While the British techniques were applied for four to five days, the GSS measures could continue for a number of weeks. Similarly, the wall-standing technique in the United Kingdom was applied for thirty hours at the most, with occasional rest breaks, whereas it was argued that on occasion the GSS implemented its painful measures for as long as sixty hours, without breaks. The British sleep deprivation technique was carried out for a period of up to four to five days with breaks, whereas the GSS prevented the suspect from sleeping for longer periods.

Terrorism did not end in the United Kingdom in the 1970s. However, since then continuous improvement has taken place in the respect shown for the rights of persons suspected of involvement in terrorist activities. In light of the recommendations of a commission chaired by Lord Bennet, the right of a person suspected of terrorist activities to meet his attorney within forty-eight hours of his detention has been anchored in statute. Similarly, interrogations are documented on video, and consequently there has been a decline in the number of complaints by detainees of cruelty and torture. In 1992 a senior lawyer was ap- pointed on behalf of the state as an external ombudsman for the prison and interrogation facilities. He was given the power to conduct surprise visits in these facilities and to be present during interrogations of sus- pects and to interview them about the conditions of their detention and the interrogations they were subjected to. In 1998 video cameras were introduced into three interrogation facilities in Northern Ireland.[58]

In contrast, there have been cases where persons remained in cus- tody for seven days—the period permitted under the old law without being required to bring the detainee before a judge—even though they were known to be innocent. The investigators were aware that there was no new information these people could disclose; however, they pre- ferred to draw out the interrogation to the end. In addition, the fear felt by suspects, deriving from the very fact of their detention and condi- tions of confinement, is exploited by the interrogators. It is also known that, in general, suspects are prevented from having access to attorneys. Transferring suspects from one police station to another in order to prevent them from identifying their location and thereby undermining their self-confidence is an accepted practice. There is also evidence that various interrogation techniques are used, such as dirty cells and sleep deprivation, in order to humiliate the suspects and break their spirit. Testimony also exists relating to the use of physical force during the interrogation of persons suspected of terrorist activities,[59] although this has not been proven.

In contrast, according to the report of the European Commission for the Prevention of Terrorism, which visited the United Kingdom in 1994, there were no accounts of cases of torture and almost no accounts of cases of brutality directed against persons arrested and interrogated.[60] Accordingly, it is perhaps possible to conclude that interrogation prac- tices degrading and torturing suspects have lessened since the 1970s. After September 11, 2001, however, the United Kingdom's approach toward the issue has become somewhat ambiguous. In August 2004 the UK Court of Appeal held in a majority opinion that evidence obtained through torture outside the United Kingdom by agencies of third coun- tries may be used to indefinitely detain foreign terrorist suspects in the United Kingdom under Part 4 of the Anti-terrorism, Crime and Secu- rity Act (ATCSA), 2001, provided that the British government has neither procured the torture nor connived at it.[61] In December 2005, this ruling was reversed by the House of Lords, which, in light of the imperative not to countenance the use of torture, stated that no court in England should admit any evidence that was extracted by torture, regardless of the place it was obtained.[62]

Part 4 of the ATCSA has been replaced by the Prevention of Terrorism Act, 2005, which imposes more-severe restrictions on detention without trial of suspected terrorists.[63] However, Britain's position in this matter remains problematical. Following the atrocities of September 11, the United States engaged in a controversial practice of extra-legal renditions—that is, the transfer of suspected terrorists (without going through formal extradition proceedings) to countries that abide by lesser interrogational restraints, with the intent to use the products of the investigations. Britain's cooperation with this practice has been ambiguous. On the one hand, the British government emphasized that it does not condone the use of torture by third parties, while on the other hand, detainees, defense attorneys, and human rights activists have argued that the British government knew about the renditions of suspected terrorists who resided in Britain by the United States authorities to countries with records of practicing torture, but did nothing to prevent it.[64]

It should be stressed that the practice of renditions employed by the United States, as well as the alleged passive cooperation by the British government, should constitute a practice as equally abhorrent as direct torture. From the moral and legal point of view, there is no difference between a country that employs interrogational techniques that amount to torture and a country that prima facie abides by the norms that prohibit torture but in fact enables the torture and enjoys its products.

The United States

In contrast to the extensive description of the variety of interrogational techniques applied to terrorists in the United Kingdom, there is no similar description available in the United States.

The prohibition on torture is entrenched in the Eighth Amendment to the Constitution, which prohibits the infliction of "cruel and unusual punishments." This prohibition originates in the historical perception of the drafters of the Constitution that a democratic society aspiring to safeguard the values it holds supreme cannot permit itself to punish the perpetrators of even the most heinous crimes in ways that amount to torture.[65] At the same time, the Eighth Amendment—as interpreted in the judgments of the Supreme Court—only spreads its net over punishments imposed in criminal proceedings and does not apply to situations in which punishment is used to extract information from a suspect concerning crimes to be committed in the future.[66]

The United States also contends with extensive terrorist activities. However, the FBI does not have the authority to apply physical pressure during interrogations of persons suspected of terrorist activities, or to deprive the suspect of his right to meet an attorney. Thus, even at the time of the bombing in Oklahoma in 1995, when Timothy McVeigh was caught and it was suspected that he had accomplices, no physical pressure whatsoever was applied to him, and none of the techniques referred to above was used on him. Moreover, after his arrest he was permitted to meet his attorney, and that attorney was present during each interrogation session. A retired senior FBI official has asserted that the GSS interrogation methods are in effect a shortcut. In his view, it is not a smart move to bring a person to interrogation and try to extract information from him with blows. The smarter step is find information through sophisticated methods—laboratory work, eavesdropping, surveillance, advanced technology, and infrared cameras. In most cases, he says, the GSS does not obtain usable or credible information by the use of violent interrogation methods.[67]

The power of the FBI is derived from the power of the attorney general to appoint people to investigate crimes committed against the United States, to help safeguard the president, and to conduct investigations concerning official matters under the supervision of the Justice Ministry and the State Department.[68] Often in the past, when the FBI implemented its wide powers, injustice was committed on the grounds of state security. Ultimately, in 1976, when this injustice was acknowledged, internal security guidelines were set for the FBI which provided particular standards and investigation procedures to prevent infringements of the rights of innocent persons. These guidelines were revised in 1983.[69] The guidelines circumscribe the boundaries of activities of the FBI, but they are not binding in court. Although these general guidelines do not have direct legal ramifications, they have a central function in protecting the constitutional rights of the citizen in the face of improper state investigations.

Some of the guidelines have not been publicized but remain under wraps. For example, the guidelines concerning how to investigate international terrorist activities have been kept secret. Executive Order 12,333 empowers the FBI to investigate such terrorist activities under the terms of these secret guidelines.[70] According to the guidelines, it is permitted to initiate an investigation on the basis of a person's words or declarations alone where these create a reasonable fear that the persons uttering them are involved or connected in some way to terrorist activity. Likewise, where there is reasonable cause for believing that two or more people have organized a group with the aim of achieving a political purpose in a manner that will breach the criminal law or make use of violence, it is possible to open a security or terrorist investigation against them.[71]

In order to open a full investigation, which can continue for a long period of time and violate a greater number of civilian rights than would an ordinary investigation, a number of requirements must be met. Only the heads of the FBI can authorize such investigations, and such investigations will be allowed only in cases where there is evidence that the persons suspected are involved, or will be involved, in violent activities contrary to federal laws. There are four additional factors that must be weighed: the damage anticipated from the violent activity, the likelihood that the activity will in fact take place, the immediacy of the threat, and the danger to freedom of speech and privacy from the implementation of the full inquiry.

With regard to the initiation of investigations before the actual commission of a crime, the guidelines (both old and new) are not conclusive. It is not clear whether certain circumstances or certain facts that meet the standards of an enterprise to commit terrorist acts also afford sufficient evidence that a criminal conspiracy exists, which enables the initiation of an investigation. It is possible that investigations of future crimes, in relation to groups that are still only suspected of being terrorist, must be based on a firmer suspicion that criminal activity will indeed be carried out. The length of time of an investigation relating to security or terrorist activity would be proportionate to the violent history of the suspected group. The investigation can continue even if at the time of the investigation the group has not been active for some time.[72]

In contrast to the policy in the United Kingdom and Israel, in the United States the credo followed until September 11, 2001, was one of professional, thorough, and comprehensive intelligence investigations, without use of any violent interrogation techniques. The attacks of September 11 were a watershed in terms of this traditional concept. In addition to the practice of renditions, described above, memorandums prepared by the Justice Department's Office of Legal Counsel and by the Defense Department during 2002–3—memorandums whose legal quality attracted broad and unusually sharp criticism—provided that the president, as commander in chief, possessed the power to permit the use of a wide range of coercive interrogation methods during the interrogation of persons suspecting of having knowledge of future terrorist attacks, without this constituting a breach of international law or of Section 2340 of Title 18, the federal law that prohibits causing severe physical or mental pain or suffering.[73]

On the basis of the groundwork laid in these memorandums, the government announced that neither Taliban nor Al Qaeda combatants detained at Guantánamo Bay were entitled to the status of prisoners of war. However, it also determined that as a matter of policy the detainees would not be subjected to physical or mental abuse or cruel treatment and would receive much of the treatment and privileges afforded to prisoners of war by the Third Geneva Convention.[74] The importance of the latter determination should not be overestimated, however, in light of the narrow interpretation given in these memos to the type of measures that amount to forbidden torture. For example, it was concluded that measures that cause the suspect severe physical pain and would therefore qualify as torture were limited to measures that might lead to his death or other serious bodily harm. A similar narrow interpretation was given to the type of measures that might amount to severe mental pain. For example, it has been held that no use can be made of drugs that profoundly disrupt the sense or the personality of the suspect, although use can be made of mind-altering drugs that do not completely disrupt a suspect's mind or cognitive abilities.[75]

On December 30, 2005, President Bush signed the Detainee Treatment Act of 2005, initiated by Senator John McCain, which prohibits any use of cruel, inhumane, or degrading treatment of detainees in custody or under physical control of the U.S. government. Nonetheless, after signing the bill, the president clarified that he still retains the executive popwer to enforce the act according to the needs of the war against terrorism.[76] Although administration officials deny that the president has ever authorized the torture of suspected terrorists, evidence that this was not exactly the state of affairs might be found in the use of a number of harsh interrogation techniques against the Guantánamo Bay detainees, including stress positions, isolation for up to thirty days, removal of clothing, and the use of unmuzzled guard dogs. The army spread these practices to other U.S. detention facilities in Afghanistan and Iraq as well, but the abuse at Abu Ghraib prison in Iraq took the permissive interrogation standards one step further. U.S. military police officers used to, among other things, force Iraqi prisoners to stand in mock sexual positions, in naked human pyramids, or in other humiliating positions. Although the government firmly denied that any official policy allowed the above practices, and asserted that a group of undisciplined soldiers had taken advantage of leadership failings in the prison, I believe that the government carries, at least, moral responsibility for the creation of an atmosphere that condoned occasional deviations from the international laws of war, from the strict adherence to the rule of law, and from the traditional military culture of moral warfare.[77]

As noted, the full implications of September 11 on the U.S. policy of interrogation are not yet fully known, but the initial indications, as described above, are not too promising.

Conclusion

International law absolutely prohibits the use of interrogational measures that cause the interrogatee serious physical or mental pain and suffering. Article 7 of the Covenant on Civil and Political Rights entrenches the absolute prohibition on torture and on cruel, inhuman, or degrading treatment or punishment. Article 4 clarifies that even though in time of public emergency member states "may take measures derogating from their obligations under the present Covenant to the extent strictly required by the exigencies of the situation," there are a number of basic rights, including the right not to be tortured, that cannot be derogated from.[78] Likewise, Article 75(2)(a)(ii) of Protocol I Additional to the Geneva Conventions places an absolute general prohibition on the parties to an armed conflict to torture persons who are in the power of a party to the conflict, and Article 12 of the First and Second Geneva Conventions emphasizes the prohibition on torturing wounded, sick, or shipwrecked combatants.[79] Article 17 of the Third Geneva Convention emphasizes the prohibition on torturing prisoners of war, and Article 32 of the Fourth Geneva Convention emphasizes the prohibition on torturing civilians.[80] Furthermore, international law perceives the absolute prohibition on torture as *jus cogens*, that is, an inviolable basic norm that supersedes contradictory international treaty and customary norms.[81] This perception is consistent with the basic principles of a democratic society in regard to its obligation to respect the rights and freedoms of the individual. At the same time, the war against terror causes the state to face situations in which, if it adheres to the principle of respect for the rights of suspects under detention and refrains from exerting physical and psychological pressure against them, it will become unable to frustrate murderous terrorist attacks leading to the death and injury of innocent civilians, who too have basic rights.

Accordingly, there are those who believe that in circumstances in which a person suspected of hostile terrorist activities refuses to reveal information to his interrogators concerning future attacks, and there is no other way to obtain the information needed to frustrate those attacks, it is justified to torture the suspect in order to prevent the occurrence of a more injurious event. The appropriate solution is therefore in the nature of a necessary evil, which a state committed to protecting the safety of its civilians has no choice but to implement.

However, like every dilemma, the issues here are not black and white. On the one hand, it is possible to understand the fears of those who completely reject the use of extraordinary investigative means on the grounds that by opening a legal chink—however small and qualified—enabling "preventive torture," that is, the torture of a person suspected of involvement in future terrorist activities, the path will be paved for enabling the torture of persons involved in security offenses that have already been committed and perhaps even of persons merely engaged in criminal activity. It is also contended that terrorists whose belief in their ideological goals is so strong that they are willing to sacrifice their lives for them will not break under interrogation, however hard and intensive, and therefore that these means can only have an impact on innocents who were mistakenly suspected and who will say anything in order to put an end to their suffering. On the other hand, it is possible to understand the special difficulties that interrogators of the security forces have to cope with when conducting interrogations of people suspected of possessing information about future terrorist strikes, difficulties that are completely unlike those encountered in the interrogation of persons suspected of ordinary criminal activities.

Neither the advocates nor the opponents of torture dispute that war against terrorism is a just war. They also do not dispute that this war often leads to situations that are more difficult and complex than those faced in other wars, both from the moral and from the legal point of view. At the same time, the war against terror—like other wars—is not waged in a vacuum, in the sense that its just purpose does not justify all means that might prove effective in its success. Every government authority—including the security branches—is obliged to respect the law. As Aharon Barak has written,

> This duty applies in times of peace and also in times of emergency. "When the cannons roar, the muses fall quiet." However, even when the cannons roar, it is necessary to preserve the rule of law. Society's strength when facing its enemies is based on its recognition that it is fighting for values which are worth protecting. The rule of law is one of these values. Indeed, there is no security without law. The rule of

law is a component in national security—the security services are creatures of the law. They must respect the law. Security considerations may occasionally influence a determination of the contents of the law. However, when these contents are decided, the (formal) rule of law requires that the law be complied with, without the security considerations providing justification for its breach.[82]

Accordingly, we can only conclude that the appropriate answer to the dilemma lies between the two aforesaid approaches. It is not practicable to prevent the security services from making use of measures that occasionally are irreplaceable, since otherwise the democratic state will not be able to meet its commitment to protect the security of its citizens and instead will be compelled to abandon them in favor of the safety of the very terrorists who seek to murder them. At the same time, in view of the great importance and far-reaching ramifications of the power to make use of drastic and extraordinary interrogational measures, the conditions for exercising that power cannot be left to internal directives of the security organizations. Rather, they should be set out in statute.

The public debate that will naturally ensue during the course of formulating the statute,[83] and the pluralism of views that will be voiced at that time, will lead to the drafting of a law that will indeed allow exceptions to conventional interrogation laws but will concurrently clearly set out the circumstances that enable such exceptions, the upper limit of the physical or psychological pressure allowed (without specifying, of course, the range of interrogational devices—a matter best left for internal operational guidelines) as well as the nature of the supervisory and control mechanisms over the exercise of those powers. Such a mechanism should be independent and autonomous, that is, it should not be enough to merely provide reports to an oversight committee answerable to the executive branch concerning the manner in which the powers are exercised, but it should also be necessary to obtain a judicial warrant prior to exercising the extraordinary measures against a suspect. In cases where the urgency of the interrogation does not permit a delay, subsequent judicial oversight should be required immediately after the disappearance of the circumstances that prevented it from taking place in advance.

I am of the opinion that public recognition of the right of a state to make use of unusual interrogational means subject to stringent normative restrictions provides a proportional balance from a legal point of view and a justifiable one from a moral point of view.

FOUR

Administrative Powers of Military Commanders in the Struggle against Terrorism

IN CHAPTER 2 we saw that the war against terror is one of those situations where the democratic state has not only a moral justification but also a moral and legal obligation to use defensive force in order to guarantee its existence, the security of its citizens, and public order within its territory. Likewise, we have seen that, after crossing the hurdle of the right to use force, we must face an even more complex issue, namely, the manner in which the state should exercise this force.

The exercise of force by a democratic state is governed by a supra-principle which ensues from its substance and character—the principle of the rule of law, which comprises both formal and substantive aspects. The formal aspect means "that all entities in the state, whether private . . . or state organs, must act according to the law . . . this is a formal principle, as we are not interested in the contents of a law but rather in the need to impose it, irrespective of its contents." The substantive aspect concerns the content of the law, and here we aspire to the formulation of "the appropriate law, which contains a balance between the needs of the public and the individual."[1]

The security forces have an absolute duty to act in accordance with and subject to the law. Every time they infringe the rule of law (in its formal sense) by relying on "compelling security interests" they undermine the stability of its foundations. Likewise, the legislative branch has an absolute duty to preserve the rule of law (in its substantive sense), not only in times of peace but also in times of emergency. Every time it gives in to the momentary temptation to negate individual rights for security reasons, it fails to fulfill its function to preserve the democratic nature of the state on behalf of the public. True, the rights and freedoms of the individual in times of peace are not the same as his rights and freedoms in times of crisis; in times of emergency they retreat before essential security needs, to the extent required to implement them, because security is an essential precondition for the individual's ability to realize his rights and freedoms. Yet this retreat must be carried out cautiously, under supervision and control aimed at ensuring its necessity, since history shows that democracy—however, strong, stable, and deeply rooted it may be—is never free of the possibility of collapse. The proper normative balance between the public interest in ensuring public order and security in times of crisis and the commitment of a democratic state to respect the rights and freedoms of every citizen, creates difficult moral and legal dilemmas. We approach the task of drawing that balance knowing in advance that the outcome will not make it easier for us to contend with the painful situation forced on us. Yet, at the same time, "This is the destiny of a democracy—it does not see all means as acceptable, and the ways of its enemies are not always open before it. A democracy must sometimes fight with one hand tied behind its back. Even so, a democracy has the upper hand. The rule of law and the liberty of an individual constitute important components in its understanding of security. At the end of the day, they strengthen its spirit and this strength allows it to overcome its difficulties."[2]

Against the background of these guiding fundamental principles, I shall now examine the proper manner in which a military commander, as part of the fight to thwart terror attacks, should apply some of the administrative tools generally at his disposal: the demolition of homes, the imposition of curfews and enclosures, and the declaration of defined areas as closed military areas.

This discussion is presented from the Israeli point of view, in the light of international laws of war. Of course, Israeli Defense Forces (IDF) commanders are not the only ones to make use of the above-mentioned administrative measures. For example, from the beginning of 2003 until sovereignty was passed to the Iraqi interim regime in 2004, the U.S. Army located in Iraq began employing these measures against guerilla organizations in the state.[3] Nonetheless, because Israel has been forced to contend with terror since its foundation, its experience in this area is richer than that gathered so far by other countries, and can provide a broad factual basis for examining the ramifications and efficiency of these practices. Further, the Supreme Court of Israel, sitting as the High Court of Justice, has been required to scrutinize the manner of implementing these practices many times, with the goal of creating clear and stable principles for their implementation. But although this discussion focuses on Israel's experience, it is applicable, with the necessary changes but with equivalent force, to every liberal democratic state faced with a similar situation.

Demolition of Homes

The period of the British Mandate over Palestine saw the enactment of the Defense (Emergency) Regulations.[4] These regulations were incorporated into Israeli law upon the establishment of the state in 1948, and they are valid and binding to this date.[5]

During the British Mandate, the Defense Regulations applied to all the territories of "Palestine," that is, they also applied to the West Bank and Gaza Strip. Following the departure of the British and the seizure of these territories by the Jordanians and Egyptians, the Defense Regulations continued to remain in effect and became part of local law. Thus in 1967, when the IDF captured these areas, the regulations were already part of local law. The military commander decided in accordance with the rules of international law and as part of the effective control of the area to leave all local laws in place as long as they did not pose an obstacle to security needs.[6]

Regulation 119(1) of the Defense Regulations provides as follows:

> A military commander may by order direct the forfeiture to the Government of Palestine of any house, structure or land form in which he has reason to suspect that any firearm has been illegally discharged, or any bomb, grenade or explosive or incendiary article illegally thrown detonated, exploded or otherwise discharged or of any house, structure or land situated in any area, town, village, quarter or street the inhabitants or some of the inhabitants of which he is satisfied have committed, or attempted to commit, or abetted the commission of, or been accessories after the fact to the commission of, any offence against these regulations involving violence or intimidation or any Military Court offence, and when any house, structure or land is forfeited as aforesaid, the Military commander may destroy the house or the structure or anything in or on the house, the structure or the land . . .

There is no doubt that "the power of the military commander under Regulation 119 is broader than broad . . . the commander has the power to order the destruction of a complete road or neighborhood."[7]

What is the purpose of this regulation? It seems that the legislature intended to enable the military commander to respond in an effective and suitable manner to every act that impairs the security of the population or threatens public order. The military commander has broad power to order the confiscation of land and thereafter the demolition of the structure or structures used by the terrorist in the commission of the offense. Moreover, the military commander may give these orders even if the act of terror was not committed from the relevant land. It is sufficient that it served as the home of the terrorist.

It is possible to understand the seizure of the structure or even its destruction if indeed it was used for the purpose of carrying out the act of terror. But is it possible to understand or justify the connection between a structure that served as the residence of a terrorist and the demolition of a house simply because he lived there? Moreover, often the terrorist does not live alone but rather with the rest of his family—wife, children, parents, or siblings. Is the demolition of the home in response to the acts of the terrorist a form of collective punishment, which is prohibited according to fundamental principles of morality and justice?

In practice, there are two aspects to an examination of the validity of this regulation: domestic law and international law.

As regards domestic law, the question is whether the regulation is lawful and whether, in the light of Basic Law: Human Dignity and Liberty (part of the Israeli Bill of Rights), it is constitutional. Even if the answer is that there is no legal or constitutional defect in the regulation, it would still be appropriate to examine the manner in which military commanders exercise it. In other words, the regulation must be tested according to administrative law, and in this context one must examine the reasonableness of a military commander's exercise of discretion when implementing his powers under this regulation.

With regard to the legality of the regulation, it has already been noted that the regulation was adopted into domestic law by virtue of being part of the prevailing law during the period of the Mandate. Although in general these regulations have been sharply criticized by libertarians and human rights activists, they have not been repealed. The late minister of justice Shmuel Tamir, however, managed to divest the power to deport a person of much of its significance—at least in relation to the territory of the State of Israel. He also succeeded in replacing the provisions relating to administrative detention with a new law which provides a better balance between human rights and security needs. At the same time, Basic Law: Human Dignity and Liberty, which raises human rights, including a man's right to property (Sec. 3), to constitutional status, does not invalidate these regulations, both because the provisions of Section 10 of the law entrench the old law and because Regulation 119 would meet the test of the limitation clause found in Section 8 of the Basic Law.[8] Nor can the regulation be said to be inconsistent with the values of the State of Israel as a Jewish and democratic state, since a democratic state must also equip its military commanders with efficient tools for fighting terrorism, and it cannot be said that such a purpose is an improper purpose. The only element that must be ensured is "proportionality," that is, that the power be exercised in a manner proportional to the gravity of the situation to which it applies.

The requirement of proportionality has been applied in the case law of the Supreme Court in a number of senses. Thus, for example, the court has instructed the military commander to conform the exercise of his power to the severity of the case and the gravity of the circumstances. Consideration must be given not only to the gravity of the acts of which the terrorist is suspected but also to the degree of participation of the rest of the household in advancing these acts. Also taken into account is the degree of influence that the demolition of the home will have on the other inhabitants.

According to the test of proportionality—which is one of the cornerstones in the examination of the reasonableness of the decision of the military commander according to administrative law—in cases where it is possible to achieve a deterrent effect by something less than demolishing the entire house, this must be done. Likewise, where it is possible to achieve the deterrence by sealing the house, this must suffice.

The second test is an examination of the manner in which the military commander exercised his discretion under the principles of administrative law. In assessing the legality of the decision, the Supreme Court—sitting as the High Court of Justice—is not a forum before which the decisions of military commanders may be appealed. The relevant question is not what the court would have decided in the military commander's place but rather whether another reasonable military commander could have adopted a decision similar to the one actually adopted. Only a severe deviation from the scope of reasonableness will justify judicial intervention.

Nonetheless, the validity of this authority is liable to be challenged for being overly broad, for being arbitrary, and for causing harm to innocent people unconnected with the terrorist act. Advocates of this claim will argue that had the terrorist used his own house for the furtherance of the terrorist attack (i.e., as a hiding place from which he fired at a passing car or threw a grenade at passersby), then authorization for seizure of the house would be both logical and just; the seizure could be justified as a preventative measure to ensure that the terrorist could not use the place again. Conceivably, it could further be argued that following the seizure, were the terrorist to remain alive and be indicted, it would be the court's role to decide whether the place should be confiscated by the state. However, as we observed above, the military commander's authority is broader, extending not only to the seizure of land but also to the authority to demolish any buildings on it. The answer to this argument would be that one cannot wait for the court ruling, given that the issue is one of an "administrative-military" response for deterrent purposes. Waiting for the trial's outcome is liable to thwart the attainment of that goal. As the president of the Supreme Court, Aharon Barak, asserted: "The power given to the military commander under Regulation 119 is not the power of collective punishment. Its exercise is not intended to punish the family members. . . . The power is administrative and its exercise is intended to deter and thereby preserve public order."[9] In fact, the courts in Israel have ruled that the authority is an administrative one, intended as a tool with which the commander can respond to terrorist acts, not only with preventative measures but also with deterrent ones.[10]

On the one hand, the difficulty with this approach is that it confers a governmental authority, such as a military commander, with power that in a democratic regime prima facie characteristically belongs to the judiciary. In other words, one of the basic human rights is not to be punished without due process. On the other hand, even a democratic state, finding itself in a state of war with terrorist organizations in territories over which it exercises military control, must equip its commanders with effective tools that can provide an immediate response to terrorist acts.

Illustrating this is the case of *Shukri v. The Minister of Defense*. In this case, the petitioner's brother confessed to the murder of a Jewish worker purely because he was Jewish; he also confessed to having attempted to cause the Tel Aviv–Jerusalem bus to fall into an abyss, again purely in order to take revenge against the Jews. The military commander issued an order for the demolition of the petitioner's house. The court responded to this by stating:

> Respondent 2 claims that this is an efficient deterrent method and we were not presented with any data that negated the reasonability of that assumption. Moreover, the fact that disruptions of the public order in

the area continue despite the use of Regulation 119 does not mean that resort thereto is not effective. We have no reason not to accept Respondent 2's claim that were it not for the use of Regulation 119, the disruptions of public order would be more numerous and more severe. All we can do is examine whether the method of demolishing a structure is reasonable in the special circumstances of the case. In assessing the reasonability of the use of Regulation 119 consideration must be given to the gravity of the actions ascribed to the inhabitants of the building and their consequences, against the background of the scope of the phenomenon and the need to adopt deterrent methods. On the other hand, the severity of the deterrent method and its affect on the inhabitants of the building and adjacent premises must also be considered. Consideration must also be given to the contributory degree of assistance provided by the building's inhabitants to the actions disturbing the public peace and the measures they actually adopted to prevent the prohibited activities that violated the public peace. The reasonability of a decision under Regulation 119 is the outcome of the balancing and weighing up of these considerations. . . . Bearing these criteria in mind, it seems to me that there is no basis for our intervention. The acts for which the Petitioner's brother was convicted are exceptionally heinous. The Petitioner's brother was convicted of murdering one person and attempting to murder 50 others. The accused cold-bloodedly planned his actions, motivated by nationalist feelings of vengeance. Under these circumstances we do not think that it was unreasonable to adopt the particularly harsh deterrent measure of demolishing a building. We are aware that the demolition of the building also damages the living quarters of the Petitioner and his mother. Admittedly, this is not the purpose of the demolition, but it is its result. This harsh result is intended to deter potential perpetrators of such acts who must understand that by their own actions, not only do they endanger public peace and security and the lives of innocent people, but also the welfare of their own relatives.[11]

For many years, the Supreme Court has seen no defect in this power being conferred on the military commander. On the contrary, the court has deemed it reasonable and just, in view of the legislative intention to provide commanders with effective legal tools for their war against terror. The assumption is that persons involved in terrorist activity will be deterred if they know that their houses will be forfeited, sealed, or perhaps even demolished and thus their families will suffer tragedy too. At the least, even if these measures do not deter the terrorists, they may deter other potential terrorists, who may reconsider their intentions, given the heavy price that their families will have to pay.

At the same time, since the State of Israel is continuing to suffer from terrorist strikes—in recent years more than in the past, as suicide bombers have joined the fray who do not hesitate to blow themselves up in civilian centers in order to cause maximum injuries—it has been argued that the demolition of homes cannot deter persons who are willing to sacrifice their lives. Further, it may be that the opposite is true. The suicide bomber carries out his mission in the belief, not that he is causing his family to suffer social stigma and economic disaster, but rather that by his murderous act he is turning his family into heroes in his people's struggle and is even enabling them to obtain generous monetary assistance from states sponsoring terrorism.[12]

While there is no doubt that a considerable number of Palestinians hold this extreme view, I think that it should not be forgotten that an equally considerable number hold a completely different view, one that, being "unpopular," is naturally not give much of a platform by the Palestinian Authority, which has become more extremist in recent years. A clear expression of this latter view may be seen in a rare public letter published in 2002 in *Al-Hayat*, the Saudi daily which is one of the most important newspapers in the Arab world. Here, the father of a suicide bomber, who refused to give his real name for fear of being killed, described his life following his son's action: "From that day I am like a ghost walking on the land, not to speak of the fact that I, my wife, and my other sons and daughters have been uprooted, following the demolition of the home in which we lived . . . the sums which are given to the families of the *shahidim* [martyrs], are more painful than healing. They cause us, the families, to feel that we receive monetary payment for the lives of our children. Do the lives of our children have a price?"[13]

The Supreme Court has no doubt about the deterrent effect of demolishing houses:

> In its responding affidavit, the Respondent explained that in deciding upon the necessity of adopting measures under Regulation 119(1), one of the customary considerations was the death of the attacker. Until that time, the general policy of the Defense establishment was to avoid adopting these measures when the terrorist-attacker had been killed. In this case too, the death of the terrorist who had committed the murderous attack was taken into account, together with all of the other factors forming the basis of the decision. However, his conclusion (shared by all of the security authorities) was that in this case there was

no escaping the adoption of measures under Regulation 119, despite the terrorist's death. There were two deciding factors. The first and principal one was that this is a case of a terrorist belonging to an extremist Islamic terrorist organization; its members "regard death in the course of a terrorist act against Israeli targets as a positive result, which ensures their place as holy martyrs in the world to come." The second consideration was gravity of the terrorist act; against the background of the wave of severe attacks over the last few months orchestrated by the extremist terrorist organizations and in view of the public declarations of these organizations that they intend to continue to perpetrate murderous terrorist attacks in the future too. Under these circumstances the Respondent saw an urgent need to deter potential candidates for suicide bombings. Security authorities consider that there will be a deterrent element in the message heard by a potential terrorist, that his death in the course of the terrorist act will result in severe consequences for his family with whom he lives. On the other hand, if it is clear that the death of the suicide terrorist will constitute a sufficient condition for leaving his house intact, he is liable to make every effort to choose to go through with the suicide attack. Thus instead of being deterred from the perpetration of murderous acts, the suicide terrorist will be encouraged to do them. I see no reason for disputing this approach. As we know, both the scope and the reasonableness of measures adopted by competent authorities for the maintenance of security can only be measured against the background of changing circumstances. . . . We all are aware and sense the extreme increase of late in the readiness of terrorist organizations to commit murderous attacks against all Israelis, soldiers and citizens alike, with the perpetrators undertaking to execute the attack by becoming suicide bombers. This is an entirely new dimension of crazy fanaticism. Given the necessity of dealing with this phenomenon, the competent authorities are entitled, *inter alia*, to adopt the measures of seizure, and demolition of the home of the suicide bomber. *Prima facie* the Respondent is justified in regarding the policy by which the security forces refrained from harming the house of the terrorist who was killed during the act as being inapplicable to suicide bombers. The reason that justified the policy in the past was the assumption that with the death of the terrorist during the act, the deterrent element was exhausted with respect to potential terrorists. On the other hand, adoption of such a policy in cases of suicide terrorists will at the very least leave a vacuum in respect of the deterrent measures open to the military commander. Furthermore, it may even preclude any chance that those living together with the terrorist, and who are aware of his intention to do a suicide bombing, will attempt to prevent him.[14]

One of the important balances that the court struck between the military interest in prompt deterrence and the inhabitants' right to protect their property came in its ruling that a person who saw himself as being harmed by the military commander's decision was entitled to petition the Supreme Court to contest the legality of the decision, and until that time the property could not be harmed. In fact, the court preferred the right to a hearing, which is a basic right, over the interest of the immediate and efficient execution of the commander's order. At the same time, the right to be heard, like any right, is relative in nature and therefore retreats before essential military needs in special and exceptional cases. This is the situation, for example, when there is a real fear that giving an advance warning to the families of terrorists regarding the decision of a military commander to demolish their home, in order to allow them sufficient time to appeal against the decision to him and to the court, would endanger the lives of the soldiers and cause the failure of the mission.[15]

The second aspect to be examined is international law.

In June 1967, during the course of the Six Days' War, the State of Israel conquered the areas of Judea and Samaria from Jordan and the Gaza Strip from Egypt. Officially, Israel has never recognized the property rights of these two states over any part of Eretz Yisrael and consequently has argued that international treaty law, such as the Fourth Geneva Convention, does not apply to them and only customary international law, such as the Fourth Hague Convention, applies, to the extent that no internal law provides to the contrary.[16]

At the same time, it would seem that this principled stand has never been put to practical effect, since over the years the various governments of Israel have declared that they undertake to act in accordance with the humanitarian provisions of the Fourth Geneva Convention. Indeed, from the beginning the premise of the High Court of Justice has been that Israel holds Judea, Samaria, and the Gaza Strip by virtue of belligerent occupation and that this occupation has never ended. Belligerent occupation ends either with the occupying power withdrawing from the territory or with the war ending, at which time international laws relating to peace come into effect. The peace treaties signed between Israel and Egypt and Jordan do not regulate the status of these territories, and therefore these treaties should not be seen as bringing about an end to the state of fighting or as an end to the belligerent occupation. Consequently, the military commander's power stems from the rules of international law concerning belligerent occupation (including the Fourth Geneva Convention, since Israel is a party to it), which are part of the laws of war.[17]

The claims that Regulation 119 contradicts international law can be summed up as follows: first, Regulation 119 violates the prohibition on collective punishment; second, it violates the prohibition on violating the right of property; third, it violates the provision of the international law that private property cannot be seized; and fourth, it violates the right to due process.

Before examining each of these claims, I will initially examine whether Israel acted justly in retaining the validity of Regulation 119 upon receiving control of the Occupied Territories.

It is a well-known principle of international law that a state conquering territory from another state is supposed to ensure the maintenance of public order and security. This principle, based on Article 43 of the Fourth Hague Convention, was the basis of the provision in Article 64 of the Fourth Geneva Convention, which stipulates: "The penal laws of the occupied territory shall remain in force, with the exception that they may be repealed or suspended by the Occupying Power in cases where they constitute a threat to its security or an obstacle to the application of the present Convention."[18] In principle, international law expects that a state that becomes the effective ruler over occupied territories should do everything in its power to ensure the security of the population and the maintenance of public order. The assumption is that these goals are attainable by preserving the domestic law to which the civilians of that state (the occupied area) are accustomed.[19]

We saw above that the expectation is that the criminal law that was previously valid will remain in force. The reservation regarding the preservation of the domestic law is that it not contradict the nature of the military occupation and the interests of the army.

This being the case, how can one justify the military commander's power to seize the house of a terrorist and perhaps even order its demolition? Clearly, when the terrorist has used that house to further his terrorist actions, then the military interest in seizing the house is understandable, at least as a preventative measure and even as a deterrent military response.

Assuming that Israel does in fact comply with the spirit of the Fourth Geneva Convention, then even according to the convention there is no absolute prohibition on harming civilian property for reasons of military necessity. This is the language of Article 53 of the convention: "Any destruction by the Occupying Power of real or personal property belonging individually or collectively to private persons or to the state, or to other public authorities, or to social or cooperative organizations, is prohibited except where such destruction is rendered absolutely necessary by military operations." In other words, even though there is a prohibition in principle against harming private property, nonetheless, if there is an absolute military necessity, such an act is valid. Can the destruction of a terrorist's house be considered as coming within the definition of a necessary military operation? The issue has been disputed. There are those who claim that the measure is an extreme one, totally unrelated to military necessity and in fact a punitive act in the guise of military need. On the other hand, Israel maintains that this is a necessary military activity, at least in those cases where it is clear that the family members of the terrorist knew about his activities and failed to report them to the authorities.

Opponents of this Israeli policy argue that, in view of the application of international law and its purpose, Article 53 was intended, from the beginning, to apply humanitarian law to the conquered territory. Broad powers of this nature granted to a military commander contradict the humanitarian goal of international law and should therefore be declared invalid and null. To this one may add the additional four claims against Regulation 119 listed above. I shall now proceed to examine each of these claims in turn.

Does the Demolition of Houses Contravene the Prohibition on Collective Punishment?

Clearly, the normative basis for the prohibition on collective punishment is found in the legal systems of all enlightened states. The ancient source is found in the Bible: "Fathers shall not be put to death for children, neither shall children be put to death for fathers: every man shall be put to death for his own sin."[20] This principle became entrenched as part of the concept of humanitarian law in at least two places: Article 50 of the Fourth Hague Convention, which states, "No general penalty, pecuniary or otherwise, shall be inflicted upon the population on account of the acts of individuals for which they cannot be regarded as jointly and severally responsible"; and Article 33 of the Fourth Geneva Convention, which states, "No protected person may be punished for an offence he or she has not personally committed. Collective penalties and likewise all measures of intimidation or of terrorism is prohibited." Is the demolition of a terrorist's house, assuming that others also used the same house, an act of collective punishment? The answer is largely dependent on the understanding of the term "collective punishment." If the intention is to inflict a punishment on a person for the act of another, then a problem exists.[21]

Whether a person will be considered an accomplice to the act of another person is dependent on how we understand the concept of criminal accomplices. In the case of a positive act, then the answer is less problematic, for a volitional act done with the intention of helping a terrorist further his purpose would certainly make that person an accomplice, and if he was also a partner in the house of the terrorist, then the demolition of that house could not be considered as collective punishment. The problem arises in the case of a family member who is aware that a member of his family is about to commit an offense against state security. In such a case, it must be stressed that the degree of involvement of the other user of the house must be taken into account and is an important factor to be considered by the military commander exercising his discretion in respect of the demolition of a house or its sealing, entirely or partially.

However, the real test is not just the language of Regulation 119 and whether it really allows collective punishment. Rather, it is the practical test, and the restrictions imposed on military commanders by Israeli courts forbid any harm to the innocent whenever this is physically possible. In this sense, I tend to think that the use generally made by military commanders of their powers under the regulation, in view of the Supreme Court supervision, does not contravene international law's prohibition on collective punishment.

Does the Demolition of Houses Contravene the Prohibition on Harming Private Property?

The prohibition on harming private property derives from the right to property, which is one of the more important basic human rights in any civilized country. It is a right that cannot be abrogated purely by reason of the state of war, unless such a violation can be explained as having been necessitated by the state of war. This prohibition is entrenched in at least three provisions of international law: Articles 23 and 46 of the Fourth Hague Convention and Article 53 of the Fourth Geneva Convention.

Article 23 of the Hague Convention makes it prohibited "[t]o destroy or seize the enemy's property, unless such destruction or seizure be imperatively demanded by the necessities of war." Article 46 adds: "Family honor and rights, the lives of persons, and private property, as well as religious convictions and practice, must be respected." And Article 53 of the Geneva Convention states: "Any destruction by the Occupying Power of real or personal property belonging individually or collectively to private persons or to the state, or to other public authorities, or to social or cooperative organizations, is prohibited except where such destruction is rendered absolutely necessary by military operations."

It is therefore forbidden to harm private property, except in those exceptional cases where such harm can be explained on the basis of military necessity.[22] Is the destruction of houses in accordance with Regulation 119 consistent with such a need? It has been argued that the demolition of a terrorist's house as a punitive act cannot be considered as a military need within the meaning of Article 53 of the said convention; this is a fortiori the case if the house does not belong exclusively to the terrorist.

In my opinion, where a military commander exercises his authority under Regulation 119, it can be considered a military necessity if indeed he exercised his discretion correctly, that is, he examined all the relevant circumstances, such as the severity of the terrorist's acts, the contributory responsibility of the other users, the degree of damage that the demolition or sealing of the house will cause to its inhabitants, and other similar considerations. Thus, the court ruled:

> This is an issue that does not admit of comprehensive, exhaustive criteria and every case will be weighed in accordance with its particular exigencies. However, generally speaking, I would include among the relevant factors to be considered by the military commander in his decision, the following considerations:
>
> a. The severity of the acts imputed to one or a few of those living in the said building, and the existence of verified proof of their involvement.
>
> b. To what extent can it be inferred that the other residents, or some of them, were aware of the activities of the suspect/s or whether they had reason to suspect the execution of such activities? It will be mentioned again, for purposes of clarification, that lack of knowledge as stated, or lack of certainty in this respect, does not, as such, prevent the adoption of the sanction. However, the factual situation in the matter may affect the scope of the commander's decision.
>
> c. Is there a practical possibility of separating the living quarters of the suspect from the other sections of the building? Does it in fact already constitute a separate unit?
>
> d. Can the residential unit of the suspect be destroyed without damaging the other parts of the building or adjacent buildings? If it is not possible, was the possibility of sealing the relevant unit considered?

e. What is the severity of the resultant damage planned to the building for those people regarding whom there is no proof of direct or indirect involvement in the terrorist activity? How many such people are there and what is the degree of their connection to the suspect resident?[23]

Thus although international law dictates full protection for the private property of the residents, it recognizes exceptions when the damage is essential for furthering military interests. Preventing terrorists from returning to use their property, as well as deterring potential terrorists from using their property, as a means for establishing a reign of terror, at the price of damage to their property, is definitely a military necessity, required to protect the army or citizens from being harmed.

Opponents of Israeli actions involving the demolition of houses point out the danger involved in granting discretionary powers to a military commander, who will tend to see a "military necessity" in situations where no such necessity exists. Dan Simon emphasizes that the term "military necessity" appearing in Article 53 refers to acts of warfare, not punishment or deterrence, and only when there are actual hostilities between the sides.[24]

I am prepared to accept that military necessity should be understood as referring to times of battle or armed activity. I am not prepared to accept the restrictive interpretation under which only seizure intended to further an act of war can justify the seizure of a house. In my opinion, demolition of a house to prevent its being used again as terrorist base, and even as part of a punitive conception that serves the war's purposes, that is, the eradication or limitation of terror, must be included within the meaning of "military necessity."

On the face of it, critics of the application of Regulation 119 in too broad a manner, with insufficient consideration for individual rights, are correct to the extent that it permits the damaging of property purely by virtue of a terrorist having lived in a certain house. In other words, in these critics' view, one cannot accept the interpretation given to the regulation in Israeli rulings, since it permits the destruction of a house just because it was the terrorist's house. The justification for this drastic measure, both in terms of domestic law—the law of the territories— and in terms of international law, must consider whether the house itself was used by the terrorist for his terrorist act; it is not sufficient that it merely served him as a place to sleep. Conceivably, if the residents provided the terrorist a hiding place or place to sleep with the knowledge that he was on his way to commit a terrorist act, their behavior would fall in the category of using property for the furtherance of terror. The situation would be different, however, if the other members of the household had no inkling as to the terrorist's actions. These critics look for a functional, substantive connection between the act of terror and the property to be seized. Such a connection must be expressed in the misuse of the property, as a tool in the terrorist's hands. Even if the connection is only indirect—that is, providing the terrorist with board on his way to the commission of an act of terror—this would be sufficient. Thus the critics do not agree with the broad interpretation given to this regulation by the majority of the judges on the Supreme Court. They are prepared to accept the comment of Justice Dalia Dorner that "one of the requirements for the exercise of the authority, which to date has not been disputed, is the existence of a causal connection between the act of violence and the demolition." But they do not concur with her conclusion that "even if the demolition of the house is not a punitive measure in the full sense of the word, but rather a deterrent measure, it should only be adopted as a direct response to a terrorist act committed by a terrorist *who lived in the house*.[25]

This criticism would seem to be correct, but only on the face of it. It appears to me that a deeper understanding of the rationale and the justification for damaging the terrorist's house shows that such destruction may lead other potential terrorists to reconsider whether to undertake terrorist activities. They are made aware that in doing so they are endangering not only themselves but also the domicile of their families. This is a just punitive measure, if indeed it proves to be a deterrent. This in fact is the accepted view.

Does the Demolition of Houses Contravene the Prohibition on Expropriating Private Property?

Regulation 119 actually contains two powers: the power to seize and expropriate private property and the power to demolish the property.

I have already dealt with the first element of damage to private property by destroying it or sealing it up. A related question is whether the less severe power of seizing and expropriating property contravenes the prohibition established by international law in this respect. Article 46 of the Fourth Hague Convention states that "private property cannot be confiscated." However, this prohibition must be read together with the qualifications laid down in Article 43 of the convention and Article 53 of the Fourth Geneva Convention. Accordingly, it can be said that military necessity dictates and justifies the seizure of private property. In terms of military interests, what could be more important than the seizure of a house that was used for the purpose of terrorist activity, or in order to deter others from violating the security of the area? It seems to me that, together with the prohibition against damaging private property, there are certain exceptions to the civilian's property rights which are dictated by military needs, whether for the maintenance of the army or in order to prevent harm to the army and to peaceful citizens.[26]

Does the Demolition of Houses Contravene the Right to Due Process?

Due process is a basic right and a precondition for any governmental violation of human rights, for example, a property right. It is generally ascribed to the judicial process, but in reality is applicable to all administrative procedures by reason of which there may be an infringement of human rights. International law, too, requires the maintenance of appropriate protection of human rights by the occupying state. Thus, under Article 71 of the Fourth Geneva Convention, a person against whom an indictment is brought is entitled to all the rights specified therein. There is no doubt that this is the Israeli practice with respect to all those against whom indictments are filed. However, our concern here is not with judicial proceedings. What bothers the critics is that Israeli application of Regulation 119 as a punitive measure is expedited not by judicial procedure but by an administrative body that is not bound by all the rules of a court.

In response to the claim that Regulation 119 conflicts with the concept of due process by allowing a person to be punished by a body other than the court, I would say that authority for the violation of basic rights does not vest exclusively in the courts. There are other governmental bodies that are statutorily authorized to impose sanctions under certain circumstances. Thus, for example, a local authority is permitted to issue an order for demolition against a resident who built without a license. There can be no doubt that the demolition of a house is a violation of a person's property rights. Does the fact that the local authority was empowered to do so conflict with the idea of due process? The answer is in the negative. Governmental bodies can also be authorized to violate a person's basic rights, provided that there is an explicit statutory authorization and that the authorization was for an appropriate purpose and not in excess of what is required.[27] However, even if the authorization complies with the requirements of constitutionality, a person nonetheless has the right to have the body exercise its authority in accordance with due process.

It is within this framework that I expect the existence of minimal guarantees to ensure that the governmental violation of rights is not arbitrary or motivated by irrelevant and illegitimate considerations. In order to ensure these guarantees, Israeli courts have forced military commanders to comply with appropriate standards. Thus, before directing the execution of a seizure or demolition order, the commanders are obligated to allow those affected to make objections to the decision. Furthermore, if the commander dismisses their objections, the Supreme Court has directed that these people be allowed to petition the court to contest the legality of the commander's decision. There are no precedents for a person in occupied territory having recourse to the supreme court of the occupying state against that state's military commander. While the Supreme Court sitting as the High Court of Justice does not function as an instance for appealing the decision of the military commander and exclusively examines the legality of his decision, nonetheless the scope for judicial review is broad and extremely restrictive. The reason for this was given by Justice Barak: "Extensive powers are concentrated in the hands of a Military Government, and for the sake of the rule of law we should apply judicial review according to the normal standards."[28] It is evident therefore that the Supreme Court was not satisfied with the retention of the affected person's right to be "heard." It added an element that is definitely not required by international law and is unprecedented—granting a person the right to contest the military commander's decision in the highest judicial instance of the state, the High Court of Justice.[29]

Furthermore, as we have observed, the Supreme Court did not hesitate to subject military commanders to compliance with the reasonability standards of other administrative bodies. The military commander must take all the relevant factors discussed above into consideration before reaching a decision.

In view of the limitations and the judicial supervision of the decisions of the military commander, I find it difficult to accept the criticism that the exercise of Regulation 119 contravenes of the concept of due process.

Even so, I am perturbed about one matter, concerning the degree of evidence and proof for the military commander. The accepted interpretation in this regard is that Regulation 119 does not require more than compliance with the standard evidentiary tests for administrative law with respect to the involvement of members of the household in terrorist activity.[30] In my opinion, it would be better to demand a higher evidentiary burden in this situation—"clear and convincing" proof, which in its nature and scope falls between the civilian and criminal standards.[31] This burden of proof is not satisfied with the reasonableness of the evidence but requires something more. The evidence submitted must clearly and unequivocally indicate that the person concerned was connected to the act of terror being examined.

Imposition of Curfews

We will now proceed to examine restrictions on freedom of movement and the individual's personal autonomy as a result of military needs connected to the war against terror. In this context, the harshest restriction is the curfew, which is the absolute restriction of freedom of movement, keeping people in their houses for whatever period of time is determined by the military commander. The encirclement or blockade is less serious in terms of restrictions on freedom of movement, for in these situations people are confined only to a particular area.

Regulation 124 of the Defense Regulations provides that

> A military commander may by order require every person within any area specified in the order, to remain within doors between such hours as may be specified in the order, and in such case, if any person is or remains out of doors within that area between such hours without a permit in writing, issued by or on behalf of the military commander or some person duly authorized by the military commander to issue such permits, he shall be guilty of an offence against the regulations.

What is the nature of this authority? It is intended to enable military commanders to discharge the duties legally imposed on them. In areas subject to military control, the intention is to allow the enforcement of the personal and public security of the military forces and the civilians. The problem with this authority is that it interferes with other rights of the civilians on whom the curfew is imposed. It restricts their freedom of movement or restricts their ability to conduct their lives as they choose. Can these severe restrictions of human rights be justified in terms of both domestic law and international law?

In terms of domestic law, the Defense Regulations are, as stated, part of the domestic law applicable in the West Bank and Gaza, and part of the domestic law of the State of Israel. This legislation has given rise to serious criticism from both jurists and public figures. But Israel is currently in control of foreign territories and responsible for their security, as well as the security of the military forces and Israeli citizens. There can be no doubt that in the current situation these regulations are justified in terms of their purpose and the tools they provide military commanders for discharging their duties.

It is also true that even if domestic law permits and recognizes these regulations, they must be implemented in a manner that has consideration for the human rights of those against whom it is applied. The period of the British Mandate in Eretz Yisrael, when these regulations were drawn up, was different from the current period of Israeli sovereignty, which waves its banner of democracy and human rights.

Even though the regulation does not restrict the military commander's discretion and allows him to decide when to impose a curfew, it is clear that his discretion is not unlimited and must comply with the criteria established by constitutional and administrative law for the exercise of governmental authority. Thus, for example, the military commander must be convinced that the imposition of the curfew is essential for the promotion of one of the goals with which he is charged, that is, the security of the area or public order. However, it is not sufficient that he regards the curfew as necessary for that goal. He must also be convinced that there is no other, less harsh way of achieving it. In other words, the commander's decision must comply with the proportionality requirement, one of whose features is reasonability.

The curfew is intended to assist the security forces in the restoration of order when order has been disturbed by illegal demonstrations, serious riots, or other such behavior. In order to allow the restoration of peace and quiet, a brief curfew is understandable. The same is true in the case of a terrorist act, when the commander knows that the terrorists have taken refuge, hiding in a house. Imposing a curfew would be an understandable measure to facilitate the location and capture of the terrorists.

A possible claim against this measure is that it harms entirely innocent people, unconnected to the disturbances or the terrorist act. In other words, the claim is that the curfew is a way of punishing innocent people. Prima facie, the result of the curfew is harm caused to innocent people who have no connection with the acts or conduct in response to which the curfew was imposed. But in fact this is the inevitable consequence of the adoption of general measures which do not admit of exceptions for innocent people.

Even so, it must be clear that the curfew should not be imposed as a punishment for conduct that disturbs public order or security of the area. The authority was not intended for that purpose, and if the military commander acts in that fashion his acts will be invalidated.

The curfew is an accepted legal tool and has also been used within Israel. On the eve of the Sinai Campaign in 1957, it was feared that some of the Israeli Arabs would attempt to help the Jordanians in the approaching war. It was therefore decided to impose a night curfew to prevent them crossing the border.

The curfew is, however, a drastic measure that severely violates human rights. It must be the last measure when there is no less-severe alternative measure available, and it must be proportional. It is forbidden to impose it for an extended period, and the military commander must reassess its necessity from time to time. Furthermore, if the curfew continues for more than a few hours, the military commander must occasionally lift it for a short time, to allow people to leave their homes for the sake of replenishing urgent food supplies needed at home. The military commander must also ensure that medical services continue to function and that sick people requiring treatment, as well as medical personnel, have freedom of movement, even during a curfew.[32]

As with any other military powers the commander has, the curfew too is subject to judicial review of the Supreme Court, sitting as the High Court of Justice. The problem is that this mode of supervision is not always efficient, for if the curfew is only of short duration, practically speaking there is no time for the resident under curfew to petition the High Court.[33] It would be more efficient to establish a speedier forum of review, for example an appeal to a military court that supervises the actions of commanders.

As stated above, the curfew constitutes a particularly grave restriction of individual liberty; it keeps the person in his house, denying him any possibility of movement outside his home. However, it is precisely the nature of the curfew that also constitutes its rationale. Keeping people in their homes facilitates the army's efforts to restore public order where it has been disrupted, or allows easier access to the homes of the residents in order to locate those suspected of being involved in terrorist activities or in possession of forbidden weapons.

Even though the curfew resembles the confiscation and demolition of homes as a means of enforcing military rule, the difference between the measures is clear. Thus, for example, Regulation 119 allows a military commander to seize the house of a person who was involved in terrorist actions, and to demolish it too, as a punitive and deterrent measure. Regulation 124, on the other hand, prohibits the use of the curfew as a punitive response, reserving it for preventative measures only.

Let us now examine the legality of Regulation 124 in terms of international law.

Even though international law does not explicitly refer to this subject, certain conclusions can be drawn from the prohibitions on collective punishments stipulated in Article 50 of the Fourth Geneva Convention and Article 33 of the Fourth Hague Convention. Accordingly, curfews cannot be imposed as a collective punishment. As we saw above, this position is also stressed in Israeli case law. On the other hand, Article 78 of the Fourth Geneva Convention empowers a military commander to detain a person in a particular place for military reasons. This article has been viewed by some as a possible framework for entrenching the power to impose a curfew.

The language of Regulation 124 does not qualify or limit the grounds for curfew, ergo it could prima facie be imposed as a punitive measure for terrorist activity, in a manner similar to the demolition of houses under Regulation 119, as we observed above. However, the courts were careful to interpret this regulation in a strict and restricted sense that would make it compatible with the requirements of international law and Israeli constitutional law.

Summing up, we can say that despite the serious nature of the curfew, and its harsh implications for individual freedom, there is no escaping the need for its existence and imposition on occasion, provided that it be done in a manner compatible with its goals, and in compliance with the restrictions imposed on it by domestic law and, to a lesser extent, international law.

Imposition of Blockades and Encirclements

The related authority of the military commander to impose blockades and encirclements derives from a number of possible sources. Thus, for example, Regulations 122 and 126 authorize a commander to limit movement in certain areas or on certain streets; Regulation 125 allows the declaration of a certain area as a closed area, with entry and exit by permit only.

Another normative source is the security legislation in the territories. This is legislation promulgated by a military commander, by virtue of his powers under international law, as the power in control of the area, which enable him, among other things, to prohibit or restrict entry into territories held by him.

These sources allow restriction on freedom of movement in a graded and geographical manner, which begins with restriction of entry or exit to all areas of the West Bank or the Gaza Strip, with the exception of those people who received special permits. In such a case, the accepted term is a "closure," imposed on these territories in order to prevent the transit of persons into the State of Israel. These closures are usually imposed when intelligence warnings have been received regarding the impending entry of terrorists into Israel in order to commit terrorist acts. Not only is the restriction of passage between the territories and Israel a restriction of movement for the residents of these areas, but more important, it prevents many of them from earning a living from their work in Israel.

This is one of the most serious problems facing the State of Israel. Many of the residents of the territories must work in Israel in order to make a living. At the same time, the moment that terrorist acts are committed in Israel by Palestinians, there is no option but to prevent entry into Israel, thereby reducing the danger of continued entry of hostile elements. Should this general closure, which is definitely a serious blow to many people who are certainly not connected to terror, be regarded as a form of collective punishment?

The answer is in the negative, for the reason that imposing the closure is not punishment but rather exclusively a means of preventing continued acts of terrorism by blocking the terrorists' passage into Israel. The accompanying result indeed harms innocent people, but there can be no way to avoid this. Furthermore, even if an inhabitant of the territories previously had a work permit allowing him to enter Israel, none of the residents have any reason to suppose that the permit is inviolable. The permit is issued subject to military necessities: "None of the Petitioners have an inherent right to enter Israel in order to work there. The Respondent has discretion to decide whether to permit their entry into Israel, be it for work or any other purpose. His discretion is exercised in accordance with fixed criteria, but the issue of the permit is always subject to the absence of any security-related reason that necessitates preventing entry."[34]

It must be remembered that the imposition of a general closure in the sense that residents of the territories are not permitted to enter Israel is reminiscent of the authority given to the minister of the interior to refuse to allow certain categories of persons to enter Israel, in the fear that they are liable to harm the public peace or public order. The authority given to the minister of the interior is intended to ensure that those seeking to enter Israel do not endanger its peace or security. The minister of the interior is entitled, for humanitarian reasons, to permit the entry of people into Israel and provide them with temporary residence permits. The same applies to a military commander. Given the economic difficulties of the Palestinian residents, when circumstances permit and the danger of terrorists coming into Israel decreases, he can sometimes permit a specific number of the residents to come to work in Israel.

In those cases in which a closure or encirclement is imposed, the court assesses that order in accordance with the same criteria that it established in the past for assessing the military commander's discretion:

> This is the response to the petition to the extent that it relates on a general level to the imposition of a curfew "from time to time" or to the imposition of other forms of restriction on "freedom of movement, occupation and work" of the local population. In all cases of the imposition of such restrictions, the competent authority must assess the degree of security needs for exercising the power given to it as compared to the harm caused to the local population, it must avoid imposition of restrictions as punitive measures and must refrain from the adoption of harsh measures which cause more harm than is required under the circumstances. This is a criterion for assessing a decision for imposing any particular restriction at any particular time or place . . . the law permits the military commander of the territories to impose a curfew and additional restrictions, as established by law, and to the extent necessitated by security considerations in every case.[35]

As stated above, the claim against the military commanders in cases of imposing a curfew on a particular village is that these measures constitute collective punishment, and cause starvation and endanger the residents' health. In other words, the criticism against the imposition of closures is that they result in the entire population being deprived of food and medicine and that, by imposing the closure, the military commanders actually intend to punish the population for having terrorists dwell among them.

None of the petitions filed to date in the Supreme Court have succeeded in proving that the encirclements or closures are intended to harm the population in general. On the contrary, the state's response is invariably that the army always takes measures to ensure the entry of sufficient quantities of food and medicine for the needs of the populace. Furthermore, the court has instructed the army to establish clear guidelines for ensuring the provision of emergency medical assistance.

It is important to stress that the measures adopted by the military commanders are the product of pressures imposed on them by terrorists who leave the residential areas in Judea and Samaria for the purpose of committing terrorist attacks, after which they return to these places. There is no other way of ensuring that they do not leave these areas again, at least until the intelligence sources have obtained the information necessary for their capture.

I will now turn to an examination of international law.

The concept of encirclement or imposing a siege is an ancient one. The original intention was to surround a city with the aim of wearing out the city's fighters until they surrendered. Clearly, this is no longer the intention when imposing a siege, and in any event Israel does not do it in order to "defeat" the residents. There is nothing in international law that prohibits such an action when it is intended to block the way for terrorists to realize their aims. This is a manifest act of self-defense that is permitted under international law.

The conceivable prohibition in this context is the prohibition against collective punishment. In other words, the tool of encirclement cannot be used if the intention is to punish the innocent for the past acts of a number of terrorists. This prohibition is stipulated in Article 50 of the Fourth Hague Convention and in Article 33 of the Fourth Geneva Convention.

In the cases of closure or encirclement orders that came to court, the State of Israel has emphasized that the measures were not being adopted with the intention of punishing the civilian population for the acts of individuals but rather as an act of defense or preventative measures. However, the conventions do impose upon the occupying power the duty of ensuring the welfare of civilians under all circumstances. Thus, Article 55 of the Fourth Geneva Convention obliges the occupying power to ensure the full provision of food and medicine. Legally speaking, however, in view of its agreements with the Palestinian Authority, it is highly unclear whether Israel has liability under this article. There are areas for which the Palestinian Authority bears full responsibility, but even so, Israel ensures the ongoing provision of food and medicines to areas around which it was forced to place a closure or encirclement.

There is one convention that raises a number of questions in the context of closures or encirclements: the International Covenant on Economic, Social and Cultural Rights.[36] This convention guarantees all persons the right to earn a living in dignity in accordance with their own decisions. Does Israel violate this right? I have serious doubts about any interpretation that ignores the security situation in the Occupied Territories. In my view, although these rights are to be respected, they are subject to those conventions that regulate the administration of occupied territory. The result is a manifest military need takes precedence over other interests, but at least the needs should be balanced in order to minimize the violation of human rights as much as possible, including economic rights.

Summing up this issue, we can say that the imposition of closures or encirclements is one of the measures at the disposal of military commanders to protect the civilian population in both the territories and Israel from repeated attacks by terrorists who flee to those areas for refuge. Because of its harshness and its effect on the civilian population, it is a last-ditch measure, to be employed in the absence of any other means for preventing additional acts of terrorism. Because of its severity, it, like the curfew, must be measured and for short periods of time, and subject to regular, periodic assessment of the necessity for it.

Designating a Closed Military Area

Earlier in this chapter I examined the restriction of freedom of movement as a result of the imposition of a curfew, closure, or encirclement. I shall now examine another restriction of movement, differing in character from these previous situations.

Regulation 125 empowers a military commander to declare a certain place or location a closed military area. It means that, for a certain period of time, both entrance and exit from the area require a special permit. The regulation states: "A military commander may by order declare any area or place to be a closed area for the purpose of these regulations. Any person who during any period in which any such order is in force, in relation to any area or place, enters or leaves that area or place without a permit in writing issued by, or on behalf of the military commander shall be guilty of an offence against these regulations." When the IDF entered the territories of the West Bank in 1967, it declared them to be a closed area, both in accordance with the Defense Regulations valid at that time and in accordance with a special directive issued by the IDF. The meaning of this declaration was that both entry into and exit from the West Bank territories required a special permit from the military commander. Consequently, people who had left the area before the Six Days' War could not return without receiving a special permit from the military commander. Likewise, those who had left temporarily but had not come back in time required permits, which were not always granted.

Even though the regulation does not specify the conditions for exercising this power, it is clear that it is subject to the rules of proper administration, as are all other administrative powers of the military commander. The discretion of the military commander must be reasonable. It must take into account the human rights of all those affected. The exercise of the power must be for a proper purpose, of an appropriate degree, and, obviously, in good faith and the product of relevant considerations only.

This regulation is intended to supervise the entry of people into the

West Bank area as well as the Gaza Strip, in the same manner as the minister of the interior is authorized to supervise those requesting to enter Israel. More pointedly, this regulation allows a military commander to restrict entry into a certain place or along a specific geographical contour. A military commander's reasons for closing an area must always be military reasons, otherwise the court is liable to rule that he exercised his discretion based on irrelevant considerations and that the action as such is void. However, military reasons may be interpreted in a variety of ways according to the circumstances of the case.

From an international perspective, there is nothing in international law that prevents the declaration of a particular area as a closed military area, under army supervision, assuming that the declaration is based on military necessities. It is clear that a declaration of this nature is liable to restrict the freedom of movement of the residents. However, considering the fact that it is an area under military control, and the correct balance between military needs and the rights of all the citizens to lead their lives in a normal manner, this power does not violate any right whatsoever of the residents.

Conclusion

In this chapter I examined a number of the legal tools available to a military commander when the democracy is engaged in a struggle with terrorist organizations. Israel finds itself in this struggle at a time when acts of terror and killing, primarily shooting attacks and suicide bombings, are committed against its citizens almost every single day, both in Israel and in the territories of the West Bank and the Gaza Strip.

The terrorist attacks carried out on U.S. land on September 11, 2001, were an awful reminder to the free world that terrorism has no clear boundaries. Although this chapter focused on the Israeli experience of many years standing concerning the use of administrative measures to fight terrorism while preserving fundamental human rights, it may provide a source of thought and inspiration for other democratic states that have been forced by circumstances to enter the territory of other countries and consequently equip their military commanders with efficient powers to deal with terrorism—for example, the United States in Afghanistan and Iraq.

The Mandate period Defense Regulations remain valid in the territory of the State of Israel, the West Bank, and the Gaza Strip. They authorize military commanders to adopt a number of measures, most of them preventative, in order to reduce as much as possible harm to peaceful citizens by acts of terrorism. While it is true that exercising these authorizations harms the local residents, the majority of whom are not involved in acts of terror, and instills in them deep feelings of resentment and frustration toward Israel, the harm caused them is unavoidable and an inevitable corollary to achieving the primary goal, which is preventing terrorist attacks.

Given that these measures affect residents finding themselves under military rule, my examination was not only of domestic law but also of international law. On both levels I found nothing wrong with the utilization of these legal tools, provided that they can be justified by manifest military needs. Furthermore, unlike other states in similar situations, the State of Israel allows the residents of the territories direct access to the Supreme Court, sitting as the High Court of Justice, in order to supervise the actions of military commanders. The Supreme Court does in fact closely and effectively supervise military commanders' exercise of their authority, even though this is a situation that does not easily admit of judicial supervision and intervention. Despite this difficulty, the court has made the commanders' work more difficult and promoted human rights for the residents. Consequently, as a rule a military commander is not entitled to implement his powers under Regulation 119 to immediately demolish a home in which a terrorist resides; rather he must wait a predetermined period of time during which the residents of the home may exhaust their right to appeal to him against his decision and even apply to the court if the military commander rejects their arguments. At the most the commander may, in urgent cases where military-operational exigencies demand immediate action, take reversible steps such as vacating the home of its residents and sealing it.

The administrative measures discussed above are drastic measures that violate the human rights of the local inhabitants. However, these rights must be balanced against the right to life of the citizens of the State of Israel, who are subject to ongoing frequent terrorist attacks by people who leave those territories and later on take refuge there again.

Democratic states, forced to fight terrorist and guerilla organizations, must be afforded the tools necessary to ensure their survival and existence. Not all ends justify the means, yet we cannot waive those democratic means, legal and legitimate, that we already have.

FIVE

Administrative Detentions
and the Use of Terrorists as Bargaining Counters

ON OCTOBER 16, 1986, a technical fault caused an Israeli Air Force plane to crash over Lebanon. The pilot was safely retrieved, but the navigator, Ron Arad, was captured and held first by the Amal movement and later by the Believers Resistance—a fanatical splinter organization. In May 1988 the latter organization delivered Arad into the hands of the Iranians, at which time Israel lost track of him.

As part of Israel's efforts to obtain information about the fate of Arad and other missing and captured Israeli soldiers, between 1986 and 1987 Israel kidnapped Lebanese citizens belonging to enemy organizations that had been involved in armed attacks against the IDF and the South Lebanese Army (SLA), which was cooperating with the IDF. In 1989 Israel kidnapped Sheikh Abd al-Karim Obeid, a Lebanese citizen who was a member of the leadership of Hezbollah and who had advocated and was also actively involved in the planning of Hezbollah's terrorist activities against the IDF and SLA. In 1994 Israel also kidnapped Mustafa Dib Mari Dirani, a Lebanese citizen who was acting as the security officer of the Amal movement when the latter captured Ron Arad, and who later established and headed the Believers Resistance and thus was responsible for transferring Arad to the Iranians.

Israel never pursued a criminal prosecution against Obeid and Dirani for their acts, but instead held them under administrative detention, in the beginning on the grounds of state security, as essential bargaining chips in negotiations for information and the release of Israel's captured and missing; and later on—following the decision in F.H. (Further Hearing) *In re Anon.*, which will be extensively discussed in the second part of this chapter—on the grounds that holding them was necessary in view of the direct danger each of them would pose to state security were he to be released. The two were not released and returned to Lebanon until January 2004, as part of a prisoner exchange between Israel and the Hezbollah. In contrast, the other Lebanese detainees were tried on criminal charges, convicted, and sentenced to varying periods of imprisonment. Upon completion of their sentences, Israel continued to hold them in detention, first by virtue of deportation orders issued against them, and afterward by administrative detention orders, issued on the grounds that state security required them to be held as bargaining chips in negotiations for information and the release of captured and missing Israeli soldiers.

In the judgment in F.H. *In re Anon.*, which was delivered in April 2000, the Supreme Court held by a majority of six to three that the prevailing laws of administrative detention in Israel did not permit the administrative detention of persons who were not themselves a danger to state security but were being held to be used as "bargaining chips"—hostages—in negotiations for the release of captured and missing soldiers.[1] Inevitably, as a result of this judgment, Israel released the eight petitioners as well as five other persons taken from Lebanon who had also been held in administrative detention for a similar purpose.

The president of the Supreme Court, Aharon Barak, who was among the majority judges, eloquently described the tragic dilemma facing the court:

> I am aware of the suffering of the families of captured and missing IDF soldiers. Their pain is great. The passing of the years and the uncertainty damage the human spirit. Even more painful is the situation of the prisoner, held in secret and in hiding, torn from his home and country. Indeed, this pain, together with the supreme interest of the State of Israel to return its sons to their borders, has not been lost to me . . . we bear the human and social tragedy of the captured and missing every day on our shoulders. Yet, however important the goal of releasing the captured and missing, it does not justify all the means. It is not possible . . . to rectify a wrong with a wrong. I am certain that the State of Israel will not be silent and will not rest until it finds the way to resolve this painful issue. As a country and as a society, our consolation will be that the path to resolution will be compatible with our basic values.[2]

This judgment clarifies the problematic nature of the use of administrative detention by a state governed by the democratic rule of law: on the one hand, administrative detention deprives a person of his freedoms by an administrative decision, without due process ending in his conviction for the commission of a criminal offense, while on the other hand, there are certain threats against state security in respect of which criminal law is incapable of providing a satisfactory solution. In these situations, the state has no choice but to employ irregular measures, such as administrative detention, in order to protect its citizens. Indeed, in light of the spreading and persistent acts of terror around the world, Western states are making increasing use of drastic devices in their struggle to thwart the threats directed against them. This trend raises the fear that excessive eagerness will lead to excessive and disproportional use of this measure, with the result that when eventually we shall look backward, we will find that it is we who have been the losers, since we have relinquished the very values for which we were fighting and have thereby fulfilled the ultimate desires of the terrorists. Put in the concise words of Alexander Hamilton, "The practice of arbitrary imprisonments, [has] been, in all ages, the favorite and most formidable instrument of tyranny."[3]

In the first part of this chapter I shall examine the purposes of administrative detention and consider the proper manner of implementing it within the context of the fight against terrorism. Thereafter, I shall turn to an analysis of how it is used in Israel, England, and the United States—three democratic countries whose citizens have been and remain desirable targets for injury by terrorist organizations. The issue of the constitutionality and legality of the most far-reaching use of administrative detention—holding a person for use as a bargaining counter—will be discussed extensively in the second part of this chapter.

What Is Administrative Detention?

The literal definition of the expression "administrative detention" is detention that is carried out by an administrative power and not by a judicial power or authority. Administrative detention, which is sometimes also termed "preventive detention," is detention in which a person is held without trial. The central purpose of such detention is not punishment for past offenses but deterring future offenses which the detainee is expected to commit. Detention is generally founded on the danger to state security or public security, posed by the particular person against whom the order is issued. Administrative detention is not a substitute for criminal arrest and should not be approached as such. As opposed to criminal arrest, where the suspect is arrested in respect of an offense he committed in the past and faces the institution of criminal proceedings, an administrative detainee does not await trial at all. Moreover, he is generally detained even though he has not committed any offense, or there is insufficient admissible and convincing evidence to enable charges to be brought against him within the framework of criminal proceedings. A person is held in administrative detention because of the fear that he may commit an offense upon being released.

This is a problematic issue. A person is put behind bars, not because of an act or offense committed by him, but because of something he may—but it is not certain that he will—do in the near or far-off future. Another distinction between arrest before trial and administrative detention is that the latter is generally indefinite, whereas the criminal remand is for a known period of time, namely, until the end of the proceedings underway.

Israeli Administrative Detention Law: A Comparison with Britain and the United States

Israel

As explained in the previous chapter, the Defense (Emergency) Regulations were promulgated by the British Mandate authorities in Eretz Yisrael and were incorporated into domestic Israeli law upon the establishment of the state. Regulations 108 and 111 empowered the high commissioner or a military commander to make an order against a person if either official was of the opinion that it was expedient in order to maintain public order, secure public safety, or secure the security of the state.

Before the declaration of the independence of the State of Israel, these regulations were primarily used by the British administration against members of Jewish underground organizations. Accordingly, a great deal of criticism was voiced when Israel itself adopted these regulations, and pressure was exerted to reform the law.

In 1979 reform was carried out, and the old regulations were replaced by the Emergency Powers (Arrest) Law.[4] True, this law was valid only within Israel, but the spirit of reform was also felt in the administered territories.[5] The new law contained a number of substantial changes. Judicial review is a cornerstone of the new law and constitutes a basic right. If the detainee is not brought before the president of the district court within forty-eight hours from the start of his detention, he must be released, unless some other ground for detaining him exists. Moreover, the detainee must be present in court during the hearing of his case, failing which he will be released from detention. The primary power to issue a detention order is conferred on the minister of defense. He may issue an order any time he has reasonable cause to believe that public security or state security would be endangered if this person is not detained. Contrary to the old regulations, these orders are limited in time; they are valid only for six months. The minister may extend the validity of the order from time to time, for additional periods of six months. Subsidiary power is conferred on the chief of the General Staff. If the chief of the General Staff has reasonable cause to believe that conditions exist permitting the minister of defense to make an order, he, and only he, may make a detention order not exceeding forty-eight hours. He has no power to extend this period at all. These powers may not be delegated.

In defense against improper exploitation of administrative detentions, the new law also adds a further level of judicial review. The detainee must be brought for periodic review, initially three months after the detention is confirmed by the district court; thereafter the decision must be reexamined by the president of the district court every three months. To enable the detainee to defend himself against the suspicions against him, there are a number of additional statutory safeguards of the detainee's rights, such as his right to legal advice and the right to know why he has been detained, unless security reasons preclude informing him of the same.

Accordingly, a detainee has a right to be present at the time of confirmation of the detention order and in the legal proceedings thereafter, unless the judge is satisfied that state security requires that proceedings continue without the detainee or his representative. Also, the order must be the sole means of achieving the desired result. If alternative measures are available, the judge must declare the detention order invalid. Difficulty in convicting a person in ordinary criminal proceedings is not a reason for favoring administrative detention. However, if the evidence against him is privileged and cannot be disclosed, administrative detention becomes an option. The Administrative Detention Law is effective only when an emergency situation prevails in Israel, declared in accordance with Section 49 of Basic Law: The Government. But this precondition has no substantive implications, because Israel has been in an emergency situation from its establishment in 1948 to the present day.

In the immediate aftermath of the establishment of the State of Israel, the Supreme Court refrained almost completely from intervening in decisions made by the various security forces, on the grounds that those responsible for security knew best what the country's security needs were and how to achieve them. Today, there is a new trend, and the judgment in the Further Hearing of the Lebanese petition may perhaps be seen as one of the milestones in the court's new approach: that it is possible to intervene in security decisions, and that there are no longer any sacrosanct issues. In order to clarify this proposition, it is necessary to turn to an examination of the various trends disclosed by Israeli case law relating to administrative detention.

Not only is effective and fair judicial review one of the basic rights in the legal system, it is also essential to the preservation of human rights and freedoms. One may say that in the case of the Lebanese petitioners, the court intervened in a security decision more than it was accustomed to doing. Today, the court's attitude is that everything is subject to judicial review; President Barak has encapsulated this approach in the phrase "Everything is justiciable."[6] There are a number of theories explaining why judges refrained from intervening in security matters in the past. One theory is that the judges were afraid that if they interfered in these issues, public confidence in the judicial system would lessen. Generally, the public displays broad interest in defense matters, as it did in this case. Public discourse has taken place and differing views voiced as to what the court should do in security cases. Although the court is not obliged to reflect public opinion in its judgments, it was afraid that if its opinion differed from that of the majority of the public, confidence in the judicial system—confidence on which the system depends—would lessen and perhaps even disappear altogether.

Since the 1979 reform, judicial review of the detention order is regarded as being constitutive,[7] although even after the reform, judges have continued to examine the legality of detention orders without investigating the reasons for the detention itself. In other words, the court has not substituted its own discretion for that of the security authority making the decision. The Knesset, Israel's parliament, provided by law that the authority issuing the order must do so on an objective and reasonable basis. Accordingly, in exercising its judicial review the court must also examine the reasonableness of the decision to issue the order.

Notwithstanding the clear modification in the scope and nature of judicial review, a number of major problems have endured. The checks and balances in the Administrative Detention Law are inadequate. There are insufficient guarantees that the detainee will know why he is being held.

Moreover, should a judge decide to examine the evidence in the absence of the detainee or his counsel—in itself a harmful procedure—in general he will be presented with written testimony and thus will not have the opportunity to observe the witnesses themselves and obtain an impression of them. Consequently, the court will not be able to establish the credibility of the witness and will have to take it for granted that the witness is credible, or rely on the impression produced by the security officer who presents the written evidence to the court.

POSSIBLE JUSTIFICATIONS FOR ADMINISTRATIVE DETENTIONS

Notwithstanding the many disadvantages of administrative detention, which shall be fully discussed below, it may be justified on a number of grounds. Administrative detention is a measure used not for punitive purposes or vengeance but for the purpose of defense. Its purpose is to fill a number of essential security needs: First, the detention prevents the detainee from reuniting with members of his organization and continuing their joint struggle against the state. Second, the detention enables the security authorities to interrogate the detainee and thus gather essential intelligence regarding the operational ability and future operational plans of the detainee's organization, as well as its structure, the identity of its members, and the source of its finances. Third, it is very difficult to prove the existence of conspiracies on the part of secret underground terrorist organizations. Most of the evidence and testimony in these cases is inadmissible in court, partly because it is considered to be hearsay evidence. In certain cases some of the evidence is privileged and cannot be disclosed in court, such as intelligence information that may expose an agent or informer and thereby imperil him. In such cases, criminal proceedings are not a possibility, and the only available options are to hold the suspect in administrative detention or set him free.

In view of these three justifications, it is possible to summarize that administrative detention is based on the idea that in deciding to detain a person society is choosing the less harmful of two possible evils. The choice is made by balancing the freedom of the individual against the harm to society that may be caused if the suspect is let free. Hence, administrative detention must be employed only when, in drawing a balance between the two situations, the scales tip toward the protection of society. The main difficulty with this argument is that there is no guarantee that the detention of the person is indeed the least harmful way of achieving the desired result, namely, precluding the disastrous outcome which may befall society. One of the difficult problems relating to administrative detention is how to ensure the credibility of the evidence, particularly when the judge himself does not see the witnesses but learns of their testimony from secondary sources or their written testimony. Further, the judge cannot know what impact the detention order will have and whether the detention will indeed prevent the outcome it is intended to foil.

In an effort to overcome this problem, the court has held that not all unsupported hearsay evidence or unchecked assumption will suffice to place a person in administrative detention; rather, well-founded evidence which every reasonable person would regard as having evidential value is necessary, even though it may not be admissible according to the ordinary laws of evidence.[8]

In yet another case, the test was held to be whether there is sufficient evidence to indicate that if the detainee is released, he will almost certainly pose a danger to public or state security.[9] The court further emphasized that the judge must not substitute himself for the function of the minister and decide against whom the order should be directed or when the detention will take place.[10] The public danger must be so grave as to leave no choice but to hold the suspect in administrative detention.

WHICH RIGHTS MAY BE DEROGATED AND WHICH SAFEGUARDED?

In declared periods of emergency, many human rights are imperiled. The most vulnerable right is the right to a fair trial. A state is prohibited from negating the basic rights of a person without a fair process. Thus, for example, a person cannot be deprived of his freedom and imprisoned without fair process of judicial review. A detainee, as such, is already limited in his rights, and we cannot deprive him completely of his remaining ones.[11] In periods of emergency, there is generally no time to institute all the usual processes and proceedings that are intended to preserve a just balance—compatible with the concept underlying the requirement of due process—between the rights of the individual and the rights of the state. In such times, the interest of the state is to make the decision-making mechanism more efficient. Thus, judicial review becomes less strict. The purpose of due process is to ensure an objective judicial process conducted by an unprejudiced judge who is committed to adjudicating in accordance with the law; this process must be open and subject to the keen eyes of the public. The hearing or trial must take place within a reasonable period of time. The person who is the subject of the process must know what charges have been made against him as well as what evidence has been gathered against him. That person must be given the opportunity to attack the veracity of the evidence brought against him and a fair opportunity to challenge it and present the court with his own version of events. The decision of the court must be reasoned and contain detailed particulars and explanations for the final outcome. There must be a right of appeal to a higher instance or to another judicial power. In all proceedings there must be a right to be represented. The same phenomena may also be seen in cases of administrative detention. There, the power to issue the detention order is conferred on the executive branch, and judicial review is conducted in a more flexible manner.

An additional question concerns whether administrative detentions in Israel accord with the standards of minimum rights. As already noted, one of the many rights that may be infringed during a state of emergency is the right to due process. A number of proposals have been made to transform this right into a right that cannot be infringed, in any manner or circumstances. However, these proposals have been rejected: no country has proved willing to accept all the aspects of the right to due process as inflexible tenets. The right to due process is problematic because it has a variety of facets. One is the right for the hearing to be conducted in public. The Fourth Geneva Convention of 1949 provides for minimum protected rights in times of emergency. Article 75 of Protocol I Additional to the Conventions, which is entitled "Fundamental Guarantees," provides a number of safeguards for the maintenance of due process, such as the obligation to promptly inform a detainee of the reasons for his detention and the obligation to release him with the minimum delay possible. These provisions apply to all persons found in the power of a party to the conflict who do not benefit from more favorable treatment under the conventions or under this protocol.

Article 9 of the International Covenant on Civil and Political Rights grants the detainee the right to be informed of the reasons for his detention and to be brought immediately before an official judicial instance. In other words, even if a person is detained, we are prohibited from preventing him from turning to the courts or other legal tribunal. Although Israel ratified this convention in 1991, it is not obliged to comply with all the requirements set out therein, since the ratification was accompanied by a reservation stating that since its establishment Israel had been subject to incessant threats of war, armed attacks, and terrorist assaults. This situation had led to the declaration of a state of emergency in May 1948, upon the establishment of the state. This state of emergency had repeatedly been extended by the Knesset for defined periods and constitutes a general public emergency within the meaning of Article 4(a) of the convention. Accordingly, Israel found it necessary to take steps in its defense but only to the extent required by the urgent needs of the situation, including the implementation of arrest and detention powers; and to the extent that these means were incompatible with Article 9 of the convention—which prohibits arbitrary detentions and arrests—the State of Israel derogated from its obligations under this provision. Thus theoretically Israel may detain a person without time limitation, without informing him of the reasons for his detention, without granting him the possibility of challenging the charges made against him—and all without breaching the convention.

It should be noted that even if the state is not subject to the article under discussion, as a result of its declaration it is still subject to humanitarian rules and domestic law. The domestic laws prohibit the deprivation of a person's basic rights, except to the extent necessary in light of the state of emergency. Thus, for example, it would be inconceivable to leave a person in administrative detention for his entire life, or even for a lengthy period of time, without reexamining at determined periods whether the detention is vital.

Apart from the right to due process, administrative detention entails the violation of other rights, such as freedom of movement, which in turn has a number of ramifications. The detainee is deprived of the right to freedom of expression and freedom of association, although he may wear his own clothes in the detention center, in contrast to other persons in remand. The Emergency Powers (Arrest) (Conditions of Detention under Administrative Detention) Regulations, 5741-1981, provide for an additional amelioration of detention conditions. While the old regulations did not contain any reference to the requisite conditions of detention, the current law introduces such requirements in order to ensure that the detainee does not feel like a convicted felon. These provisions emphasize that detention is to be preventive rather than punitive. Indeed, even the courts have reiterated that "not only should the conditions of imprisonment of administrative detainees not fall below those of prisoners, but everything should be done to ensue that conditions should be better . . . as the presumption of innocence is available to them . . . the security considerations which led to the detention of the detainees, do not justify the determination of inappropriate detention conditions."[12]

The United Kingdom

During the armed conflict between the Protestant Loyalists and the IRA, from the beginning of the 1970s to the middle of the 1990s, the swelling violence in Northern Ireland and England was directed not only against government and military targets but also against civilians and their property. Initially, the governing legislation in Britain was the Civil Authorities (Special Powers) Act (Northern Ireland), 1922, which permitted a person to be detained, in certain circumstances, even for an indefinite period of time. In 1972 Parliament began restricting the powers of the government to detain suspected terrorists. In 1974 Parliament enacted the Prevention of Terrorism (Temporary Provisions) Act (PTA), which was designed to be temporary legislation but was in fact continually renewed, becoming de facto permanent law. The PTA regulated the powers of the government to detain and interrogate suspected terrorists. The detention of a person required the presence of reasonable grounds to suspect his involvement in terrorism, a standard identical to that needed to arrest a person under the criminal law. Likewise, the act provided that the initial period of detention should not exceed forty-eight hours, and in the event that the interrogation required a longer period of time, it was necessary to obtain the authorization of the secretary of state for Northern Ireland, who could extend the detention for an additional period of five days only. The act guaranteed detainees access to counsel by the end of forty-eight hours after the original detention.

Following the ruling of the European Court of Human Rights that the arrangements set out in the act, which enabled the government to deprive a person of his liberty for seven days without judicial scrutiny of the legality of the detention, contravened Article 5(3) of the European Convention for the Protection of Human Rights and Fundamental Freedoms, 1950[13] (which compels a detainee to be brought "promptly before a judge or other officer authorized by law to exercise judicial power and shall be entitled to trial within a reasonable time or to release pending time"), Britain decided to derogate from its obligation under Article 5 of the convention in accordance with Article 15. Article 15 provides that such derogation is possible only "[i]n time of war or other public emergency threatening the life of the nation," and even then a state is required to "take measures derogating from its obligations . . . to the extent strictly required by the exigencies of the situation."

Following the publication of a series of independent inquiry reports that indicated the improper use of these arrest powers,[14] the British legislature concluded that the absence of judicial review excessively impaired the rights of the detainee, and consequently engaged in legal reform which, inter alia, incorporated arrangements ensuring increased administrative supervision and documentation regarding the implementation of the powers. Nonetheless, these reforms did not deal with the core of the problem, since they did not afford the detainee sufficient procedural guarantees of his rights. Indeed, as the years passed, it became increasingly clear that the balance set out in the statute was inappropriate, and many ensuing convictions later turned out to have been miscarriages of justice.[15] These cases in turn led to additional legislative reform, and in 2000 the PTA was replaced with the Terrorism Act,[16] which came into force in 2001 and in an inclusive, comprehensive manner regulates the powers of the executive authority to detain terrorist suspects. The statute also gives a dominant role to judicial review of the manner of implementation of the powers in a way compatible with the provisions of the European Convention on Human Rights, prohibits indefinite detention, and provides procedural guarantees of due process for detainees.

The statute empowers a constable to detain without a warrant a person reasonably suspected to be a terrorist, but the latter must be charged or released within forty-eight hours of being arrested unless a judicial authority has upheld a police application to extend the detention for a further maximum period of five days. The judicial authority is entitled to do so only if it is persuaded that there are reasonable grounds for believing that the continued detention is necessary to obtain relevant evidence and that the investigation is being conducted diligently and expeditiously. The detainee must be notified of the application to extend his detention and may respond to it before the judicial authority, by himself or through counsel.

Among the rights granted to the detainee, which as noted are intended to guarantee due process, it is possible to count the right to apply for a certain person (who may be a family member, a friend, or any other person known to the detainee or who it is reasonable to assume has an interest in the condition of the detainee) to be notified of the detention and of the transfer of the detainee from one detention facility to another. He is also granted the right to meet privately with a solicitor. Both the notification of detention and the meeting with the solicitor must be carried out as soon as is reasonably practicable; however, a police officer of at least the rank of superintendent is empowered to postpone the implementation of these rights if he has reasonable grounds to believe that they would impair the conduct of the investigation or the bodily integrity of any person, although the detainee must be allowed to realize these rights within the first forty-eight hours of his detention. Likewise, the law requires an officer who is not directly involved in the investigation to determine whether the detention is indeed essential; the first such examination to be conducted as soon as is reasonably practicable and thereafter every twelve hours during the first forty-eight hours of detention. The examining officer must put in writing the reasons why it is necessary to continue the detention and must enable the detainee or his counsel to respond before reaching a final decision.

Under the influence of the terrorist attack of September 11, 2001, on the United States, Parliament enacted the Anti-terrorism, Crime and Security Act (ATCSA),[17] which did not change the powers of detention set out in the Terrorism Act regarding British citizens but expanded the powers of detention of foreign nationals whom the government cannot prosecute criminally or deport for legal or practical reasons. The act enabled the secretary of state to issue a detention certificate for an unlimited period of time against foreign nationals who there was reasonable cause to believe were involved in international terrorist activities and whose presence in Britain therefore posed a threat to national security. The use of these powers was subject to stringent judicial supervision, under which the detainee could appeal to the Special Immigration Appeals Commission, an independent judicial body set up by the Special Immigration Appeals Commission Act, 1997, to hear appeals that involve a public-interest provision—that is, a provision by which a person's presence in the United Kingdom is considered to be not conducive to the public good for reasons of national security, or the relations between the United Kingdom and any other country, or other reasons of a political nature.[18]

If this judicial body found that there was no reasonable basis for the declaration that the detainee was a suspected international terrorist or that he posed a threat to British security, or if for any other reason there were no grounds for issuing the detention certificate, it was under a duty to nullify the certificate. If the judicial body did not nullify the detention certificate, the detainee could appeal its decision to the court of appeals and thereafter to the House of Lords. Even if the detainee had not challenged the legality of his detention, the ATCSA obligated the Special Immigration Appeals Commission to hold a periodic review of the certificate classifying the detainee as a suspected international terrorist. The first review had to be held as soon as was reasonably practicable starting six months after the date on which the certificate was issued, and thereafter as soon as was reasonably practicable after every three months.

It is important to emphasize that the power of detention vested by this act was a temporary power that required yearly renewal by the secretary of state, and in any event the act contained a sunset provision to the effect that these provisions were intended to permanently expire in November 2006. Under the detention power accorded by the ATCSA, seventeen nonnationals had been certified as suspected international terrorists. Because these arrangements were incompatible with Article 5(1)(F) of the European Convention on Human Rights, Britain notified the secretary general of the Council of Europe of a derogation from Article 5 of the convention in accordance with Article 15.

In July 2002 the Special Immigration Appeals Commission held that in light of the September 11, 2001, terrorist attacks in the United States, the government was entitled to determine that there was a public emergency threatening the life of the nation within Article 15 of the convention, even if there was no imminent threat of a terrorist attack but rather an intention and a capacity to carry out serious terrorist violence. Therefore, the commission concluded that the government had been entitled, under Article 15, to derogate from its obligations under the convention to the extent strictly required by the exigencies of the situation. Nevertheless, it granted a declaration that Section 23 of the ATCSA, which authorizes the detention of foreign nationals, was incompatible with Articles 5 and 14 of the convention insofar as it permitted the detention of suspected terrorists in a way that discriminated against them on the grounds of nationality, since there were British suspected terrorists who could not be detained under those provisions. In October 2002 the Court of Appeal reversed the commission's ruling and held that indefinite detention of foreign nationals under Section 23 of the ATCSA is compatible with British and international law.[19] An appeal on the decision has been filed, and a special nine-judge panel of the House of Lords Judicial Committee, Britain's highest court, determined (by a majority of 8 to 1) that Section 23 of the ATCSA was disproportionate and discriminatory, and that in the balance between national security and human rights Parliament had clearly attached insufficient weight to the human rights of nonnational suspected terrorists.[20]

In light of this ruling, the government initiated the enactment of the Prevention of Terrorism Act, which as of March 2005 replaces detention without trial of suspected international terrorists under Part 4 of the ATCSA.[21] The new act, which is subject to an annual renewal, applies to both foreign and British nationals. It is aimed at preventing terrorism-related activity through the imposition of derogating and nonderogating control orders on suspected terrorists. Derogating control orders deprive the individual of his liberty by subjecting him to house arrest without trial, and therefore require derogation from the European Convention on Human Rights, while nonderogating control orders impose various restrictions on the individual that do not infringe convention rights that require derogation (such as a prohibition on his being at specified places at specified times, a requirement on him to cooperate with specified arrangements for monitoring his movements by electronic or other means, and a requirement on him to report to a specified person at specified times and places).

The secretary of state may make a nonderogating control order against an individual for a period of up to twelve months, which can be renewed from time to time for additional periods of twelve months if he has reasonable grounds for suspecting that the individual is or has been involved in terrorism-related activity and that it is necessary, for purposes connected with protecting members of the public from a risk of terrorism, to make the control order. However, the secretary of state cannot make a nonderogating control order against an individual unless he first applies to the court for permission to make the order and has been granted that permission. The court may give permission to make a control order unless it determines that the decision is obviously flawed. If permission is granted, the court must give directions for a hearing in relation to the order as soon as reasonably practicable after it is made. In urgent cases where the secretary of state makes a nonderogating control order against an individual without the permission of the court, he must immediately refer the order to the court and a hearing must begin no more than seven days after the day on which the control order was made.

A derogating control order can only be made by the court, following an application by the secretary of state. In contrast to the ATCSA, which allowed the indefinite detention of foreign nationals, the new act restricts the duration of the order to a period of six months, which can be renewed from time to time for additional periods of six months. The court may make a control order against the individual upon the existence of four cumulative conditions: (a) it is satisfied, on the balance of probabilities, that the controlled person is an individual who is or has been involved in terrorism-related activity; (b) it considers that the imposition of obligations on the controlled person is necessary for purposes connected with protecting members of the public from a risk of terrorism; (c) it appears to the court that the risk is one arising out of, or is associated with, a public emergency in respect of which there is a designated derogation from the whole or a part of Article 5 of the Human Rights Convention; and (d) the obligations to be imposed by the order are or include derogating obligations of a description set out for the purposes of the designated derogation in the designation order.

The United States

The United States, too, did not go untouched by administrative detentions. While they were not always termed "administrative detentions," the nature, objectives, and characteristics of the detentions were similar to those of administrative detentions in Israel.

In 1919, in consequence of the simultaneous explosion of bombs in eight cities around the United States, the government detained a few thousand foreign nationals in what are now known as the Palmer Raids. Following their interrogation it was decided to charge them with breach of the immigration laws and prohibited association with communist elements. Hundreds were deported, but no one was found guilty of involvement in the explosions.[22]

During the Second World War, the United States again detained many of its residents. The majority of those detainees were Americans of Japanese ancestry, but some were also of German and Italian origin. However, there was an important distinction between these groups of detainees. The detainees with German or Italian roots were detained on an individual basis, on the grounds of the danger they were thought to pose. In contrast, Americans with Japanese roots were detained en masse, and without distinction, on the basis of a sweeping determination that by reason of their origins or roots they were not loyal to America. More than 110,000 American citizens and residents of Japanese ancestry were compelled to leave their homes and refused permission to stay in broad areas in the west of the country, and many of them were forcibly held in detention camps during the years of the war. The detentions relied on special temporary provisions—special procedural rules that enabled the detention of persons who posed a danger but who could not be convicted of any crime under the ordinary rules of evidence.

In the judgment in the case of *Korematsu v. United States*,[23] which over the years became one of the most important decisions relating to the restriction of the basic rights of an individual in times of emergency, the court refrained from deciding the constitutionality of placing an entire racial group in detention camps—this was not the question facing it—and focused only on the question of the constitutionality of removing them by force from their homes and transporting them to other areas. The Court held that the exclusion orders had to be examined on the basis of the situation that prevailed when they were issued, while taking into account all the problems and special circumstances surrounding their issue. The judge noted that it should not be forgotten that the coasts of the United States had been exposed to air attack by the Japanese army and that the defense against that threat had to be proportional to it.

By majority opinion—with three justices dissenting—the Court found that the exclusion was essential and therefore constitutional by reason of the legitimate security needs then prevailing.

This precedent has had a somewhat misleading effect in relation to the appropriate balance between individual rights and national security in times of emergency, since in 1982 the U.S. Commission on Wartime Relocation and Internment of Civilians concluded that the relocation and the detention were "not justified by military necessity but had been prompted instead by 'race prejudice, war hysteria and a failure of political leadership,'" and that being mistaken they would be "overruled in the court of history."[24]

ADMINISTRATIVE DETENTION AS A TOOL FOR THWARTING TERRORIST ACTS

Notwithstanding the questionable efficiency and grave constitutional consequences of the two waves of preventive mass detentions described above, the American government decided to launch an additional wave of detentions following the atrocity of September 11, 2001. As part of this operation, thousands of people were arrested—all of them Arab or of Arab origin—who were suspected of being connected in some degree to terrorist elements or who were suspected of possessing information concerning terrorism.

These persons were interviewed by the government. Against some, no further steps were taken, while others were detained on one of three grounds:[25] first, persons detained by the immigration authorities for breaching immigration laws, the vast majority of whom were deported within a few months of being detained; second, persons detained within the framework of ordinary criminal proceedings, both on suspicion of having committed terrorism-related crimes and on suspicion of having committed other federal crimes; and third, persons suspected of possessing information connected to the events of September 11, who were therefore detained as material witnesses under a judicial warrant in order to guarantee their testimony before a grand jury.

It soon became clear that the present wave of mass detentions, like the two earlier ones, had no significant benefit from a security point of view but did have serious constitutional ramifications. The government refused to disclose various details regarding many of the detainees (such as their names, the names of their attorneys, and dates and places of detention);[26] many were detained without proof of their individual complicity in an offense but rather on the basis of collective grounds for detention determined by their ethnic origin;[27] and only a few of the detainees were ultimately tried on suspicion of having committed crimes connected to terrorism, and most of those were found innocent.[28]

In addition to these detentions, the government also initiated preventive administrative detentions of foreign citizens who were captured and incarcerated outside the territory of the United States on suspicion of involvement in hostile activities against the United States, as well as U.S. citizens who were incarcerated within U.S. territory after being designated as enemy combatants.

DETENTION OF ALIENS

In the aftermath of the attack of September 11, the two houses of Congress passed a joint resolution, Authorization for Use of Military Force, which stated that acts of violence committed against the United States and its citizens "render it both necessary and appropriate that the United States exercise its rights to self-defense and to protect United States citizens."[29] Accordingly, following the decision of Congress that acts of this type constituted "an unusual and extraordinary threat to the national security and foreign policy of the United States," Congress also decided to grant the president power "to use all necessary and appropriate force against those . . . persons he determines planned, authorized, committed, or aided the terrorist attacks that occurred on September 11, 2001, . . . in order to prevent any future acts of international terrorism against the United States by such nations, organizations or persons."

By virtue of this authorization, the president sent U.S. armed forces to Afghanistan with the aim of crushing the infrastructure of Al Qaeda in that country and bringing down the Taliban regime which supported it. During the course of the military operation, the Americans captured hundreds of people whom they suspected of being Al Qaeda and Taliban followers, and incarcerated them at the Guantánamo Bay Naval Base in Cuba.

On November 13, 2001, President George W. Bush signed a military order regulating the arrest and prosecution of non-U.S. nationals, in respect of whom there is reason to believe that they were or are members of the Al Qaeda organization, or who carried out, assisted in, or conspired to carry out acts of international terrorism.[30] The military order, accompanied by the military commission order published by the Department of Defense four months later,[31] specifies the procedures to which these illegal foreign combatants are subject. The procedures provide that these persons may be detained for an indefinite period of time without being tried, that the detention may be carried out in appropriate locations in or outside the United States, as decided by the secretary of defense, and that they must be treated humanely. The detainees are not brought to trial before civilian courts or before a military court martial but before military commissions especially set up for this purpose, and they cannot seek any remedy from any other judicial tribunal whatsoever, including any international tribunal. Military commissions act according to procedural and evidentiary rules that differ from those applicable in civil or military courts, by virtue of the provision set out in Section 1(f) of the military order, which states that "it is not practicable to apply in military commissions . . . the principles of law and the rules of evidence generally recognized in the trial of criminal cases in the United States district courts." The regulations allow, for example, witnesses to testify anonymously for the prosecution. In addition, any information may be admitted into evidence if the presiding officer judges it to be "probative to a reasonable person," a standard that leaves open the question whether information obtained through torture can also be admissible. Accordingly, even though the orders purport to grant the detainees constitutional guarantees sufficient to carry out a full and fair trial, they are objectively incapable of doing so.

Furthermore, the government refuses to regard the Al Qaeda fighters as prisoners of war, within the meaning of the Third Geneva Convention, on the grounds that they do not fight on behalf of a state and consequently are not party to the convention. The Taliban fighters who belonged to the regular forces of the government are also denied the status of prisoners of war by the United States, this time on the grounds that they do not meet the necessary preconditions for being granted this status, such as the requirement to clearly separate themselves from the civilian population.[32] The American government classifies all the fighters as unlawful foreign combatants, and has declared that even though they are not entitled from a legal point of view to the protection afforded by the Geneva Convention, it will as a matter of policy grant them humane treatment compatible with the standards established by the convention, but only to the extent appropriate and consistent with military necessity.[33]

This legal perception is incompatible with the United States' oblig-ations under international law, since the fact that the status of unlawful combatants is not positively regulated by the Geneva Convention does not create a vacuum in international law wherein each state is entitled to decide how it will treat these combatants as a matter of domestic law. Rather, their detention and prosecution ought to be conducted in accor-dance with the normative principles anchored in international human-itarian law.[34]

The government has faced severe criticism about the fairness of the military commission procedures since the special tribunal was estab-lished. For example, several U.S. military prosecutors claimed that the trial system had been secretly arranged to improve the chance of con-viction and to deprive defendants of exculpatory evidence.[35] The trials were abruptly halted in November 2004 when a federal district court ruled they violated both military law and the United States' obligation to comply with the Third Geneva Convention. The Court of Appeals for the District of Columbia Circuit reversed that ruling in July 2005 and has thus cleared the way for the trials to resume.[36]

DETENTION OF U.S. CITIZENS

Unlike the preventive mass detentions of aliens, preventive detentions of American citizens classified as enemy combatants were carried out in a more measured manner. Only two individuals have been detained so far under this procedure. The authority to carry out these detentions is not statutory or found in a presidential executive order; rather, the fed-eral government has interpreted the joint resolution Authorization for Use of Military Force, combined with the constitutional power of the president as commander in chief in accordance with Article 2 of the Constitution, as empowering the president to declare a person to be an enemy combatant and to order the Defense Department to seize and arrest him and thereafter even prosecute him before a military tribunal.

The doctrine of the "enemy combatant" was born in the decision in *Ex parte Quirin*, in which the Court held that the government was enti-tled to prosecute eight German-born Nazis before a military tribunal, where one of them was presumed to hold American citizenship, and all eight had been seized on American soil on suspicion of planning to sab-otage a number of facilities being used during the war effort of the Sec-ond World War. The Court held there that "[c]itizenship in the United States of an enemy belligerent does not relieve him from the conse-quences of a belligerency which is unlawful because in violation of the law of war. Citizens who associate themselves with the military arm of the enemy government, and with its aid, guidance and direction enter this country bent on hostile acts, are enemy belligerents within the meaning of the Hague Convention and the law of war."[37] The decision of the Court relied on the distinction in international law between lawful and unlawful combatants. As explained in chapter 2, international law extensively regulates the status and rights of three defined groups during the conduct of an armed conflict: combatants, freedom fighters, and civilians. Terrorists, as follows from the name, conduct their struggle in a manner that does not permit them to be included within one of these three categories, and therefore the only conclusion is that they are unlawful combatants, that is, they belong to a category that international law has deliberately refrained from regulating.

Accordingly, one cannot complain that the Court founded the doctrine of enemy combatant contrary to federal American law. The problem lies in the law's vague nature and the absence of clear criteria for its application—two flaws which the few later judgments of the Supreme Court failed to rectify. Thus, for example, no clarification has been given as to whether and how the doctrine applies when the war is not a conventional one (i.e., one in which the enemy combatant fighting the United States belongs to another sovereign state with which the United States is at war) but rather is an armed conflict in which the enemy combatant belongs to a nonstate private terrorist guerilla organization.

Nonetheless, in contrast to Israel and the United Kingdom, which enacted legislation specifying the grounds for the administrative detention of terrorists, the mechanisms of judicial review, and procedural defense mechanisms aimed at creating a proportional balance between the right to due process and the interests of national security, the United States government chose to be satisfied with building a shaky legal construction relying, on the one hand, on a vague judgment given during the Second World War—which was confined by the judges to the concrete circumstances of the case before them and which it is doubtful they ever thought would be stretched so far—and, on the other hand, on the decision of Congress granting the president sweeping power to administratively detain a person, with the criteria for exercising this power placed absolutely within the discretion of the executive authority.[38]

The result of this combination is dangerous to liberal values lying at the core of modern democracy. The power granted to the president is so expansive and comprehensive that it enables him to indefinitely detain a person incommunicado as an enemy combatant without informing him whether and when charges will be brought against him. The vagueness of the legal criteria for classifying the detainee as an enemy combatant do not enable him to attack the legality of their implementation, and he does not enjoy the benefit of any procedural guarantees—such as the right to know the charges and evidence against him and the right to meet with a legal representative—that ensure the existence of due process. The constitutive designation of an individual as an unlawful enemy combatant deprives him of all the rights granted to him by the Constitution by virtue of his status as an American citizen, thereby severing him completely from his life prior to being detained. The right to be held in proper conditions, to meet family members, and even the most basic right of appeal against the legality of the detention within the framework of habeas corpus proceedings no longer accrue to him. The moment the government classifies him as an "enemy combatant," he becomes entitled only to the rights granted to him by the president. Indeed, even if the government makes cautious use of these powers, the issue is one of such constitutional importance that it is too great to be left to the complete discretion of the government.[39] The rule of law requires, therefore, that these powers be anchored in statute and accompanied by stringent provisions for judicial review, which would minimize as much as possible not just the potential for improper exploitation of these powers but primarily their exercise in an inappropriate and defective manner.

Some of the significant constitutional difficulties arising from the two types of administrative detention were considered by the Supreme Court. In relation to the Guantánamo Bay detainees, the government insisted that they were not entitled to apply to the federal courts within the United States in order to challenge their detention, and stated that under the legal construction explained above, it had the power to detain and imprison them for an unlimited period of time without granting them any rights, apart from those which the president considered appropriate.[40] This argument was asserted on the basis that the courts in the United States did not have the power to issue a writ of habeas corpus in relation to aliens detained by American military forces outside the borders of the United States.

The Supreme Court dismissed this argument, and by a majority of 6 to 3 held that U.S. federal courts have jurisdiction to consider challenges to the legality of the executive detention of foreign nationals captured abroad in connection with hostilities and incarcerated at Guantánamo Bay. The rationale was that the detainees were being held in territory over which the United States had exercised plenary and exclusive jurisdiction for more than a hundred years and was likely to retain such control in the foreseeable future, notwithstanding its lack of ultimate sovereignty over the territory. The Court did not consider the merits of the petitioners' claims, since it held that these would be heard by the district court to which the case would be returned by virtue of the finding that it had jurisdiction to hear the detainees' petitions.

Regarding the detention of American citizens designated as enemy combatants, the government argued that the principle of the separation of powers obliged the judicial authority to refrain from intervening in the military considerations of the executive branch in connection with an ongoing conflict, and that all the courts were entitled to examine was whether legal authorization existed for the broader detention scheme.[41] At most, the government argued, the courts were entitled to examine the executive decision that a particular American citizen was an enemy combatant, albeit this examination had to be conducted under a very deferential "some evidence" standard. Applying this standard, the court was to engage in judicial review on the assumption that the facts underlying the classification of the individual as an enemy combatant, as presented to it by representatives of the executive, were true and accurate, so that judicial scrutiny was to be confined, in practice, to considering whether the facts presented to the court provided a legitimate basis for a constitutive declaration that a U.S. citizen was an enemy combatant.

Justice Sandra Day O'Connor, who wrote the majority opinion in *Hamdi v. Rumsfeld*, found that the congressional resolution Authorization for Use of Military Force indeed empowered the president in his capacity as commander in chief—as argued by the government—to detain a U.S. citizen as an enemy combatant. However, she dismissed the doctrine of judicial review proposed by the government as failing to satisfy the constitutional requirement for due process. The Court found that the detention of a U.S. citizen as an enemy combatant led to a confrontation between two weighty legitimate interests. The first interest was in granting autonomy of action to the executive, in order to enable it to effectively realize the essential goal of safeguarding national security and the safety of U.S. citizens. The seizure and administrative detention of those citizens who had betrayed their country and joined the enemy ranks during an armed conflict was essential in order to prevent them from rejoining the enemy in its war against the country. The more the Court tilted the balance in favor of a more comprehensive judicial process regarding alleged enemy combatants, the heavier the burden imposed on the government would be, causing harm to the war effort and therefore to national and public security. The second interest was in ensuring due process for every citizen, irrespective of the gravity of the charges against him, before his country negated his constitutional rights. In an enlightened democratic regime, it was an exceptional step for the executive to negate the physical liberty of a person, and one that had to be exercised with great care, since the detainee was not being tried in a criminal process for commission of an offense and the question of his guilt was not subject to examination by a judicial body. Consequently, there was always the danger of mistaken deprivation of his liberty.

The proper manner in which to resolve this clash of interests was by maintaining a constitutional balance that took into account, on the one hand, the risk of an erroneous deprivation of the private interest if the process were reduced and, on the other hand, the probable value, if any, of additional or substitute safeguards. The Court held that "striking the proper constitutional balance here is of great importance to the Nation during this period of ongoing combat. But it is equally vital that our calculus not give short shrift to the values that this country holds dear or to the privilege that is American citizenship. It is during our most challenging and uncertain moments that our Nation's commitment to due process is most severely tested; and it is in those times that we must preserve our commitment at home to the principles for which we fight abroad."[42]

The operational significance of this finding is that every citizen detainee who seeks to challenge his classification as an enemy combatant is entitled to do so and is also entitled to have access to counsel in connection with the proceedings on remand; the government is obliged to give him notice of the factual basis for his classification and a fair opportunity to rebut the government's factual assertions before a neutral decision maker. At the same time, regarding the scope of judicial review, the Court emphasized that although the idea of a judicial review that operated on the assumption that all the assertions put before the court by the executive's representatives are fact is derisory, since the court must enable the detainee to present his factual case with the aim of repudiating the government's case, nonetheless

> the exigencies of the circumstances may demand that, aside from
> thesecore elements, enemy combatant proceedings may be tailored
> to alleviate their uncommon potential to burden the executive at a
> time of ongoing military conflict. Hearsay, for example, may need to
> be accepted as the most reliable available evidence from the Government in such a proceeding. Likewise, the Constitution would not be
> offended by a presumption in favor of the Government's evidence,
> so long as that presumption remained a rebuttable one and fair oppor-

tunity for rebuttal were provided. Thus, once the Government puts forth credible evidence that the habeas petitioner meets the enemy-combatant criteria, the onus could shift to the petitioner to rebut that evidence with more persuasive evidence that he falls outside the criteria. A burden-shifting scheme of this sort would meet the goal of ensuring that the errant tourist, embedded journalist, or local aid worker has a chance to prove military error while giving due regard to the executive once it has put forth meaningful support for its conclusion that the detainee is in fact an enemy combatant.[43]

These determinations by the Supreme Court demonstrate an extremely important policy of checks and balances regarding the scope and manner of operation of the powers of incarceration taken by the president under the banner of the war against terror. The determinations unequivocally clarify that, both in time of emergency and in time of peace, the president is not above the law, and no man is ever beneath the contemplation of the law.[44] They strengthen the commitment of the judicial branch to guaranteeing the fundamental nature of an individual's right to be free from involuntary confinement without due process of law; but more important even than this, they testify to the fact that the judiciary has learned the lessons of the past and chosen not to fall into the same errors in the future, however pressing the time of emergency. As Justice O'Connor wrote: "As critical as the Government's interest may be in detaining those who actually pose an immediate threat to the national security of the United States during ongoing international conflict, history and common sense teach us that an unchecked system of detention carries the potential to become a means for oppression and abuse of others who do not present that sort of threat."[45]

However, without detracting from the great constitutional importance of these judgments, it should be emphasized that they do not provide an answer to some equally important constitutional issues.[46] Thus, for example, while it was held that an American citizen who has been classified as an enemy combatant has the right to attack the factual basis for the classification before a neutral decision maker, it is unclear whether this is a right to apply to the federal court or whether the right is more confined, namely, to apply to a military tribunal only, where the procedures for guaranteeing an individual due process are inferior to those implemented in the civilian courts.[47] Likewise, the Court refrained from deciding the question whether the presidential power of administrative detention also applies to perpetual executive preventive detentions;[48] whether and in what circumstances it is possible to prevent immediate access to counsel following detention; and what restrictions may be imposed on the meeting between the detainee and counsel.[49] It should also be noted that these judgments do not reflect a constitutional breakthrough, but merely an important clarification of the positive constitutional position in the United States. From the territorial point of view, the constitutional norms apply to every individual found within the borders of the United States, and from the personal point of view, they apply to American citizens wherever located who come into contact with any purported administrative authority of the United States.[50] Consequently, the Court reached the inevitable conclusion that every American citizen detained within the United States is entitled, except in the rarest of circumstances, to file a petition for a writ of habeas corpus and obtain substantive and effective judicial review in order to ensure due process as required by the Fifth Amendment of the Constitution.

The case law in which the constitutional and statutory entitlement of the Guantánamo Bay detainees to appeal against the constitutionality of their detention before the federal courts was determined, was rooted in the fact that the detainees were located in territory subject to foreign sovereignty but under plenary and exclusive U.S. jurisdiction—that is, de facto American territory. The majority judges emphasized that in contrast to an individual detained on American soil, not in every case where officials of the United States were empowered to deprive an alien of his liberty and detain him in foreign territory was that alien entitled to argue before the American courts that his detention was unconstitutional. This right was much more limited and accorded to the Guantánamo Bay detainees because of the plenary and exclusive U.S. jurisdiction over the foreign sovereign territory in which they were being forcibly held.[51]

Whereas, as noted, the laws of administrative detention in Israel and Britain vest every foreign national with the right to appeal to a judicial body against the constitutionality of his detention and provide that, even in the absence of such an appeal, periodic judicial review must be undertaken, the majority judges in *Rasul v. Bush* reached their conclusion after distinguishing the features of the Guantánamo Bay detentions from those of the detainees in *Eisentrager v. Johnson*.[52] In the latter case it was held that twenty-one German nationals captured by U.S. forces in China, tried and convicted for war crimes by the American military commission in Nanking, and incarcerated in occupied Germany were not entitled to be heard by the American courts. The three minority judges, however, were of the opinion that the *Eisentrager* ruling also applied to the Guantánamo Bay detainees, who were therefore not entitled to petition the American courts at all. Since the *Eisentrager* ruling was not overturned but merely distinguished, it is not clear whether every foreign detainee held outside the borders of the United States is entitled to petition the courts within the United States merely because he has been detained by an American executive authority, and on the basis of the careful and qualified reasoning of the majority judges it would seem that the answer to this question is almost certainly no. Since the *Eisentrager* ruling was not overturned, and it was not held that the actions of every American soldier are governed by American constitutional law and that therefore every detainee, whatever his nationality, is entitled to his day in the American courts, the Supreme Court did not provide the necessary and hoped-for innovation, and the United States has not yet reached the same vital level of judicial review that already exists in Israel and Great Britain.

The Lawfulness of Holding Terrorists as Bargaining Counters

The Normative Dimension

In the Further Hearing relating to the Lebanese detainees, whose circumstances were described at the beginning of this chapter, the majority of the judges held that the legality of their detention had to be determined according to the Administrative Detention Law. As noted, this law will remain in effect so long as the emergency situation in Israel continues to prevail.

To examine whether the detainees were being held in accordance with the Administrative Detention Law, President Barak attempted in the Further Hearing to elucidate the meaning of the "reasons of state security or public security" which require a particular person to be detained and which are referred to in the Administrative Detention Law. President Barak held that the term was sufficiently broad to embrace events where the danger to the security of the state or the public did not ensue from the particular person himself. But he did not content himself with a linguistic interpretation of the term—a first stage—but further tried to determine the purpose of the law underlying the words.

The purpose behind every law is twofold: objective and subjective. On the subjective level, after examining the history of the draft bill in the Knesset, President Barak concluded that it did not teach anything regarding the intention of the legislature as to whether the law enables a person to be detained even if he does not pose a direct danger to state or public security. The comments of the members of the Knesset during the drafting hearings indicated that they had not considered this situation at all and had concentrated solely on the classic situation in which the detainee himself posed a danger to state or public security. The objective purpose of the law, on the other hand, was the outcome of the balance between the values it was intended to realize and the values it infringed. It followed that administrative detention was intended to protect state security and cause the least possible harm to the basic rights of those injured by the detention.

President Barak noted that when we seek to understand the scope of these basic values and the proper balance to be drawn between them in cases of administrative detention, we encounter a genuine, difficult, and intense conflict, since "freedom ends where detention begins," and in light of its unique characteristics, administrative detention has a particularly radical impact on human rights. Since the person is detained without trial, he may be held in detention for a lengthy period of time, and he may be prevented from knowing the nature of the evidence against him, if that evidence is classified as secret.[53]

Notwithstanding the supreme importance of human rights in a free society, a "balance is needed—a sensitive and difficult balance—between the freedom and dignity of the individual and state and public security."[54] This need for balance supported the argument that a democratic society could hold a person in administrative detention only if he posed a real danger to the state. Therefore, it did not enable and did not authorize the detention of a person who did not pose a direct danger or threat to state security and was being held solely as a bargaining counter.

This conclusion was based on the same reasoning applied by President Barak in his contrary decision in the initial appeal:

> Administrative detention violates the freedom of the individual. When the detention is carried out in circumstances in which the detainee provides a "bargaining counter," this constitutes a serious infringement of human dignity, since the detainee is perceived as a means of achieving an objective and not as an objective in himself. In these circumstances, the detention infringes the autonomy of will, and the concept that a person is the master of himself and responsible for the outcome of his actions. The detention of the appellants is nothing other than a situation in which the key to a person's prison is not held by him but by others. This is a difficult situation.[55]

A state that detains a person merely with the intention of negotiating his release with the opposing party creates a situation that leads to violations of rights, human dignity, and freedom which a free state should not permit or abet, notwithstanding prevailing security exigencies.

This conclusion is also supported by international treaty law, which prohibits the detention of persons as hostages, a term that also embraces the detention of persons to turn them into bargaining counters.

In his judgment in the initial appeal, President Barak had held that he was convinced "that the detention of individuals for the purpose of the release of our missing and captured [soldiers] . . . is conferred on the respondent (the state) within the framework of the Detention Law,"[56] contrary to his later judgment in the Further Hearing: "The return of captured and missing [soldiers] is an integral part of the security of the state and fulfills an important function in relation to the morale of the army and its values. Accordingly . . . holding the detainees in this case falls within the boundaries of reasons of state security, and where it is proved that their release will harm the efforts to release the captured and missing [soldiers], the detention order becomes valid."[57]

In the initial judgment President Barak had also held that, relying on the secret information presented to him, he was persuaded that there was a near certainty that if the Lebanese petitioners were released, Israel's negotiations with the enemy for the release of the captured and missing soldiers would be undermined. With regard to the question of proportionality—in other words, whether there was a less harmful way of achieving the desired goal—he held that at the present time there was no such alternative means.

In the same initial judgment, Justice Dorner, in a dissenting opinion, held that the Administrative Detention Law did not permit persons to be held in administrative detention for the sole purpose of being used as negotiating counters for the release of missing and captured soldiers where the detainees themselves posed no real danger. Justice Dorner based this opinion on a number of factors. First was her understanding of the appropriate interpretation of the Administrative Detention Law, according to the intention of the legislature. Second, Justice Dorner dismissed the contention that if the law did not prohibit detention when the risk did not arise from the detainee himself, then the detention was permitted. In her view, failure to anchor the prohibition in the law was immaterial. Third, according to the law, the court had to confirm the validity of the order. In her view, such confirmation could not be regarded as part of routine judicial review in which consideration was given to whether the decision fell within the ambit of logical reasonableness, but rather it was an instruction to the court to determine whether the decision reached was an appropriate decision in the particular circumstances. Finally, the regulations preceding the new Administrative Detention Law were aimed at deterrence and not at providing a supplementary war measure. In her view, the majority opinion "leads to an interpretation of the law which enables the detention, for an unlimited period of time, of a particular person, provided that the detention is of, even indirect, benefit to state security. Such inclusive and unlimited power is unrecognized even by the laws of war in the sphere of international law."[58]

After the finding in the initial judgment on appeal that the detainees could be left in detention, sharp criticism was voiced against the Supreme Court. It was said that the court had refrained from intervening in a matter of great sensitivity out of fear of losing public confidence if it delivered a judgment contrary to the prevailing public mood. An additional criticism was that the court was not and should not be the keeper of the public's morals. Rather, the function of the court was to protect human rights in Israel. The court was not empowered to determine whether the emergency situation, required for the validity of the Administrative Detention Law, indeed existed in the state. Further, a different interpretation of the Administrative Detention Law might have led the court to an outcome contrary to that obtained in the initial judgment. It is impossible to know whether this criticism influenced the thinking of the court. One may reasonably assume that it did not, but it is a fact that the decision was later overturned.

In the Further Hearing, President Barak changed his mind and joined another five judges in forming the majority opinion.[59] The three dissenting judges wrote three separate opinions. Each objected to their colleagues' conclusion that the Administrative Detention Law did not embrace a situation such as that represented by the instant case. They also objected to the finding in that case that the Lebanese detainees were in fact innocent civilians. In their opinion, the detainees were members of terrorist groups fighting against Israel. What, then, was the status of these Lebanese petitioners? Justice Cheshin, one of the dissenting judges, referred to them as "*quasi* prisoners of war."

In his judgment Justice Cheshin also considered the terms "hostages" and "bargaining counters," which had been employed by the majority judges, and held that these terms were incompatible with the facts of the matter brought before the court:

> Indeed, in the same way as holding prisoners of war is regarded as holding persons for a legitimate and appropriate purpose—and therefore prisoners of war are not described as either "hostages" or "bargaining counters"—so to, by analogy, [is holding] the Hizbullah fighters, whom we hold for the legitimate and appropriate purpose of state

security. The petitioners do not possess the attributes of "hostages"—or even of "bargaining counters"—and in any event we know that they are not "hostages" or "bargaining counters."

We must remember: the petitioners are not innocent villagers who were taken by force to a country which is not theirs. It is true that the petitioners were merely simple fighters in the forces of the Hizbullah. At the same time, they themselves joined the enemies' forces and accordingly they are neither "hostages" nor "bargaining counters."[60]

The Legal Status of the Detainees

ARE THE DETAINEES LEBANESE CIVILIANS?

As explained in chapter 2, to be a person who does not belong to fighting forces and who is not a combatant is one thing, and to be a person who fights against someone whom he regards as his enemy is something totally different.

The majority opinion in the Further Hearing considered the petitioners as civilians protected by international law. However, these citizens were not innocent civilians but were terrorists. They were convicted and had completed their sentences. However, does the fact of their conviction and completion of sentence by itself affect their legal status? Must they now be regarded as mere civilians, who are protected by the Fourth Geneva Convention? I tend to the view that the answer to this question should be no.

The Four Geneva Conventions and the Additional Protocols do not refer to the legal status of civilians who do not fall within the term "lawful combatants" but nonetheless take an active part in the fighting. The silence of the conventions regarding this situation, as explained in chapter 2, should be understood, not as a lacuna, but as a negative arrangement. The petitioners did not meet the necessary requirements for being recognized as combatants, entitled to the rights of prisoners of war, and therefore they should be treated as unlawful combatants.

It is indisputable that the petitioners were indeed affiliated with terrorist organizations. The terrorists' persistent desire over the years to be regarded as freedom fighters, and therefore entitled to the status of prisoners of war, has been consistently rejected by the Israeli courts, since they did not conduct their warfare in accordance with the international law of war.

Accordingly, if it is not appropriate to regard terrorists as combatants, a fortiori they also cannot be regarded as civilians who are not combatants, thereby entitling them to even greater rights. In our case, since the Lebanese petitioners were guerilla fighters—some of whom had even been tried in a criminal process for terrorist acts—there was no need to regard them as civilians after they completed their sentences. The fact that they were convicted and imprisoned did not modify their status as terrorists. Accordingly, I do not agree with the majority opinion, which regarded the petitioners purely as innocent civilians.

ARE THE DETAINEES HOSTAGES?

After the majority judges in the Further Hearing reached the conclusion that the petitioners were in fact Lebanese civilians, and that they were being held in detention solely for the purpose of bringing about the release of missing Israeli soldiers, it was a short next step to the conclusion that they were, in fact, also hostages.

In the past there was no clear prohibition on taking and holding hostages. During the Second World War, the Nazis took hostages and executed them, both in reprisal and to frighten the population into obedience. Execution of innocent persons being held as hostages in retaliation for attacks on military commanders had become customary during the previous century. Surprisingly, the taking of hostages was not prohibited by customary international law. Only after the Second World War did the Geneva Conventions expressly prohibit the taking of hostages, although this prohibition referred to persons taking no active part in the hostilities, especially the civilian population. Thus, interning combatants does not fall within the definition of taking hostages. The prohibition on taking hostages was regulated with greater specificity in 1979 in the International Convention against the Taking of Hostages. In addition to reiterating the prohibition on taking hostages, the Convention defines a person who will be regarded as a hostage.[61]

In my opinion, holding civilians in detention exclusively for the purpose of exerting pressure on a third party to release soldiers or to provide information about their condition and whereabouts does amount to hostage taking. Article 1 of the Convention against the Taking of Hostages expressly provides that such a situation will be regarded as taking a person hostage.

The real problem is whether a detained person who is an unlawful combatant, and therefore not entitled to the status of a prisoner of war, on the one hand, or that of a civilian, on the other, may be regarded— while still in detention—as a "hostage."

The Geneva Conventions are silent on this issue. We may assume that the drafters of these conventions did not intend to protect terrorists as civilians or to include them within the definition of lawful combatants. It is more reasonable to assume that the Geneva Conventions regarded these terrorists as criminals and therefore left regulation of their status to individual states.

If, as I argue, the Lebanese petitioners were terrorists who were not protected by the Geneva Conventions, then Israel was clearly entitled to try them as criminals and imprison them. Nonetheless, this determination does not solve the problem and does not supply an answer to the question whether Israel was entitled to continue holding the petitioners after they completed their sentences, and on what legal basis it could do so.

The state contended before the Supreme Court in the Further Hearing that it was entitled to hold the petitioners in order to bargain for the release of the missing soldiers. President Barak emphasized that counsel for the State of Israel had admitted that the petitioners did not pose any danger to state security and that in the normal course would have been released upon completing their sentences.

This declaration by counsel for the state is surprising and in my view unacceptable in view of the likelihood that upon release the terrorist fighters would return to their units and resume their previous activities. Accordingly, the contention that they did not pose a danger to security was implausible.

The completely illogical character of the description of the petitioners, following completion of their sentences, as harmless persons yearning for peace may also be seen by reference to international law. The Third Geneva Convention Relative to the Treatment of Prisoners of War allows a party to an armed conflict to detain combatants as prisoners of war; only upon cessation of the conflict must the parties release the prisoners in their custody. What is the logic underlying the internment of a combatant as a prisoner for the duration of the conflict? In my opinion, the central reason for taking this measure is to prevent the combatant from returning to his unit and continuing to fight. I assume that a fighter by his nature poses a danger to the opposing party, and therefore that party is entitled to intern the fighter until the danger passes and the armed conflict ends. The danger will cease when, and only when, the conflict ends. What is the difference between an interned combatant and a terrorist in relation to the question of the moment when he ceases to pose a danger? Both endanger the security of the other party, and both cease to pose a danger when the conflict ends. Therefore, in principle, there can be no significant distinction between the two types of combatants.

Nonetheless, there is at least one exception to the distinctions drawn so far. It is not possible to hold a person in detention for an indefinite period of time. It cannot be said that the danger posed by a person after a long period of imprisonment, say ten years, is equivalent to the danger posed by him at the start of his detention:

> With the passage of time the measure of administrative detention becomes so onerous as to cease being proportional. Indeed, even when there is power to infringe freedom by means of a warrant of arrest, use of this power must be proportional. The "breaking point" must not be passed beyond which the administrative detention is again disproportional. The location of the "breaking point" varies with the circumstances. Everything depends upon the importance of the goal which the administrative detention seeks to achieve; everything depends upon the likelihood of achieving the goal by using the detention, and the compatibility of the administrative detention with the achievement of the goal; everything is connected with the existence of alternative means for achieving the goal which causes less injury to the freedom of the individual; everything ensues from the severity of the injury to the freedom of the individual against the background of the appropriate purpose which it is hoped to achieve. Indeed, we are concerned with a complex range of considerations, which differ from case to case, and from time to time.[62]

I do not dispute the conclusion of the Supreme Court regarding the legality of the detentions, on the assumption that the interpretation of the Administrative Detention Law is not mistaken. Had that been the case, the state would have had the task of directing the court to another legal source for the detention, and this the state could not do. However, I do disagree with the majority opinion's finding that the Administrative Detention Law does not contemplate situations such as that involved in the instant case.

ARE THE DETAINEES BARGAINING COUNTERS?

President Barak concluded that the use of a person as a bargaining counter is prohibited under the Administrative Detention Law. I wish to challenge this finding. Who should properly and necessarily be regarded as a bargaining counter? The primary factor is the principle of the guilt of the concerned person himself. We must not exploit an innocent man in order to achieve an appropriate purpose.

A democratic state cannot, in any circumstances, detain a person who is totally guiltless. I agree that a country that behaves in this way offends against the minimal standards that have been established by cultured communities. Indeed, the grounds for this absolute prohibition ensue from the distinction between what is just and what is wrong. Every person must pay for his own sins.

In my opinion, in view of the normative analysis conducted above, these Lebanese detainees had to be regarded as unlawful combatants, who do not have the status of prisoners of war and are not entitled to the rights conferred on prisoners of war, but who, from the point of view of the ability to hold them until the cessation of the dispute and to receive appropriate treatment during the detention itself, are analogous to prisoner of war combatants. Thus it was possible to detain the Lebanese petitioners under the Administrative Detention Law applicable in Israel, irrespective of the ability to try them for their activities. In other words, in my view, there is a third status, in addition to that of civilian or combatant, a status that refers to terrorists and members of guerilla organizations. This status of terrorists—unlawful combatants—will be accompanied by rights relating to appropriate detention conditions. However, alongside these rights, it will be possible to hold the terrorists until the cessation of the conflict.

Conclusion

In the Further Hearing regarding the Lebanese detainees, the Supreme Court overturned its earlier decision and held that the detainees had to be released. Within a short period, they were indeed released and returned to Lebanon.

As I argued, I do not agree with the factual assertion, either of the state or of some of the justices, that these Lebanese detainees would not pose a real danger to Israel upon their release. I agree with the claim that the level of danger had lessened with the years, but in my opinion it was necessary to examine, within the framework of the Further Hearing, what danger still ensued from these Lebanese detainees. The state should have raised this point from the beginning. From the normative point of view, I do not accept the majority view of the justices of the Supreme Court in the Further Hearing to the effect that the Lebanese petitioners were merely "bargaining counters" or "hostages." Some of these men had been convicted in the past for terrorist offenses. It is not possible to assert that they were untainted, innocent civilians. Since I do not regard them as civilians taken hostage or as combatants—as defined in international conventions—but as terrorists, those international conventions that concern civilians in time of war or to combatants do not apply to them. As I pointed out, in my view a deliberate negative arrangement exists in these conventions with regard to terrorists, which enables each state to regulate its stance toward terrorists as it sees fit in the light of its domestic constitutional regime. However, it is possible to determine by analogy, a fortiori, about the treatment of unlawful combatants from the treatment of lawful combatants permitted by international law.

Thus, in the same way that it is possible to hold prisoners of war until the cessation of active hostilities and at that time to exchange them for prisoners held by the other side, it is also possible to hold terrorists until the cessation of the armed conflict, when they will be exchanged for Israeli missing and captured soldiers. As I suggested, these terrorists must be granted a third status—of unlawful combatants, who are neither lawful combatants nor freedom fighters and are certainly not mere civilians.

The outcome of the judgment in the Further Hearing was the enactment of the Imprisonment of Illegal Combatants Law.[63] The purpose of this law is "to anchor the imprisonment of members of hostile forces who are not entitled to the status of prisoners of war in Israeli law, in a manner which is compatible with the provisions of international humanitarian law."[64]

In view of my assertion above that we must learn by way of analogy from the provisions of international law regarding prisoners of war and thus regulate the detention of terrorists and guerilla fighters, this law is superfluous. It is possible to hold the persons the law refers to in administrative detention so long as Israel has not recovered its missing and captured soldiers or so long as no end has been declared to the struggle waged by terrorist forces against Israel. At the most, this law may be seen as a more explicit arrangement that confers statutory validity on the existing position.

However, apart from the general similarities between this new law and the Administrative Detention Law, there are also substantive points of difference. For example, the judicial review referred to in the law is not as broad as the judicial review prevailing under the Administrative Detention Law. First, the detention order need not be authorized immediately, but only within fourteen days from its promulgation, whereas the Administrative Detention Law refers to an examination of the order within forty-eight hours. Second, the only issue that must be decided by the court is whether or not the person indeed falls within the definition of "an illegal combatant" in Article 2 of the law.

It is doubtful whether these distinctions between the two laws can be satisfactorily explained, and I doubt whether the new law would meet the test of constitutionality.

In conclusion, a democratic country, such as Israel, which is forced to confront terrorist and guerilla organizations must have to hand the tools that will enable it to survive. Since it is a democratic country, it is true that not all means can justify the end, but it would be a mistake to insist on grasping an idealism that is apt in times of peace but that would prevent us from building efficient defenses against our enemies in times of emergency. As I've explained, I am not asserting that in times of crisis these ideals cease to exist, indeed "[w]hile the need for society to protect itself against acts of terrorism is self-evident, it remains of the greatest importance that, in a society which upholds the rule of law, if . . . the detention . . . is not lawful, then [the detainee] has to be released."[65]

Yet, we must not forgo those democratic, lawful, and legitimate measures that are available to us.

The Supreme Court, too, did not regard this matter lightly, as can be seen in the judgments in both the appeal and the Further Hearing. The court required two complex legal hearings in order to reach its conclusions and formulate its final decision. I must disagree with some of those conclusions.

SIX

The Right to Privacy in
Times of Terrorism

A TERRORIST ATTACK cannot be defined solely as the accomplishment of the terrorist's aspirations. A terrorist act is the completed external expression of a catalogue of preliminary activities—planning, preparatory work, financing, training, and qualification—clandestinely carried out by the terrorists while exploiting the state's lack of watchfulness over activities carried out in the realm of its citizens' private lives.

Accordingly, it is easy to understand why after every attack, and more compellingly after an attack that produces multiple casualties, the question that echoes in every quarter is why the intelligence services failed to identify those preliminary activities: Was it because modern surveillance measures were not sufficiently sophisticated? Was it because despite the availability of sophisticated intelligence devices constitutional restrictions prevented their use? Or was it perhaps that, despite the efficacy of the measures and the absence of constitutional obstacles to their implementation, the intelligence personnel were simply negligent in the performance of their duties?

History teaches us that the erosion in the public's sense of personal safety brought about by the sights of carnage and destruction, combined with feelings of pain, anger, and the desire for revenge, generally lead the public to assign the blame for the tragedy to the constitutional restrictions and therefore to conclude that those restrictions must be removed and a new balance drawn between human rights and the public interest in national security. However, history also teaches that after the security crisis has passed, it generally becomes evident that there was no factual basis for sacrificing rights in favor of security needs, and that the lifting of the constitutional restrictions was no more than the emotional product of panic, paranoia, and fear.

What, therefore, is the proper rational balance between the protection of the privacy of the citizens of a state on the one hand and the security interest in invading the public's privacy on the other to allow the security authorities to identify those few who would exploit the right to privacy in order to plan and execute acts of terror?

The Moral and Legal Nature of the Clash between the Right to Privacy and National Security Interests

At all times, in every society, the individual desires to maintain a certain amount of distance from the rest of society. Even though, or perhaps because, privacy is such a deeply rooted value in human culture, the vast literature in this field teaches us that it is one of those concepts which everyone understands but which cannot be defined in an objective and descriptive way that clearly expresses the scope of its application. Over the years, numerous efforts have been made to define the term. The most important and influential definitions may generally be placed in one of three categories: First, privacy is defined in terms of moral rights and claims. For example, it is described as the right of the individual to be left alone;[1] as a claim to the freedom to decide in what circumstances and to what extent information about the person will be divulged to others;[2] and, as a corollary, the person's right to live part of his life far away from the prying eyes of the public.[3] Second, privacy is defined in terms of control. Among other things, it is described as the individual's control over the dissemination of information about himself;[4] his control over the quantity and quality of the information concerning himself which is made known to others;[5] his control over his body, his place of residence, his identity;[6] and his control over the extent of the public's knowledge of his private affairs.[7] Third, privacy is defined in terms of accessibility. For example, it is described as that which prevents the unwanted access of the public to the individual on three levels: the level of secrecy (access of the public to information concerning the individual), the level of segregation (access of the public to the body and premises of the individual), and the level of anonymity (physical, as opposed to mental, attention of the public to the individual).[8]

The grounds for privacy are instrumental in nature and are twofold: individual and collective.[9] On the individual level, privacy plays a central, and sometimes critical, role in realizing the aspirations, desires, hopes, and goals of the individual. First, privacy is an essential condition for formulating the individual's personality: a person's ability to comprehend the uniqueness of his existence relative to that of other people is dependent on his capacity to personally experience physical and psychological events and thereby conceive his separateness from the whole.

Second, privacy is an expression of human dignity: open invasion of a person's privacy compels him to plan his actions while taking into account the public, which has been forced on him and which judges those actions. Clandestine invasion of his privacy changes the state of affairs on the basis of which he acts and prevents him from making considered behavioral choices in the light of existing objective circumstances. In both situations, lack of respect for the individual's desire to distance himself from others (in the absence of justifiable reasons) expresses disrespect for him.

Third, privacy is an essential condition for the creation of interpersonal relations in general and deeper relations based on feelings of love, friendship, trust, and respect in particular. Accepted social mores dictate the type and scope of sharing of information which are appropriate to different types of personal relations. Without privacy, everyone has the same quantity and quality of knowledge about a person, with the result that he will not be able to create different relationships on different strata. Deep relationships rely on the individual's exposing certain facets of his personality to another party. Lack of privacy prevents him from concealing these facets from the outset, and thereby prevents him from creating a relationship that is separate from and deeper than those relations he normally has with the public at large.

Fourth, privacy is an essential condition for intimacy. A person who participates in an intimate experience submerges himself in it, whereas an inherent aspect of an onlooker's perception is the sense of relative detachment from the event being observed. Awareness of the presence or the possible presence of an uncalled-for spectator compels a person to examine his acts from the perspective of the onlooker, and the detachment this causes prevents him from plunging into the intimate experience.

Fifth, privacy helps an individual to concentrate, to be calm, and to refrain from criticism and ridicule, because the absence of uncalled-for observers frees him from the distraction inherent in being watched. Privacy will make it easier for the person to focus on the range of creative human activities, by virtue of which he can enrich his spiritual world, acquire knowledge and skills, and develop his intellectual abilities.

Sixth, privacy is important for the mental health of the individual. In the absence of the capacity to perform acts known only by himself, a person is forced to continuously conform to social standards, since any deviation from those standards will attract social condemnation. The inhibitions and isolation entailed by this may cause the person psychological harm.

The second type of grounds for privacy are collective. On this level, privacy plays a critical role in shaping the character of society. True, in the absence of privacy many wrongful, fraudulent, and hypocritical acts might not be committed; moreover, the proponents of communitarian theory question the liberal ideal that the individual is an island able to form his personality in isolation from the rest of society and argue instead that a surplus of privacy impairs his ability to form an independent personality. Yet, the individualistic grounds for privacy make it clear that the essential contribution privacy makes to the formulation of personal autonomy, and consequently to the existence of the democratic regime, has a positive value that considerably outweighs its negative aspects. Recognition of the individual as a complex separate entity worthy of respect enables him to develop a personality possessing independent moral judgment. A society whose members possess conformist personalities based on submissive acceptance of social norms does not encourage the pluralism necessary to create the democratic experience.

A key condition for conducting an intelligent discussion is understanding the fundamental concepts involved. Since the concept of privacy is difficult to define, there is an inherent risk that it will be perceived on an intuitive, nonrational level, which would undermine our ability to conduct a pertinent discussion of the proper balance to be drawn between the right to privacy and the national security interest in the war against terror. When on the one hand we are witnesses to concrete atrocities, scenes of streets and malls transformed into arenas of death, and on the other we are faced with an abstract right, our intuition tilts the balance unequivocally in favor of national security. The clarification of the concept of the right to privacy given above should prove helpful in a discussion of the legal and moral aspects of this issue.

Means of Infringing the Right to Privacy

Privacy may be invaded in a wide variety of ways. Human detectives have been at work since time immemorial. There are clear benefits to be gained by surveillance of the activities of a person suspected of terrorist activities, searching his person and property, interrogating his contacts, and eavesdropping on his conversations. Yet, the limitations inherent in human surveillance—that is, the fact that it entails the allocation of enormous human and economic resources, that it is dependent on the skills and expertise of the persons performing the surveillance, the difficulty in disguising the trackers, and the risks they face—has led over the years to a decrease in the use of people and greater reliance on technological surveillance measures.

Technological surveillance measures may be divided into six categories:

1. Technologies for Intercepting Communications. Visual surveillance is carried out by positioning in public places (e.g., on the street or at bus stops) or private places (e.g., in houses and vehicles) closed-circuit television (CCTV) cameras relaying live pictures to a control center. Visual documentation has multiple advantages, including assisting us in identifying terrorists seeking an "ideal" place to carry out a suicide bombing or conceal an explosive package, as well as spotting collaborators collecting intelligence for future attacks. Likewise, documentation produced during a "successful" terrorist event enables the security forces to determine the nature of security flaws, which can then be rectified to avoid similar attacks. Following the London terrorist attacks in July 2005, for example, the police were able to identify the suicide bombers and arrest other members affiliated to the group that planned and committed the bombings, primarily thanks to CCTV photographs of the bombers.[10] Audio surveillance is carried out by means of audiotape devices or telephone taps.[11]

Electronic wiretapping can be carried out by a range of devices. In relation to the Internet, the best known tool is the American Carnivore program, which is able to scan the Internet transmissions of all the subscribers of a provider on whose server the program is installed and register both identities (such as the Internet sites visited by the surfer or the e-mail addresses of his contacts) and content (record the surfer's activities at the Internet sites he visits, such as purchases at an online auction, information sought using a search engine, and the contents of his communications) of transmissions which fall within certain defined parameters.[12] Scanning Internet transmissions enables the security authorities to track individual terrorist suspects and to engage in more general surveillance aimed at identifying user practices or cybercommunications characteristic of terrorists. However, a terrorist can adopt a variety of measures to camouflage his activities, such as using encryption programs to convert his electronic communications into indecipherable code. All the addressee need do is tap in the password, while the security authority is forced to try to breach the encryption program—a complex, time-consuming, and often impossible process. The solution is a program installed on the computer, of either the sender or the receiver of the communication, which records all the key strokes typed by someone using the computer (including the encryption program's password) and then sends that information to a defined e-mail address. Installation of the program (known as Key-Logger) may be performed manually—which requires physical access to the computer—or by means of a virus (known as Magic Lantern), which is operated when a person opens an e-mail attachment or visits a certain site.

2. Technologies for Enhancing the Quality of Information Obtained by Natural Senses. "Normal enhancement" refers to ways of enhancing information that the human senses are capable of discerning without technological assistance (e.g., binoculars, telescopes, night vision glasses, and satellite photographs improve the quality of information obtained visually), whereas "abnormal enhancement" refers to information that the human senses are not capable of discerning without technological assistance. For example, a metal detector enables the detection of metal weapons concealed under clothing or in baggage. A thermal imager detects the infrared heat waves emitted by every object and presents them as a visual image colored according to the degree of heat of the object, while advanced devices can even detect heat waves through closed walls. Such an imager can detect traditional weapons and explosives on the body or in a person's property, but it can also aid in the rescue of hostages, since it is capable of revealing the location of the terrorists and their physical condition at any given moment. The passive millimeter wave imager detects electromagnetic radiation naturally emitted by objects and presents it as high-resolution images that allow the contours of a person to be detected through his clothes or baggage (such as weapons or explosives but also pens and coins). The radar skin scanner produces even more precise images, which can detect any object larger than a millimeter and consequently reveal the most intimate details of a person. Likewise, a broad range of X-ray cameras image the naked body of a person through his clothes at different levels of resolution; the most advanced of these cameras provide an image that leaves no room for the imagination. At the same time, these devices may be equipped with accessories that reduce the degree of infringement on a person's privacy, such as accessories that distort the face of the subject or systems that are programmed not to show the operator an image unless it detects items with the shape of weapons or explosives.[13]

3. Technologies for Mapping Location. n electronic tracking device, generally called a beeper, is a miniature radio transmitter that broadcasts signals on a cyclical basis. The signals are received by a compatible device that maps its location and consequently the movements of the object in which it is placed. So long as the beeper remains within the range of the mapping device, the tracked object cannot be lost. If the beeper moves out of range, it is easier to relocate it than in the case of physical tracking.[14] Technologically more sophisticated tracking procedures enable the operator to ascertain a person's location by means of his cellular telephone by mapping the cyclical signals broadcast by every cellular telephone linked to a communications network.[15]

4. Identification Technologies. Passwords and magnetic cards are not reliable means of identifying people, since these can be borrowed or stolen. Biometric measures, however, identify the individual through unique, nontransferable physical characteristics.[16]

The various biometric techniques, such as DNA fingerprinting, retinal scanning, iris recognition, fingerprinting, hand geometry, face recognition, and voice recognition, follow an identical process. Each system first scans the characteristic on which it focuses. The data are converted into digital code, which is entered into a computerized data bank. The data on the scanned person can then be used either to determine identity, by checking them against all the codes in the data bank, or to verify identity, by checking them against the code of a person whose identity has been claimed.

Biometric techniques also have the potential to reveal information concerning the health of the person. For example, the human genome might indicate a predisposition to a particular disease; the structure of the iris and the retina point to possible diseases such as diabetes, high blood pressure, and AIDS; and certain studies claim that the geometrical structure of the hand points to a person's sexual orientation and his predisposition to chromosomal disorders. Accordingly, the important question arises whether, after the biometric characteristic has been converted into a digital code, obstacles should be placed on examining this kind of information or whether the system should allow it to be analyzed.

The biometric systems are of great importance in the fight against terrorism, since they can be positioned at the entrance to security sites or at sites containing dangerous materials, such as fuel and gas depots, to prevent terrorists from infiltrating. Likewise, they can be positioned in public places, to locate known terrorists whose details have already been scanned into the system. Their potential can be enhanced by integrating them into other kinds of systems. For example, a voice recognition system integrated with a system for intercepting telephone calls would significantly increase the likelihood of intercepting conversations between terrorists. Similarly, a face recognition system combined with a CCTV data bank would make it easier to locate wanted persons.

5. Technologies for Integrating Information. Information collected using the measures described above can be recorded and stored in computerized data banks. Uniting these data banks into a super data bank enables the compilation of a detailed portrait of the habits and lifestyle of the subject. Thus, for example, uniting data banks managed by governmental authorities (such as registries of criminal records, family status, education, health) with data banks managed by private business enterprises (such as financial registries, telephone records, public library lending records, records of searches, and purchases at public online auctions) would create a central data bank that would allow the identification of persons whose actions or lifestyles are characteristic of terrorists or supporters of terrorist organizations.[17]

6. Terrorism Profiling. Since good management of popular public places precludes the stringent application of the measures described above to all those entering the premises, and since taking such security measures entails significant costs, it has become increasingly necessary to shift from zeroing in on individual terrorist suspects to locating suspect groups, whose members are then subject to much more stringent scrutiny than the rest of the public.

Terrorist profiling operates in a three-stage process. In the first stage, the intelligence services collect the maximum amount of data about known terrorists (their country of birth, gender, age, family status, socioeconomic status, religious affiliation, religious commitment, education, lifestyle, etc.). Next, a statistical analysis is carried out, and the most frequent characteristics are established as criteria for the profile of a potential terrorist. People fitting this profile are considered more likely to be terrorists than people who do not. In the second stage, methods are established for identifying people who fit the profile. While most of the details about this process of identification are secret, it can be said that they are based both on a subjective test, involving an examination of the person's behavior in the relevant situation (nervousness, sweating, impatience, dishevelment, excessive neatness, etc.), and on an objective test, involving factors that are independent of behavior (such as gender, age, nationality, religion, and skin color). In the third stage, those persons found to comply with the profile are subjected to prolonged and stringent investigative processes, which include interrogations and searches of their persons and property.

Profiling is used in four situations. The most well known is the profiling of passengers in sea- and airports (passenger profiling). The first plane hijacking took place in 1931, when Peruvian revolutionaries took control of an airplane in order to distribute propaganda leaflets. The first criminal-caused crash of a commercial aircraft occurred in 1949, when a woman hired two released convicts to hide a bomb in a Philippines Airline plane in which her husband was to fly.

These events showed the world the enormity of the catastrophe that could occur to sea and air transport. The efforts by a number of countries to eradicate this phenomenon led to the invention of a series of safety measures, which included variations on the profiling system.[18] Usually, a defined group of people who are more strongly suspected of involvement in terrorist activities is exempt from the profiling system described above, since their names in any event appear on a border control list operated by the state's security services.[19]

The second situation in which profiling is used is at the entry to a public place. The checks conducted of persons entering places such as restaurants and bus stations is much less thorough than that conducted in ports and is chiefly based on subjective behavioral characteristics and objective data such as external appearance, sometimes aided by information drawn from various data banks.

The third situation concerns profiling of passersby. Responding to security alerts about the infiltration of terrorists or as part of routine security measures, the security forces place road barriers and patrol city streets with the object of delaying, questioning, and sometimes even searching the persons, vehicles, and property of people fitting the profile criteria. Identification is based on suspect behavior, external appearance, possession of a vehicle suspected of being stolen or carrying foreign license plates, and the like.

The fourth situation in which profiling is used has both a preventive and an investigative purpose, in that it takes place subsequent to a terrorist attack. Following every terrorist incident, the security forces not only question witnesses but also detain for interrogation or arrest persons found at the site of the attack (including, on occasion, people who themselves have been injured) or people seen in the vicinity shortly after the attack, if they conform to the profile of persons suspected of involvement in the incident.[20]

If, in the past, George Orwell's ominous prophesy concerning Big Brother's tracking and recording every facet of the lives of the populace was regarded as unrealistic because of the technological impossibility of actualizing that goal, the above remarks show that today we live in a society where there is no such impediment. The issue of the restrictions that a state in fact sets for itself and those which it should properly set for itself—when required to safeguard state security yet continue to preserve the privacy of its citizens—is the subject of the next section.

The Legal Situation in Israel

In 1966 Israel signed the International Covenant on Civil and Political Rights, which provides in Article 17(1): "No one shall be subjected to arbitrary or unlawful interference with his privacy, family, home or correspondence, nor to unlawful attacks on his honour and reputation."[21] In Israeli domestic law, recognition of the right to privacy was initially implied from a line of statutory provisions that qualified the right to search the person and premises of the individual, enter his property, disseminate information about him, and so on. However, over the years, as the methods of invading a person's private life grew in quantity and sophistication, the force of the traditional protections eroded, and statutes were enacted that entrenched various aspects of the right to privacy, such as protection against monitoring and human and electronic surveillance.

The contribution of Basic Law: Human Dignity and Liberty, adopted in 1992, to the protection of privacy was twofold. First, privacy was recognized as an integral part of the human right to dignity, and therefore it was granted the status of a constitutional basic right which every governmental authority must respect. Second, for the first time a statute entrenched a *general* right to privacy—not one confined to the specific issues that had up to then been established by statute.[22] At the same time, since the concept of privacy was incapable of exhaustive definition, the courts found it difficult to clearly delineate the boundaries of the right and satisfied themselves with a general statement of principle: "Now, as it has been given an enacted constitutional basis, it must be interpreted from a 'wide perspective' . . . and out of an understanding that we are concerned with a provision which establishes a way of life. We are concerned with human experience which must conform itself to a changing reality."[23] It has been recognized that even in places where the human right to privacy does apply, the legal protection of that right is not absolute, and there will be cases where the right will be superseded by more important interests, including the public interest in national security.[24]

The relativism of the right to privacy, like the relativism of all human rights, ensues from the individual's obligation to sacrifice his rights for the benefit of the community in which he lives to the extent necessary to ensure its continued existence, since that existence is a prerequisite for the individual's ability to actualize his rights. In the Israeli situation, sacrificing these rights is constitutional only if carried out according to a valid law that is compatible with the values of the State of Israel as a Jewish and democratic state and that has a proper purpose, and where the violation of the right does not exceed what is necessary.[25]

There is no doubt that a violation of privacy aimed at preventing a terrorist attack on innocent people has a worthy purpose in accordance with the values of Judaism and democracy, both of which recognize the need to curtail individual rights in times of crisis in order to protect the state. Consequently, the primary problem centers on the extent to which these standards must be reduced, that is, on finding the line that separates permissible constitutional violations of privacy from excessive violations.

The case law has held that finding this line involves a threefold test:[26] (a) The compatibility test: the infringing measure must lead rationally to the achievement of the purpose of the infringement. (b) The least harm test: among all the measures suitable for achieving the purpose, the selected measure must be the one that causes the least harm to the right. (c) The proportionality test: there must be a reasonable relationship between the benefit accrued and the damage caused to the individual as a result of the violation of his constitutional right.

When we seek to determine whether violations of privacy satisfy these conditions, we must take into account the basic premises underpinning democratic society: on the one hand, not in every case where it would assist the state does the war against terrorism justify abandoning basic values. On the other hand, while human rights sometimes require a democracy to struggle with one hand tied behind its back, those rights are not a springboard for national ruin.[27] Accordingly, national security will permit the proportional violation of human rights for the sake of those rights and in order to ensure their continued preservation.

I shall now turn to an examination of the scope of the protection accorded by Israeli law to the right to privacy in cases where it clashes with the national security interest.

Security Searches

The general arrangement regarding the power to search premises provides that a police officer is entitled to conduct a search in a house or place without a warrant if he has reason to believe that a felony is being committed or has recently been committed there.[28] In every other case, a search may be conducted only with a warrant, which a judge has the discretion to grant if he has reason to believe that the place is intended to be used for an illegal purpose.[29]

The law distinguishes among three types of body searches.[30] The most invasive type, which is defined as an "internal search," includes blood tests; imaging the interior of the body using supersonic devices, X-rays, ultrasounds; and gynecological examinations. The intermediate type, which is defined as an "external search," includes a frontal examination of the naked body, fingerprinting all aspects of the body, removing material from under the suspect's fingernails, cutting his fingernails, removing material from his nostrils, taking hair samples including root samples, removing material from the surface of the body, skin tests, buccal (cheek) cell samples, and urine, saliva, and air samples. The least invasive type, defined as a "search over the body of a person," comprises those searches which are neither internal nor external, such as the power to search the clothes and personal effects of the individual.

A police officer is empowered to search above the body of a person being arrested. He may conduct an external search if he has reasonable cause to suspect that the suspect's body contains proof of the commission of a felony or misdemeanor or proof of a connection between the suspect and the commission of an offense. Internal searches may only be authorized by a police commander who has reasonable cause to suspect that the suspect's body contains proof of the commission of a felony (or in the case of a blood test—a misdemeanor) or proof of a connection between the suspect and the commission of an offense.

This arrangement provides the police—but not other enforcement agencies—with tools for preempting or investigating crimes generally, although clearly it cannot provide a sufficient answer to the threats posed by terrorism. Consequently, a number of statutory provisions have expanded and increased the flexibility of the powers they confer. First, in relation to the power to search premises, Regulation 75 of the Defense (Emergency) Regulations empowers any soldier or police officer to conduct a search in any place—including vehicles, aircraft, and sea vessels— if he has reasonable cause to suspect that it is being used or will soon be used for a purpose that harms public order or national security.

The General Security Service Law (hereafter, the GSS Law) grants GSS operatives the right to search the vehicle of a person who crosses Israel's border points if it is necessary to foil unlawful acts intended to harm national security; to safeguard people, information, or places as determined by the government; or for other purposes directed at safeguarding or promoting national interests essential to the national security of the state.[31] If a GSS operative has reasonable cause to believe that the vehicle contains an item whose seizure is essential to carrying out the operations of the GSS, he is entitled to conduct a search even without the presence or knowledge of its owner. Likewise, the law provides that the prime minister is entitled to provide written authorization to GSS operatives to search vehicles or premises in the absence and without the knowledge of their owners (i.e., a "covert search") if he is persuaded that they contain information vital to carrying out the operations of the GSS and that there is no other reasonable method of achieving the purposes of the search. In cases where the search cannot be delayed, the head of the GSS is empowered to authorize the search, but he must notify the prime minister within seventy-two hours of granting such authorization.

The Civil Aviation Law confers discretion on a security officer, a police officer, a soldier, or a member of the Civil Defense Force (i.e., "authorized examiners") to search the vehicle of a person entering or present at an airfield if the search is necessary in his opinion to ensure public safety.[32]

The Powers of Search (Emergency) Law provides that when a state of emergency exists in the state by virtue of a declaration made under Basic Law: The Government, the authorized examiners may carry out a search of a person's vehicle upon his entry into any building or enclosed premises, or while present in a seaport, if in their opinion such a search is necessary in order to protect public security.[33] Likewise, the law enables authorized examiners to carry out a search of vessels upon their entry into a seaport or while present there if in their opinion such a search is necessary to protect public security. Additionally, power is granted to search vehicles or vessels irrespective of where located when it is suspected that there are arms or explosives unlawfully present in those vehicles or vessels.

Second, in relation to the power to search a suspect's body, Section 9 of the Civil Aviation Law empowers authorized examiners to search the body of any person entering or present in any airfield or aircraft if in their opinion the search is necessary to protect the security of the public. If a person refuses to allow his body to be searched, the law categorically prohibits him from being transported and vests discretion to carry out the search despite the person's refusal, to prevent the person from entering or leaving the airfield, or to remove him from the airfield.

Section 3 of the Powers of Search (Emergency) (Temporary Provision) Law empowers authorized examiners to search the body of a person upon his entering a building or enclosed premises, or while present in a seaport, if in their opinion such a search is necessary to protect public security. Likewise, the law enables authorized examiners to carry out a search of a person's body—irrespective of where he is located—if it is suspected that he is unlawfully carrying arms or explosives.

Section 9 of the GSS Law grants GSS operatives the power to search the body of a person, his personal effects and goods, if this is necessary in order to carry out one of the activities referred to above in relation to the power to search premises. In the event that the GSS operative has reasonable cause to believe that a person's effects contain an item whose seizure is essential to carry out these activities, he is entitled to search them even in the absence and without the knowledge of their owner.

As the above review shows, the set of powers of search—both in premises and on the body of a person—are extremely broad and comprehensive. This brings us, then, to the principal question: Is this an appropriate arrangement?

To answer this question, we must now turn to an examination of the criteria used in applying the various search powers.

PROFILING

Although security considerations preclude disclosure of the internal directives guiding the application of these wide powers, reports issued by human rights organizations and journalistic accounts show the crucial role of profiling. Those who fit the criteria of a potential terrorist are suspected of involvement in terrorist activities and are therefore subject to a prolonged and intensive process of questioning and searches of their bodies, effects, and premises, while those who do not conform to the profile are exempt from examination in certain circumstances (e.g., where roadblocks are set up) or are subject to merely perfunctory searches in other circumstances (e.g., when passing through sea- and airports).

Implementing wide-ranging search powers on the basis of profiling entails numerous moral and legal dilemmas. On the moral level, there is an obvious difficulty in determining an individual's treatment based on his affiliation with a particular group, since, at least prima facie, perception of him as part of a collective, as opposed to an independent entity worthy of separate consideration, might undermine the most basic tenets of the liberal ideal that forms one of the pillars of the democratic regime.

On the legal level, the constitutionality of the use of profiling is doubtful, even though it has not been the subject of judicial attention. The first doubt concerns the basic question whether, as a matter of law, it is even possible to exercise the power to conduct a security search in this manner. Administrative law provides that the power must be exercised fairly, equally, reasonably, honestly, and in good faith.[34] The central issue, therefore, is whether profiling is discriminatory and consequently prohibited.

The principle of equality is a fundamental tenet of Israeli law which has its origin in the Declaration of Independence, in which the State of Israel undertook to guarantee the equality of all its citizens without distinction by religion, race, or gender. The principle of equality is not entrenched in Basic Law: Human Dignity and Liberty, but case law has recognized its transformation into a constitutional supralegal right within the framework of human dignity.[35] Equality means the neutral and uniform implementation of normative powers in respect to all individuals unless there is a relevant substantive difference between them, in which case differences in implementation will not amount to unlawful discrimination but will instead be regarded as a lawful distinction.

In my opinion, use of profiling—subject to the restrictions described below—cannot be described as a form of prohibited discrimination. As noted, a terrorist profile comprises a collection of characteristics known to be commonly present in terrorists. When the frequency of a particular characteristic—such as nationality, religion, gender, age, family status, or socioeconomic level—is clearly disproportionally high among terrorists relative to the rest of the population, the state, in view of the huge importance of preventing acts of terror, is justified and even obliged to take extra precautions against those who possess this characteristic.[36]

The second doubt concerns the question whether every characteristic may be used as a profiling criterion or whether certain basic characteristics in the democratic experience—particularly of race, nationality, and religion—ought to be rejected as legitimate criteria.

Here too I believe that the test for regarding *any* characteristic as a relevant and therefore legitimate factor is its incidence among terrorists. At the same time, one cannot disregard the risk of sliding down the slippery slope inherent in dependence on these characteristics and creating a stereotypical social climate that legitimizes the racist and degrading treatment of groups in the population, the majority of whose members abhor the acts of killing.

My view is that, in order to negate this risk, profiles based solely on these characteristics should not be permitted; rather, these factors should be integrated into a broader range of criteria, thereby guaranteeing that not all those affiliated with the particular groups concerned will automatically be subject to such serious violations of their privacy.

The third doubt concerns the efficiency of the profiling system. The theory on which this system is based is that the statistical incidence of particular characteristics possessed by known terrorists is relevant to the identification of potential terrorists. Skeptics argue that because every person follows unique, sometimes strange, practices, it is not possible to identify suspicious patterns of behavior based solely on statistical characteristics. Thus, for example, in the United States, profiling in the air transport sector began at the end of the 1960s in the aftermath of a wave of airplane hijackings; however, it was stopped in 1972, when it was proved to be ineffective. When profiling was brought back into use in 1998, this time in a computerized version (Computer Assisted Passenger Prescreening System, or CAPPS), it succeeded in identifying only two of the seven aircraft hijackers of the September 11, 2001, attacks.[37]

While it has achieved some success, profiling has on occasion proved defective, both in falsely identifying innocent persons and in failing to identify terrorists. At the same time, no alternative currently available offers a better solution. Avoiding the use of profiling would entail establishing uniform security arrangements for the entire population. Inevitably, in order to allow people to pursue a normal way of life, the standard of implementation would have to be lower than it is now. On the other hand, the injury caused to the privacy of the entire population would be uniform, even though interpretation of the provisions of the search laws in the spirit of the Basic Laws requires that the degree of injury to each individual be compatible with the level of risk posed by each individual.

THE CONSTITUTIONALITY OF SEARCH PROCEDURES

We have seen that every person may be subjected to a routine search above his body. The search may be conducted by a police officer, soldier, a member of the Civil Defense Force, or security officer, whereas persons suspected of involvement in terrorism are subject to internal and external searches by virtue of the general search power accorded by the Criminal Procedure Law, a power that has been conferred solely on the Israel police force. Likewise, we have seen that suspicion is formulated by use of profiling methods. In short, every person is subject to routine search of the surface of his body, his clothing, and personal effects, but only terrorist suspects are subject to more extensive bodily searches.

This principle, while proportional, entails a number of arrangements that infringe the person's privacy in an excessive manner. First, the power to conduct a covert search of the premises and vehicle of a person is not confined to persons suspected of involvement in terrorist activities and, moreover, is not subject to prior judicial review (by means of applying to the court for a search warrant, in cases where the search can be delayed) or even retrospective review (in cases where the search is required immediately). It is sufficient for the prime minister to give his approval or, in urgent cases, for the head of the GSS to give his approval.

Judicial review in these circumstances is particularly important. Whereas normally witnesses are allowed to be present while the search is carried out so that they can supervise its performance and prevent the warrant from being overstepped,[38] this right is negated when covert searches are performed. Moreover, the law does not determine whether and when a person whose premises or vehicle is being searched is entitled to know of that search, and consequently that person is deprived of the ability to challenge its validity.

The power to conduct a covert search of the personal effects and vehicle of a person who crosses a border checkpoint is even more far-reaching, since it does not contain any requirement for authorization of the search, and service personnel may exercise that power at their discretion.

There may indeed be security investigations that will be frustrated if certain persons learn of searches before they are conducted or while they are underway. However, it would seem that there can be no justification for allowing such a severe violation of privacy—particularly in cases where the person is not suspected of involvement in an offense—without first applying to a court for a search warrant and thereby guaranteeing its propriety. In cases where there is insufficient time for an application, the search should be permitted only upon authorization by the prime minister or the head of the GSS (and this would be appropriate even in relation to covert searches at border checkpoints), subject to the obligation to apply to the court for a retroactive warrant affirming the legality of the search.

Likewise, the silence of the law relating to notification should not be interpreted as a negative arrangement exempting the security authorities from the principles of administrative law regarding fairness and reasonableness. Under those principles, notification must be made within a reasonable period of time from the moment the security grounds for secrecy disappear, since it is evident that had the legislature wished to establish an exception in relation to these basic principles, and thereby cause indirect harm to the individual's right to be heard, it would have been done by express legislative provision.

Second, when the question of the constitutionality of the border checkpoint lists was made the subject of judicial consideration, the court held that the GSS had to allow those included in the list to challenge the decision in court and, in the event that their application was rejected, to file an administrative petition to the High Court of Justice against the decision. The court left open the possibility of applying prior judicial review, that is, establishing a rule whereby it is a precondition for including a person in the list that an ex parte application has been made to the court for authorization of this action.[39] The broad language of Section 98 of the GSS Law, which, as noted, permits service personnel to search the body, cargo, or vehicle of a person who crosses a border checkpoint, in practice permits use of this list, but without establishing criteria for including or excluding names from the list or, indeed, an alternative mechanism for judicial review.

Since, by its nature, the list is determined in advance, it would seem that there is no relevant obstacle to the imposition of prior judicial review, except in cases where there are urgent security grounds for swiftly including the name of a person in the list, in which case it is appropriate that the judicial review be conducted retrospectively, as soon as possible after its inclusion.

Secret Monitoring during Security Investigations

The Secret Monitoring Law regulates the laws applicable to the use of devices for listening in to the conversations of others without the consent of at least one of the speakers.[40] A "conversation," for the purposes of this law, is defined broadly and includes conversation by word of mouth or by a land line or wireless telephone, and communication by fax or computer.

For our purposes, three types of monitoring are relevant. First, monitoring the conversations of a person in the public domain may take place only with authorization by the head of a security authority for reasons of national security.

Second, monitoring the conversations of a person in private may be conducted only with written permission from the prime minister or the minister of defense, if they are satisfied that it is necessary to do so for reasons of state security. In cases that require secret monitoring to be carried out without delay and there is no time to obtain a permit, the head of a security authority is empowered to authorize such monitoring in writing, but must notify the prime minister or minister of defense immediately, and the latter may cancel or modify the permit.

The relative ease with which secret monitoring may be carried out in the public domain—compared to that carried out in private—requires that these terms be explained. "Public domain" is defined in Section 8 of the Secret Monitoring Law as "a place where a reasonable person could have expected that his conversations would be monitored without his consent." It follows that the "private domain" is a place where a reasonable person would expect that his conversations would not be monitored. The law provides a substantive, objective test: when a person's subjective expectation of privacy (disclosed by his conduct) is reasonable, that is, legitimate in the eyes of the public, his conversations must be monitored in accordance with rules applicable to monitoring in the private domain. An expectation of privacy may be reasonable not only in a place where a person has a proprietary interest (such as in his house or vehicle) but in a public place. Thus, for example, two persons secluding themselves in an isolated spot in a café or a person talking in a public telephone box, all have a legitimate expectation of privacy in the eyes of the public, and therefore their communications should be monitored in accordance with the rules applicable to monitoring in the private domain.

The third type is the monitoring of those conversations—in the public or private domain—which are privileged under the Evidence Ordinance, such as conversations between attorney and client or between doctor and patient. Such monitoring is permitted under three cumulative conditions. First, it must be essential for reasons of national security for the purpose of investigating a felony. Second, there must be reasonable cause to suspect that the professional (e.g., the attorney or doctor) is involved in the offense. Third, the two preceding conditions having been met, the president of the district court has decided to grant permission for the monitoring. It should be emphasized that only when this type of monitoring is involved does the law require judicial scrutiny.

There is no doubt that secret monitoring offers great advantages in the investigation of acts of terror, and the fact that the power to monitor is limited solely to the Intelligence Branch of the IDF and to the GSS reduces the potential for harm. At the same time, this does not justify the absence of a requirement for judicial scrutiny prior to monitoring being carried out—save in those cases where the urgency of the matter precludes such scrutiny, in which event retroactive judicial scrutiny must suffice.

Surveillance, Monitoring, and Photography

The Protection of Privacy Law establishes the rules applicable to about eleven aspects of the right to privacy. The relevant ones for our purposes are external surveillance of the movements of a person, listening in to the conversations of a person without the assistance of technological devices, and photographing a person while he is in the private domain.[41]

Whereas the rule is that an infringement of privacy is both a criminal offense and a civil tort, Section 19(b) of the law provides that a security authority "shall bear no responsibility under this Law for an infringement reasonably committed within the scope of its or his functions and for the purpose of carrying them out." From this provision it follows that an infringement of privacy for security reasons may also be directed against a person who is not suspected of involvement in terrorist activities. It also follows that the test of the reasonableness of the infringement, which is a precondition for a discharge from liability, is amorphous and lacks any real meaning, and indeed to date the courts have refrained from establishing standards for its application. It seems to me that the reasonableness of the infringement of privacy should be established in the light of all the circumstances of the specific case, with special emphasis on the manner and severity of the infringement.

As noted, the law is applicable to many of the devices for infringing privacy described above. At the same time, these devices differ from each other not only in the gravity of the infringement but also in their level of efficiency. Thus, for example, not all biometric devices have high levels of reliability. Likewise, studies have raised doubts about the efficiency of CCTV cameras in preventing crime, including acts of terrorism. Studies have shown that the monotony involved in watching the television screens leads to a decrease in concentration in the personnel manning the control centers to below average levels after only twenty minutes of watching, and therefore the likelihood of identifying suspect movements is extremely low.[42] Consequently, the greater the harm caused by a device to an individual's privacy, and the darker the shadow hovering over the compatibility of the device with the purpose of the investigation, the more stringent should be the conditions for the application of the defense of reasonableness.

It also follows from Section 19(b) that since the law does not grant affirmative powers to perform acts that infringe privacy but merely a retroactive discharge from liability, there is no requirement for judicial review or for accountability, prior to or subsequent to the infringement. Review, so it seems, will only take place in those cases where the subject appeals against the legality of the injury. This process is largely a fiction, since many of the infringements of privacy take place without the knowledge of the injured individual, who is consequently unaware of the possibility of appealing against it. These problems are particularly serious in view of the doubtful efficiency of many of these infringing devices.

Accordingly, I believe that it would be right to set qualifications on the protection accorded by the above all-encompassing exemption so that it will only apply under the following conditions:

(a) Since the exemption cannot be regarded as an affirmative authorization to infringe privacy, it is not possible to compel the security authority to apply to the court in advance for a judicial warrant permitting the infringement but merely to compel it to apply to the court shortly *after* commission of the infringement (or in the event of a continuing infringement, shortly after the commencement of the infringement).

(b) It is necessary to establish a duty to make an accounting at regular intervals, including details of the number, nature, objectives, and results of the infringements committed during the period of time being reported.

(c) As stated in relation to the power to conduct covert searches, here too it is necessary to apply the rule whereby the subject of the search is notified of the infringement after the security grounds justifying absence of notification have ceased to exist.

Other Infringements of Privacy

ENTERING PREMISES WITHOUT SEARCH

I. Section 6 of the Civil Aviation Law empowers the minister of transport to order measures to be taken to safeguard an aviation facility on land adjacent to the facility, and those carrying out these measures may enter the land, set up equipment, and enclose it. These measures do not require the consent of the occupier of the land or judicial scrutiny, and a person who believes that he has been injured by these orders is entitled to apply to an appeals committee.

II. The GSS Law empowers GSS operatives to enter premises that are not closed private buildings in order to carry out activities necessary to protect persons, places, or information within the responsibility of the GSS. Entry for up to twelve hours does not require the consent of the occupier of the premises or authorization by a court. Entry for a longer period of time requires the consent of the occupier, and in its absence authorization by the court.

In my opinion, it is highly doubtful whether the infringement permitted by these two provisions is proportional. Section 7 of the Basic Law prohibits entry into the private domain of an individual without his consent—whether the private domain is closed (e.g., a house) or whether it is open (e.g., a yard). An all-embracing power to enter open premises without the consent of the occupier and without judicial scrutiny for up to twelve hours (in the GSS Law), and a fortiori without time limitation (in the Civil Aviation Law) is not proportional, because in the vast majority of cases entry into premises is planned in advance and there is ample time to apply to the court for a warrant. Consequently, it would be appropriate to modify these provisions and provide that every entry into premises requires the consent of the occupier or alternatively a judicial warrant, save in urgent circumstances where it is necessary to effect immediate entry into the premises and time does not permit an application to the court for a warrant—in which case entry into the premises should be permitted subject to the obligation to apply to the court for a permit to remain in the premises.

RECEIPT OF COMMUNICATION DATA

Section 11 of the GSS Law enables the head of the GSS to demand statutory communication license holders (such as telephone and cable companies) to transmit to the GSS information located in data banks under their control, if this is necessary to fulfill the functions of the GSS.[43] The law requires the head of the GSS to report periodically to the prime minister, the attorney general, and the Knesset committee overseeing the GSS. The application of Section 11 is dependent on the establishment of regulations regarding the types of information and the details of the report; these regulations have not yet been promulgated. Likewise, Section 13 of the Telecommunications Law requires the licensee—upon being given an order by the minister of communication—to provide telecommunication services to the security services, if considerations of national security or public safety so require.[44] Thus, for example, the minister may require cellular telephone companies to install broadcasting antennas in certain areas in order to allow the movements of their subscribers to be tracked.

Over many years the State of Israel shaped its array of constitutional balances between national security and individual rights, including the right to privacy, under the shadow of continuous security threats. Accordingly, it is not surprising that while the events of September 11 led many democratic countries to carry out far-reaching changes to their traditional array of balances, in Israel no real constitutional changes were undertaken. Nonetheless, as we have seen, this alone is not evidence of the appropriateness of the balances currently in place.

From the procedural point of view, the fact that current regulations are spread over a large number of statutes makes it difficult to draw an overall picture of the powers infringing privacy on grounds of national security. The substantive danger arising from this eclectic arrangement lies in the necessity of examining the need for each power from the micro perspective of the statute within whose framework the specific power is granted (one tree in a wood), instead of from the macro perspective of the entire body of powers granted by the various laws (the wood as a whole). The outcome is the granting of gratuitous powers that infringe privacy to an unnecessary extent.

In addition to the conferral of gratuitous powers, the laws occasionally permit the infringement of privacy without establishing mechanisms for prior judicial review or even retroactive oversight mechanisms, and also fail to prescribe arrangements for notifying the individual of the infringement of his rights.

An additional issue concerns the lack of transparency regarding the manner of exercising these powers. The Freedom of Information Law expressly prohibits a public authority from transmitting information to a citizen or a resident of the state which may cause harm to national security or to the safety of the public.[45] Democracies, it is said, die behind closed doors,[46] because unrestrained power tends to corrupt. The absence of transparency makes it more difficult both for the individual who has been harmed and for human rights organizations to bring these weighty issues before the courts. Consequently, despite the importance and critical character of these provisions, they should not be interpreted overbroadly.

A Comparative View

The United States

The right of a person to legal protection from having his privacy interfered with by law enforcement agencies is not expressly entrenched in the constitutional documents of the United States—the Constitution and the Bill of Rights. Nonetheless, over the years the Supreme Court has interpreted the amendments to the Constitution, and chiefly the Fourth Amendment, as granting express or implied constitutional protection to certain aspects of privacy.[47]

Even though, prima facie, the Constitution establishes absolute human rights, the fact that it does not refer to conditions for infringing those rights has led the courts to recognize that they may be limited to serve critical public interests.

The Fourth Amendment to the Constitution provides, "The right of the people to be secure in their persons, houses, papers, and effects, against unreasonable searches and seizures, shall not be violated, and no warrants shall issue, but upon probable cause, supported by oath or affirmation, and particularly describing the place to be searched, and the persons or things to be seized." Unlike Israeli law, American law does not define the term "search" in the Fourth Amendment. Until the *Katz* case in 1967, the courts interpreted this term in the light of the trespass doctrine, so that a search was conducted whenever a person's property rights in his body or concrete assets were violated.[48]

The more sophisticated developments in electronic surveillance technology became, the less this doctrine proved adequate to grant the individual proper protection against the state's invasion of his private life. For example, monitoring the conversations of a person by means that did not require physical entry into his premises was not regarded as a search and therefore was not subject to the restrictions of the Fourth Amendment. In order to remain loyal to the rationale underlying the Fourth Amendment, the Court adapted its interpretation to the changing times and in the *Katz* case abolished the trespass doctrine and replaced it with the doctrine of reasonable expectation of privacy. Holding that "the Fourth Amendment protects people not places," the Court stated that "search" means infringement of a person's protected interest in the privacy of his life: "What a person knowingly exposes to the public, even in his own home or office, is not a subject of Fourth Amendment protection. . . . But what he seeks to preserve as private, even in an area accessible to the public, may be constitutionally protected."[49]

In an opinion that later case law adopted as the guiding principle of law, Justice John Marshall Harlan interpreted this principle as comprising two cumulative conditions: "First that a person have exhibited an actual (subjective) expectation of privacy and, second, that the expectation be one that society is prepared to recognize as 'reasonable.'"[50] In view of this ruling it has been held that a person's subjective expectation that air surveillance will not be carried out of movements in the private domain is not reasonable, at least as long as the tracker is not assisted by sophisticated technological aids or observes intimate activities.[51] Similarly, tracking the location of a person by means of a beeper is not a search as long as the article in which the device has been placed is located in the public domain so that the person's movements can be tracked without technological assistance. Conversely, when the article is placed within a private home, continued tracking will be deemed to be a search.[52] Similarly, use of a thermal imager in order to detect the amount of heat emitted from a person's house is regarded as a search, since the information acquired by the tracker could only have been acquired by physical entry into its boundaries.[53] Regarding the use of biometric measures, the Court has held that "[f]ingerprinting involves none of the probing into an individual's private life and thoughts that marks an interrogation or search."[54] And also: "The physical characteristics of a person's voice, its tone and manner, as opposed to the content of a specific conversation, are constantly exposed to the public. Like a man's facial characteristics, or handwriting, his voice is repeatedly produced for others to hear. No person can have a reasonable expectation that others will not know the sound of his voice, any more than he can reasonably expect that his face will be a mystery to the world."[55]

It follows from this reasoning that means of identification using voice, signature, features, palm print, and fingerprints are not in the nature of a search. However, in the *Skinner* case (1989) the Court held that activities that entail entry into a person's body (such as a blood test) and activities that lead to the disclosure of a person's medical information violate the individual's reasonable expectation of privacy and consequently constitute a search.[56] In view of this subsequent reasoning, all biometric measures—including identification by means of voice, signature, features, palm print, and fingerprints—that meet at least one of these two criteria are in the nature of a search.

Once it is decided that a particular act constitutes a search, it must satisfy the conditions of the Fourth Amendment in order to be regarded as constitutional—that is, it must be reasonable and be carried out under a judicial warrant clearly defining the article being sought. The person applying for the search warrant must have sworn an affidavit showing probable cause for the involvement of the person who is the subject of the warrant in an offense that has been committed or is about to be committed.

However, over the years, case law has established a number of exceptions to the requirement for a warrant. The two relevant exceptions for our purposes are:

Stop-and-frisk Search. Law enforcement agencies are empowered to detain any person who gives rise to a reasonable suspicion that he is involved in criminal activities. During the course of the detention, the law enforcement agent is entitled to search the person's clothes if he has reasonable cause to believe that the latter is armed and therefore poses a danger to him or to the public.[57]

Administrative Search. Since the previous exception is limited to situations where there is reasonable cause to suspect that a person is dangerous, it does not provide an answer to situations where locating weapons and explosives requires routine searches to be carried out (e.g., searches of the person and baggage of all the passengers in a plane or visitors to a tourist site). In order to enable preventive searches to be carried out, case law has developed the doctrine of the administrative search, which has been defined as a search that is conducted "as part of a general regulatory scheme in furtherance of an administrative purpose, rather than as part of a criminal investigation to secure evidence of crime."[58]

Consequently, in order for a search to be regarded as administrative, the reason for it must be compelling. This is undoubtedly the case in relation to security searches aimed at uncovering weapons and explosives. The search must be confined to achieving this purpose, and it must be conducted following the exercise of discretion based solely on relevant considerations.[59]

Even after establishing this doctrine, the courts remained cognizant of the severe injury caused to the privacy of innocent persons: "The unavoidable consequence of this exhaustive search for weapons is that security personnel will become aware of many personal items that do not pose a danger to air safety."[60] However, in view of the huge devastation that terrorist attacks may potentially cause, it has been held that the benefits arising from conducting the search outweigh the inherent damage entailed by the search, and accordingly the constitutional test of reasonableness is satisfied.[61]

In cases in which a search warrant is required, the Fourth Amendment provides that the court may issue a warrant if the requirements of reasonableness and probable cause are satisfied. In this context, the Court has held that, first, "[w]hether a particular search meets the reasonableness standard is judged by balancing its intrusion on the individual's Fourth Amendment interests against its promotion of legitimate government interests."[62] And second, that "'[p]robable cause' is the standard by which a particular decision to search is tested against the constitutional mandate of reasonableness. . . . In determining whether a particular inspection is reasonable—and thus in determining whether there is probable cause to issue a warrant for that inspection—the need for the inspection must be weighed in terms of these reasonable goals of code enforcement."[63]

Based on these pronouncements, it may be stated that in times of emergency it is possible to lower the standards for determining probable cause below the level of proof needed to obtain a search warrant for ordinary criminal offenses. However, care must be taken not to lower the standard of proof so excessively as to make the requirement of proof of probable cause meaningless.

Against this backdrop, I shall now turn to an examination of the federal antiterrorism legislation prevailing before the attacks of September 11, 2001.

Title III of the Omnibus Crime Control and Safe Street Act and the

Electronic Communications Privacy Act (ECPA) regulate the law applying to the monitoring of verbal communications and the monitoring of
electronic and wire communications.[64] Monitoring is dependent on a
judicial warrant, which may be granted only if the monitoring is sought
as part of a criminal investigation of an offense listed in the law, and if
the applicant has satisfied the stringent standard of proof, which requires
"probable cause for belief that an individual is committing, has committed, or is about to commit a particular offense . . . probable cause for
belief that particular communications concerning that offense will be
obtained through such interception . . . normal investigative procedures
have been tried and have failed or reasonably appear to be unlikely to
succeed if tried or to be too dangerous."[65]

Monitoring by means of pen register and trap-and-trace devices is
conducted by virtue of judicial warrants issued under the Foreign Intelligence Surveillance Act (FISA) or the Pen/Trap Statute.[66] Probable
cause need not be shown to obtain a warrant; rather, it must be proved
that the information to be seized is relevant to a criminal investigation
or to an investigation of international terrorism or foreign intelligence.
Apart from engaging in pen/trap monitoring during investigations aimed
at defending national security or gathering foreign intelligence, FISA
controls the legal regime applicable to electronic tapping, physical entry
into premises, and obtaining records, when these activities are required
for investigating the issues mentioned above. Unlike the stringent standard that Title III requires for obtaining a judicial warrant, FISA requires a lower standard, except if the suspect is a citizen of the United
States, in which case probable cause is required of his involvement in
activities contravening the criminal law.

The Anti-Terrorism and Effective Death Penalty Act was enacted in
the aftermath of the first terrorist attack on the Twin Towers in 1993
and the terrorist attack on the federal office building in Oklahoma City
in 1995.[67] Among its provisions, Section 804 allows governmental bodies
to compel communication providers to preserve their records regarding customers who are suspected of having committed offenses for an
initial period of ninety days, subject to an option to extend the period
for an additional ninety days.

Section 303 of the act requires every financial institution that knows
it is in possession of monies associated with a foreign terrorist organization to continue to hold those funds and concurrently report their
existence to the authorities. Section 701 removes from the application
of Title III information stored in communication systems that are used
for storing and transferring monies, thereby lessening the standard of

proof that has to be met by the authorities when seeking information about bank accounts.

On September 11, 2001, the full force of terror struck at the heart of the United States. History will not record the attack of September 11 as the first hostile action taken against the American people; however, in terms of the number of victims, the extent of the destruction, the methods by which it was carried out, and the degree of defiance it exposed, it was an assault more threatening than any that had preceded it. The American government responded to this threat in part by initiating the legislation of the Patriot Act, which severely shifted the long-standing constitutional balance in favor of national security needs at the expense of the individual's right to privacy.[68]

Even though the purpose of the act is to strengthen the ability of law enforcement agencies to fight terrorism, many of the statutory provisions may be used in ordinary criminal investigations. Likewise, in a number of situations the statutory provisions negate the court's discretion and turn it into a rubber stamp engaging purely in symbolic judicial review. The examples of this are many, and I shall confine myself here to the outstanding ones.

Before the enactment of the law, the rules of criminal procedure and the judgments of the state courts interpreted the Fourth Amendment as compelling law enforcement agencies to notify a person of a search that was about to be carried out on his premises (knock-and-announce principle), with certain exceptions that varied from state to state and that allowed covert searches to be carried out subject to retroactive notification.[69] As a result of claims by law enforcement agencies that the variations in the laws of the various states undermined interstate investigations, including investigations of terrorism, the Patriot Act established a uniform federal standard. Under this standard, in criminal investigations the court is empowered to authorize a search without prior notice being given, upon reasonable proof that notice would have a deleterious effect on the investigation (e.g., it might endanger the life or well-being of a person, allow a person to abscond, interfere with evidence, or frighten witnesses).[70]

Before this law, FISA granted the FBI power to apply to the court for an order compelling a closed list of bodies to hand over records in their possession regarding a person in respect of whom there were "specific and articulable facts giving reason to believe that the person to whom the records pertain is a foreign power or an agent of a foreign power."[71] Section 215 of the Patriot Act significantly expands this power by enabling the FBI to demand not only records but also "any tangible things," not only from the closed list of bodies but from any body or person (such as a bookshop or Internet service provider), and not only in cases where there is reason to believe that the subject of the information request is a foreign agent but in cases where any person is involved. Judicial supervision of the exercise of this power is a pretense, since once the FBI has informed the court that it needs the information as part of an authorized investigation relating to international terrorism or secret foreign intelligence, the judge has no discretion to refuse. Moreover, the body or person obliged to hand over the information is prohibited from telling this to anyone else, even in cases where there is no security justification for secrecy, and consequently the person whose privacy has been infringed will never know of it and naturally will not be able to challenge the legality of the search.[72]

As we have seen, even before the Patriot Act, the obstacle to obtaining a judicial pen/trap order was overcome relatively easily. Section 216 of the act expands this power even further, in three respects.[73] First, whereas in the past the validity of the warrant was limited to the area of jurisdiction of the court issuing the order, now courts are entitled to issue warrants valid throughout the United States, and there is no requirement to identify the article that is the subject of the search. Second, the act clarifies that it is possible to monitor not only telephone communication networks but also a range of other communication technologies—a previously contentious issue. Third, the act expands the types of pen/trap information that may be made the subject of the order; however, because it does not contain an explicit definition distinguishing between content and pen/trap information, there is room here for an expansive interpretation. Thus, for example, there is a dispute whether the addresses of Internet sites should be seen as purely technical information or as information relating to content, since they have the potential to disclose personal information about the user's areas of interest.

In the past, during an ongoing criminal investigation, law enforcement agencies could issue an administrative subpoena compelling suppliers of electronic communication services to hand over limited information regarding their subscribers (such as name, address, telephone account). Section 210 of the Patriot Act expands the type of information that may be sought under the subpoena, so as to include information regarding the means of payment of the subscriber (such as credit card number or bank account number) and records of the dates and hours of surfing on the Internet.

In the past it was possible to apply under FISA for a warrant for electronic surveillance and search of premises in respect of investigations that had the *sole* purpose of gathering foreign intelligence. Section 218 expands the application of FISA to investigations where intelligence gathering is a significant purpose but not the sole purpose. Since the ground for application is vague, there is a danger that it will be construed broadly so that the easier statutory standard will also be used for criminal investigations.

In light of the ongoing terrorist operations around the globe since September 11, the government has concluded that the threat to the security of the American people has not receded and that the need to detect and disrupt terrorist activity before it occurs has remained as compelling as before. Thus, on July 2005 the U.S. House of Representatives and the Senate voted to extend permanently fourteen of the sixteen Patriot Act provisions that were set to expire at the end of 2005, and to extend the two other provisions (Section 206 concerning "roving wiretaps" and Section 215 dealing with access to certain business records under FISA) for an additional period of ten years, according to the House bill, or four years unless renewed by Congress again, according to the Senate bill. Section 215, described above, has been one of the most controversial provisions of the Patriot Act. Among other things, the proposed reenactment tightens the requirements that must be met to seize business records and requires greater judicial oversight.[74]

It should be pointed out that, despite the significant expansion of its powers, the government remains of the opinion that it is insufficiently equipped to wage its war against terror. Accordingly, it is also seeking to augment its powers by enacting the Domestic Enhancement Security Act. This act would infringe the right to privacy—as well as other fundamental rights—even more severely than its predecessor. Among other things, Section 101 expands the application of FISA by amending the definition of people included in the term "foreign power." Section 103 provides that electronic surveillance, physical searches, or pen registers may be used for a period of fifteen days following a congressional declaration of war or terrorist attack—without obtaining a search order. Sections 128 and 129 enable the authorities to issue administrative subpoenas when a terrorist investigation is underway, requiring any person or body to divulge information in his possession without a court order. The final version of the revised Patriot Act, known as the "act to extend and modify authorities needed to combat terrorism," was approved by both houses of Congress and signed by President Bush in March, 2006. Recently, following the findings of the 9/11 Commission, the intelligence services have been recognized by the Intelligence Reform and

Terrorism Prevention Act of 2004, which affects more severely the right to privacy.

United Kingdom

Despite possessing a democratic tradition going back over hundreds of years, the United Kingdom has refrained from entrenching its commitment to individual rights and freedoms in a written constitutional document.

In 1998 Parliament passed the Human Rights Act, which gave domestic effect to the provisions of the European Convention on Human Rights.[75] Thus, the right to privacy, which is explicitly protected in Article 8 of the convention, acquired binding legal force in the United Kingdom.

A number of statutes protect various aspects of the right to privacy. The most important of these is the Data Protection Act, which establishes the legal regime for data held by public and private bodies.[76] According to the act, these bodies must register the type of data held by them, the purpose for collecting it, and its use with the Office of the Information Commissioner, an independent public body that is responsible for the management of the register and enforcing the statutory provisions. Likewise, the act grants every person the right to request to be notified whenever action is taken to collect or use data relating to him, and prohibits the bodies subject to the act from collecting, using, or disclosing data outside the framework of the means and purposes established for collecting and managing it. However, these provisions do not apply when to do so would harm national security.

In the year 2000 the Regulation of Investigatory Powers Act was passed.[77] This act grants the investigatory bodies extremely broad powers, without the need to obtain judicial warrants. The extent to which this act is compatible with the provisions of the European Convention on Human Rights is open to grave question. For example, the act enables the secretary of state for defense to authorize the interception of communications transferred by means of the postal service or telecommunication systems if this is necessary for reasons of national security, as part of the investigation of serious crimes, or to safeguard the economic well-being of the United Kingdom. Likewise, the act enables the defense secretary to require these service providers to adjust their systems in order to permit monitoring.

Section 22 allows these service providers to be ordered to disclose identifying communication data—as opposed to content information—relating to the users of their services to the legal authorities if this is necessary on grounds of national security, public safety, the investigation of serious crime, or safeguarding the economic well-being of the state. Likewise, the act enables the defense secretary or other officials to authorize human surveillance on grounds of national security.

A number of statutes grant the police wide powers to search the body and premises of a person. Section 1 of the Police and Criminal Evidence Act enables a constable, without a search warrant, to search any vehicle or person in a public place if the constable has reasonable cause to suspect that weapons, explosives, or equipment intended for use in the commission of a crime are unlawfully present there.[78] Section 8 authorizes a justice of the peace to issue a search warrant for premises if he is satisfied that there are reasonable grounds for believing that a serious arrestable offense has been committed and that there is material in the premises which is likely to be of "substantial value" to the investigation of the offense.

Section 17 authorizes a constable to enter and search any premises for the purpose of arresting a person for an arrestable offense if he has reasonable grounds for believing that the person he is seeking is on the premises. Similarly, Section 18 authorizes a constable to enter and search, without a search warrant, any premises occupied by a person who is under arrest if he has reasonable grounds for suspecting that there is evidence on the premises that relates to that offense, or to some other arrestable offense that is connected with or similar to that offense. Section 60 enables police commanders to authorize their subordinates to search every vehicle or person located in a cordoned area if there is reasonable cause to believe that serious violent offenses will be committed there.

In the year 2000 the Terrorism Act was passed, incorporating numerous provisions that significantly infringe the right to privacy.[79] For example, Section 19 provides that a person commits an offense if he does not disclose to a constable as soon as is reasonably practicable that information has come to his attention in the course of his business that has led him to reasonably suspect that another person is supporting terrorists financially, is assisting in obtaining financial support for terrorists, is performing actions aimed at money laundering for terrorist purposes, or knowingly holds property intended for terrorist purposes. Section 20 permits—but does not compel—a person to disclose to a constable that he suspects that money or other property is terrorist property, and Section 21 provides that a person who participates in activities supporting terrorist acts shall not be liable for his involvement if he makes a disclosure on his own initiative to the police as soon as he begins suspecting that he was involved in prohibited activities.

Likewise, the Terrorism Act states that during the course of terrorist investigations, a constable may apply for a judicial warrant authorizing him to search premises and any person found therein. The judge may only give this order if he is persuaded that there is reasonable cause to believe that in the said premises there are articles of substantive value in advancing the investigation and that the grant of the warrant is essential in the circumstances.

In addition, during the course of investigating terror, a judge is entitled to issue an order requiring a financial institution to divulge certain customer information in its possession, such as the customer's account number, full name, date of birth, address, and the date on which a business relationship between the financial institution and the customer begins or ends. The order will only be granted on proof that the order will enhance the effectiveness of the investigation.

Section 42 provides that a judge may, on the application of a constable, issue a warrant in relation to specified premises if he is satisfied that there are reasonable grounds for suspecting that a person whom the constable reasonably suspects to be a person who is or has been concerned in the commission, preparation, or instigation of acts of terrorism is to be found there.

Likewise, the act provides that a constable may arrest without a warrant a person whom he reasonably suspects to be a terrorist; moreover, he may search a person arrested under Section 41 to discover whether he has in his possession anything that may constitute evidence that he is a terrorist. A constable may also search a person suspected of being a terrorist, even without arresting him.

A particularly draconian power set out in the law enables police commanders to authorize constables to search every vessel or person located in a defined area if they believe that this is expedient for the prevention of acts of terrorism. Even though this power allows the invasion of the privacy of people who are not suspected of having committed any offense, the act does not require prior judicial scrutiny, or even retroactive scrutiny, of the exercise of the power. Only two restrictions are imposed on this power. First, that the commander reports the grant of authorization to the secretary of state for defense as soon as is reasonably practicable; the secretary of state may then modify or cancel the authorization. Second, the authorization will be valid for a maximum period of twenty-eight days, following which it must be renewed in a new process.

The terrorist attack on the United States also had an impact on the United Kingdom. Like the government of the United States, which hastened to initiate legal legislative action clearly according superiority to security interests over individual rights, the United Kingdom also believed that the balance of interests established in its statutes failed to provide it with sufficient tools to defend the country against terrorists. Consequently, even though the Terrorism Act had come into force only a few months before, the Anti-Terrorism, Crime and Security Act was passed in 2001.[80]

Among its provisions, the latter act broadens the range of customer information which financial institutions must divulge under the Terrorism Act to also include information regarding the customer's account in that institution. Section 17 of the act expands the duty of disclosure of certain public authorities to cases where the information is sought in the context of an investigation or criminal procedure. Section 19 permits the tax authorities to voluntarily disclose information in their possession, if such disclosure is not prohibited under the Data Protection Act, for the purpose of facilitating the carrying out by any of the intelligence services of any of that service's functions or for the purposes of any criminal investigation or criminal proceedings.

Conclusion

Unlike those in the past who believed that the ideological struggle between democratic theory and its challengers had ended with the clear victory of democracy,[81] today—after the events of the last century and in particular the transformation of Germany from a state boasting a long democratic tradition to one embracing Nazism—we can no longer delude ourselves into thinking that the ideological battle has ended and that our society is guaranteed an abiding democratic future. On the contrary, we understand that "the democratic regimes throughout the world . . . are not primeval rock the existence of which is guaranteed after it is created. Without vigilance and persistent activity democracies may collapse in a gradual manner and occasionally also in the blink of an eye. We must be aware of this potential for fragility and understand that it is possible to overcome the danger only by means of openness and watchfulness and taking a firm stand on safeguarding freedoms."[82]

A comparative examination of the formulas balancing security needs and privacy shows that even before the terrorist attack on the United States in September 2001, the Western democratic states had granted the security authorities broad powers to invade a person's privacy. After that attack, the United States and the United Kingdom engaged in hasty and far-reaching legislative changes to these formulas which significantly limited the protection of privacy. Is it true that the previous array of checks and balances limited the effectiveness of the tools available to the security authorities to fight terrorism, and that therefore the legislative changes were legitimate and inescapable measures forced on demo-cratic states seeking to defend themselves? Or, were these measures the outcome of panic and paranoia?

An answer to these questions requires us to examine a number of points.

First, the tool available to a democratic state which most seriously denies and restricts freedoms is its criminal law, and consequently the state must use the utmost care to comply with procedural rules designed to ensure that the individual against whom this tool is directed enjoys fair process. Even though security offenses are at the same time crimi-nal offenses, the harm they cause to national security, public safety, and the fabric of social life is much more destructive. Therefore, investiga-tive powers that would cause disproportionate harm to an individual in an ordinary criminal process—such as a covert search of his premises or personal effects—are acceptable as a constitutional exception in the security arena.

In situations where the Israeli legislature was careful to refrain from expanding the scope of application of special security legislation to the criminal process as a whole, the legislatures of the United States and the United Kingdom—even before the new antiterrorist acts but more so subsequently—abstained from drawing a clear distinction of principle between the two areas. The application of security legislation to ordi-nary criminal offenses does not lead rationally to achieving the purpose of the infringement—that is, prevention of acts of terrorism—and therefore violates the individual's right to a fair criminal trial in a dis-proportionate manner.

Second, while every power requires the establishment of effective supervisory mechanisms over the manner in which investigative powers are exercised in order to ensure that they are not improperly exploited or used unnecessarily, this requirement is even more important in secu-rity related matters, where the scope of the powers and the relative ease with which they can be exercised lead to a much greater possibility of abuse. Moreover, difficulty in defining the term "terror" has led every country to adopt a broad and vague definition of this concept. While there is no doubt that the purpose of the vagueness is to ensure that the term will catch such terrorist organizations as Al Qaeda and Hamas within its net, a by-product is that many of the legitimate acts of civil protest carried out under the banner of freedom of speech and associa-tion may fall within its precincts, and therefore it is conceivable that one day political opponents will pervert the purpose of the vagueness in an effort to neutralize each another.

Notwithstanding the immense potential risks, and notwithstanding that establishing restraining and controlling mechanisms—such as substantive, as opposed to symbolic, prior judicial scrutiny, or at least retrospective scrutiny; or the establishment of supervisory bodies or ensuring public transparency by requiring periodic reports—would not necessarily undermine the effective implementation of the powers, it is apparent that all the states have on occasion renounced these mechanisms. This is particularly true in the aftermath of the September 11 attacks.

Third, a system of balances between security and freedom has existed from time immemorial, although each era has sought to adapt those balances to changing reality. Today, technologies exist that can image the body of a person under his clothes, track his movements using satellite pictures and CCTV cameras, pinpoint his location with the aid of beepers or cellular telephones, cross-check vast quantities of data to determine whether a person fits the profile of a terrorist, track his movements on the Internet, and perform many other functions that enable a state to create a detailed and comprehensive portrait of the lives of its citizens. While it is inappropriate to latch onto outdated checks and balances that would prevent security authorities from using technological innovations on the grounds of the severe, sometimes mortal, harm caused to the privacy of masses of innocent persons, the state—if it wishes to be faithful to its democratic values—cannot permit unrestrained use of these technologies, even if they have the potential to assist in the prevention of acts of terrorism.

We have seen that a number of arrangements in Israeli law fail to meet these core principles. The events of September 2001 led the United States and the United Kingdom to sharply tilt the scales toward security needs, on the grounds that their previous checks-and-balances formulas had been wrong and had given excessive weight to the individual's privacy. In my opinion, this argument is factually unfounded, since our examination of the statutory amendments has revealed that most of the amendments did not grant the security authorities new powers but rather removed or eased the oversight mechanisms of past powers—a process that does not increase the efficiency of the war against terrorism at all but only creates a danger of unlawful implementation of those powers.

Emergency times pose a dual challenge to a democracy: on the one hand, it must protect its citizens and ensure their security, and for this purpose it must restrict their rights. On the other hand, a democracy must safeguard itself against blindly sacrificing the values of freedom and justice on the altar of national security.

This task is not easy, either legally or morally, since in times of crisis the individual tends to accord greater weight to the collective interest in security than to individual rights. The legislature—an elected body dependent on public support—is likely to exploit this temporary public mandate to engage in unnecessary, destructive, and irreversible violations of the individual's rights.

As democratic states, "we have always placed our trust in the fact that here the voice of the law is not silent even in the tumult of the hostility which surrounds us,"[83] and therefore we must be careful not to enact laws that turn the individual from an end into a means to achieve a security objective.

The State of Israel, which since its establishment has been contending with persistent security threats, and the democratic Western states, which since September 2001 have understood that they too must live under the shadow of terrorist threats, have more than once surrendered to the temptation to see the individual as a tool, and consequently to suspend his right to privacy on imaginary and factually baseless security grounds—a phenomenon that is particularly noticeable today in the United States and the United Kingdom.

All those who argue that any infringement whatsoever on a person's privacy can be tolerated only in times of crisis, and that immediately upon the arrival of a time of peace it must be removed, are suffering from self-delusion. The boundary line separating the protection of the rights of the individual in times of emergency and their protection in times of peace is extremely fine and hard to perceive, and therefore there is a danger that unnecessary restrictions imposed in times of emergency, and their moral impact, will remain long after the cessation of that emergency; and we will find ourselves living in an abyss into which we have thrown ourselves unnecessarily.[84]

Particularly in its hour of trouble, against the background of gunfire and scenes of destruction, it is vital for the state to take honest stock and examine whether it has remained faithful to its democratic character and to the values for which it is fighting. Without this, at the end of the battle, when the veil of smoke lifts, we may discover that not only were the symbols of democracy destroyed by the terrorist attacks, but so was democracy itself.

SEVEN

Use of Civilians as Human Shields

ONE OF THE most difficult and complex questions, from both a moral and a legal point of view, arising out of the battle between democratic states and guerilla terrorist organizations concerns the treatment of innocent civilians on both sides when they voluntarily or involuntarily become human shields used to protect the lives and prevent the capture of terrorists. Whereas the state complies with the law when it fights and employs only those measures falling within the rule of law, terrorist organizations violate the law in their fight and are not deterred from any methods that, in their view, can contribute to the effective advancement of their goals, including the use of civilians as human shields. This is done in two primary ways: First, terrorists hide among their own civilians, who are volunteered willingly or unwillingly to preserve the terrorists' safety. Second, the terrorists seize the civilians of the state against which they are fighting as hostages either to assist their safe escape from the scene of an attack or to be used for negotiation purposes. What, therefore, is the scope of the protection which the state is obliged to afford to those civilians who are used as human covers for terrorists?

International Law Regarding the Protection of Civilians in Times of Hostilities

In chapter 2, I considered the problems involved in classifying terrorist attacks as armed attacks vesting the state under attack with the inherent right to protect itself and make use of force. I concluded that in view of the unique characteristics of the terrorist act, it is possible and even proper to categorize it in this way. I then turned to the issue of the choice of law that applies to the way the attacked state implements its defensive powers in these circumstances, and here too I concluded that while in the majority of cases there is insufficient evidence to attribute the activities of nonstate terrorist organizations to sovereign states supporting their actions, and consequently apply all the international laws of war regulating the conduct of international armed conflicts, it is still right to regard terrorist attacks as amounting to armed conflicts not of an international character. Consequently, it would be right to apply Article 3 common to all the Geneva Conventions of 1949, which establishes minimum humanitarian norms binding on all parties to a conflict, and indirectly—by way of analogy—all the *jus in bello* applicable to the conduct of international armed conflicts, which restrict the freedoms of the parties when waging war and prevent them from making use of some of the means at their disposal.

While it is true that all these laws are based on the principle of reciprocity, according to which both parties to the dispute take upon themselves the duty to comply with the restrictions on the use of force, and in the war against terrorist organizations only one party—the targeted democratic state—agrees to comply with these restrictions, the democratic nature of the state and the rule of law to which it is committed impose on it an absolute obligation to abide by these restraints. In other words, the fact that its opponent sees itself as unfettered by these restrictions does not allow the state to also see itself as free of restraints, as this would be incompatible with its character and values.

The restrictions on the freedoms of the combatant parties are principally set out in the Hague Conventions of 1899 and 1907, the Geneva Conventions of 1949, and the Additional Protocols to the Geneva Conventions of 1977. Some of these laws have also obtained the status of customary law over the years. As stated in chapter 2, the guiding principle underlying these laws is the distinction between combatants and noncombatants: warfare must be conducted solely between combatants, who are required to refrain from causing each other unnecessary suffering and to treat captured combatants as prisoners of war, and who are also required to refrain as far as possible from harming the civilian population and civilian property of the opposing side as well as to safeguard the rights of the civilian population which finds itself under enemy occupation.

Below I shall consider in more detail the norms of the laws of war relevant to the issue of using civilians as human shields.

Protecting Civilians against Enemy Attacks

Article 3(1) common to the four Geneva Conventions of 1949 provides:

> Persons taking no active part in the hostilities . . . shall in all circumstances be treated humanely, without any adverse distinction founded on race, colour, religion or faith, sex, birth or wealth, or any other similar criteria.
>
> To this end, the following acts are and shall remain prohibited at any time and in any place whatsoever with respect to the above-mentioned persons:
> (a) violence to life and person, in particular murder of all kinds, mutilation, cruel treatment and torture;
> (b) taking of hostages;
> (c) outrages upon personal dignity, in particular humiliating and degrading treatment;
> (d) the passing of sentences and the carrying out of executions without previous judgment pronounced by a regularly constituted court, affording all the judicial guarantees which are recognized as indispensable by civilized peoples.[1]

Article 48 of Protocol I Additional to the Geneva Conventions provides: "In order to ensure respect for and protection of the civilian population and civilian objects, the Parties to the conflict shall at all times distinguish between the civilian population and combatants and between civilian objects and military objectives and accordingly shall direct their operations only against military objectives."[2] Article 51(2) emphasizes that an attack whose primary purpose is to spread terror among the civilian population is prohibited.

Terrorist organizations by definition operate in a manner completely contrary to this basic rule, since their acts of murderous violence are in fact aimed at harming innocent civilians in order to provoke dread and panic.

In contrast, the democratic state by definition acts to foil terror attacks while remaining subject to moral and legal norms that require it to distinguish between harm to innocent civilians and harm to terrorists operating from the center of civilian populations. Accordingly, it is precluded from dropping aerial bombs onto civilian centers where terrorists have found cover, since doing so would violate the basic prohibition referred to above, as well as the provisions of Article 51(4) of Protocol I regarding the prohibition on indiscriminate attacks, that is, attacks that are not directed at a specific military objective or that employ a method or means of combat which cannot, or whose effects cannot, be directed at a specific military objective. Article 51(5)(b) expands the protection given to civilians and defines as indiscriminate and therefore prohibited even an attack directed at a specific military objective if that attack may be expected to cause incidental loss of life or injuries to civilians or damage to civilian property that would be excessive in relation to the concrete and direct anticipated military advantage. At the same time, we should note that Article 51(5)(a) defines as indiscriminate and therefore prohibits an attack by bombardment by any method or means that treats as a single military objective a number of clearly separated and distinct objectives located in an area containing a concentration of civilians or civilian property. In other words, if the military objectives are not distinct and the civilian objects are not concentrated as required, the area may be treated as a single large military objective. Such an interpretation erodes the protection given to civilians and may justify causing them harm during the course of an attempted assault on terrorists deliberately merging with them.

Article 23 of the Second and Fourth Hague Conventions of 1907 prohibits the destruction of enemy property unless such destruction be imperatively demanded by the necessities of war. Article 54(2) and (3) of Protocol I further prohibits attacking, destroying, or rendering useless objects indispensable to the survival of the civilian population which are not clearly used for the military purposes of the adverse party. Article 57(1) demands: "In the conduct of military operations, constant care shall be taken to spare the civilian population, civilians and civilian objects."

Article 51(6) of Protocol I provides that attacks against the civilian population as acts of reprisal are prohibited. The analogy that can be drawn from this paragraph in relation to the state's war against terrorist organizations is particularly relevant, since prima facie it shows that the fact that the terrorist enemy harms civilians cannot justify the state's killing of civilians surrounding the terrorists. As I shall show below, the proper construction of this article is that it prohibits a deliberate and knowing attack against the civilian population of the adverse party as an act of reprisal for the killing of the state's own civilians. The article does not prohibit an attack against the killers themselves, even though in consequence injury is caused to civilians whose presence in the same location as the terrorists is unknown to the democratic state, to civilians who freely choose to support the terrorists by providing them shelter in their own homes in order to deliberately blur the distinction between civilian and terrorist objectives, and in some circumstances to innocent civilians who are being held against their will by the terrorists.

Article 26 of the Second and Fourth Hague Conventions provides that the commander of an attacking force must, before commencing a bombardment, do all in his power to warn the local authorities.

This obligation is designed to prevent undue suffering to the civilian population, to enable them to find shelter and protect themselves.[3] Nonetheless, the duty to give effective advance warning, as it has developed in customary international law, is not an absolute duty. A state may depart from it if "the circumstances do not permit advance warning."[4]

This review of the various provisions clearly highlights the differences between the parties in a war being waged between a democratic state and terrorists. The democratic state regards itself as subject to these provisions on both a legal and a moral level, whereas the other side does not.

Protecting Civilians against Being Turned into Human Shields by Combatants from the Same Side

Article 28 of the Fourth Geneva Convention provides: "The presence of a protected person may not be used to render certain points or areas immune from military operations."[5]

Article 51(7) of Protocol I prohibits the parties from using the civilian population as a human shield or as a means of achieving immunity from military attack. Accordingly, Article 58(b) requires the parties to the conflict to avoid as far as possible locating military objectives within or near densely populated areas. Article 44(3) of Protocol I recognizes an exception in circumstances where "owing to the nature of the hostilities an armed combatant cannot so distinguish himself" from the civilian population. In such cases, a combatant need only carry his arms openly "during each military engagement" and "during such time as he is visible to the adversary while he is engaged in a military deployment preceding the launching of an attack in which he is to participate."

A violation by one side of these prohibitions does not entitle the other side to cause harm to the civilians of the other side.

Article 50(3) of Protocol I provides that the presence within the civilian population of individuals who do not come within the definition of civilians does not deprive the population of its civilian character. Accordingly, Article 51(8) emphasizes that even if one party takes shelter behind civilians, this does not release the other party from its legal obligations with respect to the civilian population.

Terrorists situate themselves among the civilian population with the improper sole purpose of using those civilians as a means of achieving immunity from attack by the democratic state. Terrorists are not directly committed to Protocol I, but the prohibition on the use of civilians is not only a legal prohibition. First and foremost, it is a moral prohibition. A man is never just a means; he is always an end in himself.[6] Turning civilians from their own people and religion into human shields is an immoral act that frustrates the efforts of the democratic state to leave this population outside the arena of war. Thus, the terrorists violate an additional prohibition of international law, set out in Article 34 of the Fourth Geneva Convention and of the International Convention against the Taking of Hostages of 1979, which prohibits civilians being taken as hostages.

The situation under discussion here—terrorists' use of their own people as *involuntary* human shields—should be distinguished from the situation where the civilians of their *own will* participate in the fighting effort, and as part of that process shelter the terrorists and introduce into their territory legitimate targets for attack, such as weapons factories. In the latter case, as we shall see below, the civilians may lose their immunity to attack and become legitimate targets.

The cynical use made by the terrorists of civilians—at times even of children, who are incapable of understanding how they are being used—presents the democratic law-abiding state with an extremely difficult legal and moral dilemma, requiring it to choose between its duty to protect its own citizens by engaging in military operations against terrorist strongholds located in the heart of population centers where every attack will entail harm to those civilians, and its duty not to harm innocent civilians who are used against their will to shield terrorists. On occasion, refraining from harming civilian shields during the course of pursuing terrorists will lead to the deaths of soldiers which might otherwise have been avoided. Such incidents introduce a new element into the moral equation, namely, the right of soldiers to defend their own lives. Is it right to ask them to sacrifice their right to self-defense in favor of protecting the lives of enemy civilians?

Should, therefore, the duty of the state to protect its citizens by engaging in military operations in the course of which soldiers are entitled to perform essential actions to protect themselves retreat before the moral and legal imperative that seeks to distinguish between civilians and combatants, or should the legal and moral duty of the state to do everything in its power to protects its citizens supersede?

The Moral Dilemmas

A democratic state is required to fight terrorism in accordance with principles and values that are derived from its democratic nature, first among which are the preservation of the rule of law and respect for human rights. Notwithstanding their importance, an individual's rights are not a springboard for national destruction, and an individual is therefore required to sacrifice those rights to the extent necessary to ensure the proper existence of his state, since that existence is an essential precondition to his ability to implement those rights. It follows that we are dealing with a *moral duty* on the part of the democratic state to protect its citizens by using the means necessary to frustrate activities endangering their security in general, and their lives in particular.

Before turning to an examination of the specific moral dilemmas at issue in this chapter, it is necessary to provide a brief general explanation of the nature and characteristics of a moral dilemma and the ways of resolving it.

A moral dilemma consists of a clash of values that makes it difficult to act, since choosing any of the alternatives will be inconsistent with the decision maker's obligations and values. In this case, we are speaking of a situation in which a person (or state) is obliged to choose between performing a particular act (protecting the lives of the citizens of the state and those of its soldiers) which entails a bad outcome (harm to innocent civilians of the adverse party), and performing a different act (refraining from causing harm to the civilians of the adverse party) which also entails a bad outcome (endangering the security and safety of the citizens and soldiers of the state).

In a situation with two clashing obligations, there are those who believe that only one of them, depending on the circumstances, is real and the other is imaginary.[7] However, this would be too easy an answer, since moral obligations often clash, and if we were to believe than in every such situation one of the obligations is imaginary, most moral obligations would lack any effect. Consequently, the solution must be more complex, and it is difficult to guarantee that it will be moral per se.

This conclusion receives added force when we speak of the moral dilemma confronting a state under attack which is required to choose between the lives of its citizens and soldiers, on the one hand, and the lives of the compatriots of the attacking terrorists, on the other.

Kant was of the opinion that dilemmas of this type are insoluble, since there is a moral imperative that human beings are equal in value and every person must be treated as having his own value and being an end in himself.[8] But I think that the absolute character of Kant's approach makes it overly extreme. History has shown that the maintenance of a regular and orderly life requires that we refrain from the absolute and replace it with realistic considerations, which often lead to human life being superseded as a value by other values. If this were not the case we would not be able to explain why a state does not allocate all the budget necessary to ensure that its health services are able to grant every patient the best possible treatment, and all the budget necessary for maximum security, education, and efforts to reduce road traffic fatalities.

True, the argument that human life is not an absolute value and that in particular circumstances it is possible to prefer the life of one person to that of another does not necessarily release us from a sense of moral guilt. Having this sense indicates to us that even though the choice is "correct," it involves undesirable results that are regrettable. The sense of moral guilt reflects moral character. It does not reflect the absolute nature of a moral duty.

In a clash between the state's duty to protect its citizens and soldiers and the duty to avoid harm to innocent civilians held against their will, the former is likely to prevail. True, the killing of innocent persons is an act that is legally prohibited and morally reprehensible; "however, it would seem that only a few would be willing to accept in simple terms the duty never to kill innocent persons. Someone who is not a pacifist and who is not blind to the modern reality of war which inevitably entails injury to the innocent, will find it difficult to argue in favor of the principle that the killing of innocent persons is always absolutely prohibited."[9] As we shall see below, moral and legal justification may be found for the killing of innocent persons within the context of military operations.

If we agree that there are no absolute moral obligations, we might ask on what basis we ought to determine the prevailing moral obligation. In this chapter I shall focus on two primary moral theories: the utilitarian-consequential doctrine and the deontological doctrine.

According to the utilitarian doctrine, the moral value of an act is determined in accordance with its impact on aggregate world happiness. Therefore, the moral action is the one that brings about the greatest happiness.[10] It follows that if harming the human shield is an essential precondition to harming the terrorists, and consequently to causing real damage to their ability to carry out their destructive missions, the measure of the positive outcome (preventing terrorist attacks) will be greater than the negative outcome (harming the innocent persons used as human shields); social happiness will increase and consequently also the moral justification for the act. In contrast, according to the deontological approach, the moral value of an act is determined by its internal nature and not by its outcome. An anticipated positive outcome is not relevant to assessing its moral value, and therefore does not justify harming innocent persons.

These two doctrines will assist us in resolving the moral dilemmas that inherently arise when innocent civilians are being used by terrorists as human shields.

We are concerned with a war that is consistent with the "theory of just war" by virtue of the fact that it is a war of self-defense. Terrorism is not a onetime passing phenomenon. It consists of a series of prolonged, numerous, and brutal attacks that threaten the existence of states of the free world and thereby afford these states the legal and moral right to self-defense.

As noted, I am of the opinion that not every war is wrong from a moral point of view, and there are occasions when the state is under an obligation to fight those seeking to destroy it. However, this moral duty, like all moral duties, is not absolute in the sense that it is not morally justified to use all means in order to fulfill it, and there may well be circumstances where this moral duty will retreat before other, more important moral obligations.

The dilemmas with which we are concerned here arise within the context of a war against an enemy inspired by uncompromising radical ideologies. The price paid by the citizens of the state under attack from terrorism is unbearable. Thus, it would not be moral to demand that the state refrain completely from military activities against the attacker. The dilemma, therefore, is not whether or not to go to war, but which military measures are moral.

Since the current laws of war do not delineate a normative framework for the state's battle against a terrorist organization, it follows that even if we were to agree with Herbert L. A. Hart's approach whereby the law is a microcosm of prevailing social and public morality,[11] we would not be able to find a positive objective solution to the moral dilemmas arising within the framework of this war. The solution to every dilemma is a subjective solution which must be adjusted to a varying reality and its diverse situations.

In my view we should completely reject the assertion that soldiers fighting a just war are entitled to do everything that might prove useful in that war on the grounds that it is the enemy who is responsible for the war. Such unrestricted freedom of action is dangerous, for it transfers responsibility entirely onto the shoulders of the enemy, and it improperly regards the rights of the just as unqualified.[12] In no war, however just, can the adverse party bear responsibility for the moral wrongdoings of the first party.

As a rule, killing during the course of a war is permitted when it is an essential means of self-defense. Legal and moral principles require us to distinguish between combatants and civilians, and only the former may be harmed. According to Michael Walzer, civilians who are not combatants are in a certain sense innocent and therefore entitled to a moral immunity to which combatants are not entitled.[13] This distinction between civilians and combatants is a basic rule of the laws of war and has special importance in a war being waged by a democratic state against terror.

However, there are those who believe that there is no moral basis for the distinction between civilians and combatants but only a consensual basis. In other words, the distinction reflects the common desire of the parties to limit the destructive consequences of the war—it expresses *mutual consent* to avoid inflicting harm on the civilian population.[14] According to this approach, if one of the parties deviates from the principle of mutuality, the other party will also be released from his duty to abide by the distinction. I do not agree with this approach. We have seen that according to the laws of war and in particular according to moral imperatives, a democratic state is not discharged from its duty to avoid inflicting harm on the civilian population merely because the adverse party, the terrorists, deliberately targets civilians.

Moral Dilemmas in the War against Terror

DILEMMA I

As noted above, terrorists tend to protect themselves by burying themselves among members of their own people who are not active participants in the fighting, a practice that makes it very difficult for the state's security forces to operate, and makes it impossible for them to respect the rules of war except by acting in a way that poses a real danger to their own lives. Is it really right to ask them to pay this price?

Certainly, a state's repudiation of moral values—and at their heart, respect for the life of every person—is incompatible with its obligation to preserve the fundamental principles of democracy and is therefore not legitimate. Consequently, it is not inconceivable for it to ask its soldiers to risk their lives because of the moral imperative prohibiting causing harm to the innocent. This is a justified risk: "[T]he army of a democratic state recognizes two types of situations in which a soldier is permitted to risk his own life and the lives of his soldiers: in the face of the enemy and in order to save human life."[15]

However, is it right to draw a parallel between (a) the situation where terrorists create a dangerous circumstance that poses a risk to the lives of the citizens of the state, thereby requiring the state to protect them and consequently put soldiers lives at risk, and (b) a situation where the terrorists create a dangerous situation that poses a risk to the lives of the citizens of their own group, which compels the democratic state to protect the citizens of the enemy and to this end put its own soldiers' lives at risk? In my opinion, the two situations are not fully analogous.

In the first case, the soldiers risk their lives in order to protect the citizens of their own state, whereas in the second they risk their lives to protect the citizens of the enemy against a danger which the enemy itself has created. If the state were to endanger its soldiers in order to avoid harming enemy civilians, and as a result make it easier for the terrorists to fight and thereafter to flee, the state would soon find itself locked in a circle where its forces would be injured and its citizens continue to be threatened—that is, it would not be able to effectively pursue its just war. In circumstances of combat against an enemy operating out of a civilian population which supports it, it may be argued that "if the guerrilla fighters and the population that supports them do not keep the distinction between combatants and noncombatants, why should the enemy be committed to this distinction?"[16]

As explained, there are no absolute duties. There is no absolute duty not to endanger the lives of our soldiers in order to protect the citizens of the enemy, and there is no absolute duty not to injure those citizens. The moral thing to do depends on finding the correct balance in accordance with the circumstances of each case. In my opinion, as a rule, it is not proportional to aerially bombard places that are known to house terrorists alongside innocent civilians. It is necessary to choose less lethal means, even if they are less certain and may endanger the state's military forces. The operation must be precise, rigorous, and surgical, in order to create the greatest possible distinction between the terrorists and the civilians among whom they are concealed.

Thus, for example, during the coalition war led by the United States and Great Britain to bring down the regime of Saddam Hussein in 2003, many precautions were taken to protect the Iraqi civilian population during the aerial bombardment of targets located in or near population centers. Precision guided munitions were used, much of the bombardment was carried out at night when most civilians were at home, penetrating

munitions and delayed fuses were used to ensure that most blast and frag-
mentation damage was kept within the impact area, and attack angles
took into account the locations of civilian facilities such as schools and
hospitals. Despite all this, a number of the air attacks did cause damage
to the civilian population that far exceeded what was necessary in order
to achieve essential military objectives, since it was known in advance that
both the proximity of the targets to civilian concentrations and the munitions chosen to increase the likelihood of success (such as air-delivered
cluster bombs) would amount in practice to indiscriminate attacks.[17]

Guilty Civilians versus Innocent Civilians. The classic approach entails
a distinction between combatants and noncombatants, from which it follows that protection of "innocents" is actually protection of all those
who are not called "combatants." A more correct approach from a legal,
and particularly a moral, point of view distinguishes between the guilty
and the innocent, so that there may be soldiers who are innocent and
civilians who are guilty.[18] Since in the case of terrorists we are not referring to soldiers in the accepted sense of the word who are comparable
to soldiers of a state, there can be no terrorist who is not guilty. Accordingly, we need only distinguish between civilians who are guilty and
civilians who are innocent, and only the latter merit protection.

The effort must thus be directed at distinguishing between civilians
who have lost their rights by virtue of their involvement in the warfare
and those who have not. The distinction that interests us is not between
the participants in the war effort and those who have not contributed to
it, but between those who supply the combatants with whatever is
needed to fight and those who supply them with whatever is needed to
live, in effect all the rest. The innocent are those do nothing that would
lead them to be deprived of their rights.

On the other hand, "What is required for the people attacked to be
non-innocent in the relevant sense, is that they should themselves be
engaged in an objectively unjust proceeding which the attacker has the
right to make his concern."[19] This is the case with civilians who freely
choose to provide shelter to terrorists, allow them to operate from their
homes, and provide them with protection. These civilians are none
other than collaborators with the terrorists and as such lose their immunity from harm. Is it conceivable to demand that a soldier risk his own
life to avoid injuring civilians who have supplied shelter and protection
to terrorists and permitted them to shoot at and otherwise operate
against the soldiers from their homes? This serves the policy of terror.
Accordingly, in my opinion, it would be improper to demand that such
civilians be protected merely because they take cover under the formal

title "civilian." The title "civilian" is not an empty phrase, and even though the protection of enemy civilians is a valuable moral and legal rule, it does not apply when the civilians collaborate and assist in bringing about the terrorists' objectives. By doing so, these civilians become participants in the actual fighting and pose a danger to the military forces of the state and indirectly to that state's citizens.

In practice, civilians who assist terrorists to carry out their missions must be regarded as guiltier than the terrorists themselves. Guilty civilians are not entitled to the protection to which innocent civilians are entitled.

The purpose of recognizing a state's right to self-defense is to enable it to defend itself against those who pose a threat to it or attack it—such as the terrorists and the civilians who collaborate with them. Nonetheless, I do not argue that it is necessary to deliberately attack civilians involved in combat with the aim of killing them if it is possible to bring their activities to a halt in another way without creating great risk to our forces. Only when such an option does not exist will the obligation of a democratic state to avoid harm to these civilians be canceled.

We should note that Article 52 of Protocol I Additional to the Geneva Conventions defines military objectives—which are legal objectives for attack—as objects which by their nature, location, purpose, or use make an effective contribution to military action and whose total or partial destruction, capture, or neutralization, in the circumstances ruling at the time, would offer a definite military advantage. The definition is flexible and highly relative. The same objective may at one and the same time be regarded as civilian and military. Consequently, the article provides that in cases where doubt exists whether an object that is normally dedicated to civilian purposes is being used to make an effective contribution to military action, it should continue to be regarded as a civilian object. This presumption may be rebutted if contrary evidence is adduced.

My comments in this discussion apply solely to those cases where the security forces have a credible evidentiary basis for concluding that the civilian object has indeed undergone a change of character and has become a military objective. In such a situation, the object attacked is not civilian, legal authorization exists for striking at it, and the killing of civilians located there is not a moral wrong, since they are no longer "innocent."

When fighting is conducted on a house-to-house basis in an urban area and the civilians have been warned before the attack to vacate the area but have nonetheless chosen to remain, it becomes necessary for us to distinguish between two situations. In the first situation, the civilians freely choose to remain in their homes with the aim of enabling the terrorists to conceal themselves among them, since they know that the moral and legal fetters binding the state prohibit civilians from being harmed, and consequently also the terrorists to whom they have provided shelter.

Civilians who provide shelter to terrorists are differentiated in only one way from civilians who are physically involved with the terrorists in fighting from their homes. Whereas the former are passively involved, the latter are actively involved; however, their involvement exists, and it causes them to lose their moral immunity from harm. When they choose not to escape from the battle arena (assuming that they were warned in advance and could have escaped) and prefer to supply the terrorists with shelter, they incur moral blame. Their deaths will not be the deaths of innocents, and the moral duty to protect the lives of the soldiers will take priority.

In the second situation, in contrast, the terrorists hold the civilians against their will as hostages, and make use of their homes and property for their fighting purposes. It follows that these civilians are innocent and free of any moral wrongdoing. This is sufficient, in my view, to give rise to a moral justification for not harming them, even at the price of endangering the state's soldiers. As Walzer puts it:

> It is forbidden to kill any person for trivial reasons. Civilians have rights which supersede even this. And if the saving of civilian life means the risking of soldiers' lives, such a risk must be accepted. Nonetheless, there is a limit to the risks which we demand. We are talking, after all, of death caused by mistake and by legitimate military action and the absolute rule against attacking civilians does not apply here. War necessarily endangers civilians; that is another aspect of the inferno. We can only demand of the soldiers that they limit the risks which they impose.[20]

DILEMMA II

In the situation under consideration, when terrorists are using innocent persons as human shields, the right to self-defense will not provide moral and legal justification for injuring these civilians. The relevant legal defense here is the defense of necessity. Yet, the defense of necessity only discharges a person from criminal liability, it will not necessarily transform his action into a moral one. Our purpose is not to identify the legal defense for an action whose outcome was injury to innocents, but rather to focus on the moral justification (if one can speak of such justification at all) for the end result of harm to innocents in situations analogous to situations of necessity in criminal law, that is, in situations where clear danger to the lives of the soldiers and civilians of the state cannot be avoided save by harming innocent people.

The central concept that may assist us to draw a proper balance between the duty to fight the terrorist enemy and the duty to avoid causing harm to innocent civilians is the principle of *Tohar Haneshek*, a Hebrew term which loosely translates as "use of weapons in a virtuous manner" or "moral warfare," and which refers to scrupulously abiding by an appropriate moral system of values during the course of fighting.[21] *Tohar Haneshek* requires the security forces to restrain themselves and avoid using their military might beyond what is necessary. The fact that the adverse party does not regard itself as bound to comply with similar principles does not release the democratic state from respecting such moral values.

Accordingly, it is clear that security forces are absolutely prohibited from using the compatriots of the terrorists as human shields for the purpose of safeguarding soldiers' lives during the course of their military operations. This point—although fairly obvious—is worth emphasizing, since events in the field have proven that the principle is not always adhered to. For example, until recently, Israeli forces that operated in the Gaza Strip and in Judea and Samaria with the mission of catching terrorists who had gone into hiding in highly populated civilian Palestinian centers on occasion seized civilian passersby who were not suspected of any terrorist involvement and forced them to carry out a range of dangerous tasks, such as removing from the roads items suspected of being booby-trapped to clear traffic routes, entering abandoned buildings suspected of being booby-trapped, and marching in front of soldiers or sitting on the hoods of their vehicles in order to protect them from snipers. In other cases, after the army had encircled homes in which wanted terrorists were hiding, the soldiers carried out what they termed the "neighbor routine": one of the Palestinian residents living close to the encircled house would be taken from his home, dressed in a protective vest, and forced to march toward the targeted house to warn its residents, those who were not wanted, of the risks to them if they did not leave immediately and to ask the wanted men to surrender without bloodshed. The reason given for employing this practice was that whereas the wanted terrorist would not hesitate to shoot at soldiers, he would avoid harming one of his own people. Many times this presumption was proved wrong, and terrorists in fact did not hesitate to shoot and kill their neighbors.[22]

These methods, which reflect the cheapness of the lives of Palestinian civilians in the eyes of the army, are not only wrong morally but also clearly contrary to domestic law, in that they seriously violate the constitutional rights to human dignity, freedom, and life of these civilians, and to international humanitarian law, in that they contravene Article 27 of the Fourth Geneva Convention, which provides that "[p]rotected persons are entitled, in all circumstances, to respect for their persons, their honour. . . . They shall at all times be humanely treated, and shall be protected especially against all acts of violence or threats thereof and against insults and public curiosity." Further, the exception set out in the article to the effect that "the Parties to the conflict may take such measures of control and security in regard to protected persons as may be necessary as a result of the war" cannot permit use of innocent civilians as human shields against terrorists, since this does not comply with the precondition of necessity. The army can achieve the objectives for which it uses civilians by alternative, less harmful means, such as bringing demolition experts to deal with suspected booby traps and using loudspeakers to warn the residents of encircled houses. Even in cases where there are no less-harmful methods or it is impossible to use them, and the choice is between endangering the lives of the soldiers and endangering the lives of the local innocent civilians, the army is not entitled to prefer the lives of its soldiers over the lives of persons unconnected with terrorism who merely happen to pass by.

In addition, use of civilians as human shields violates Article 51 of the convention, which provides that "[t]he Occupying Power may not compel protected persons to serve in its armed or auxiliary forces," since by turning civilians into human shields, the soldiers are in effect forcing them to participate against their will in military missions against their own people. In response to a petition filed with the High Court of Justice by several human rights organizations,[23] the army has issued an operational directive that strictly forbids assigning protected persons to military operations (such as opening traffic routes or entering abandoned buildings suspected of being booby-trapped) or using them as human shields.[24] However, the directive does allow the army to be aided by protected persons during military operations aimed at apprehending suspected terrorists if such persons voluntarily agree to provide the requested assistance, and if the force operating in the area reasonably believes that their personal safety will not be endangered by providing such assistance.

Even though this new procedure is undoubtedly an improvement over the previous situation, many difficulties still remain, the most prominent of which concerns the element of free will. According to the directive, the local civilian must express willingness to provide the occupying power with the requested assistance, and the army has an absolute obligation to refrain from "encouraging" him to consent with threats, violence, detention, and so on. In other words, the directive is based on the premise that if the army requests assistance from a protected person and that person agrees to perform the task without undue influence, his willingness is sincere, and therefore it is legally and morally justified to use him for the task, unless his personal safety would be endangered in the process.

This assumption, in my opinion, is inherently incorrect. Interactions between an occupying power and the civilian population of a conquered territory are highly delicate, since the local population is not bound to the occupying power by duty of allegiance but rather perceives it as the "enemy." Hence, when armed soldiers of the occupying power appear at the doorstep of a local civilian during an ongoing military operation and request his assistance in capturing one of his own people, the likelihood is that he would agree to provide it, but not out of free will, rather out of fear, since he knows that the occupying power has complete control over every facet of his daily life. Only in the rarest of circumstances would a local civilian truly desire to assist the occupying power, and that situation is when he has a significant *personal* interest in reducing the danger of injury to innocent civilians and to the wanted persons—that is, when close family members of his are in the targeted house. Indeed, this was also the opinion of the Supreme Court in concluding that this procedure was illegal.

However, what is the law when the state army does not initiate the use of the local population as human shields but is faced with the situation where it cannot overcome the terrorists save by killing civilians in circumstances where it is extremely difficult to distinguish them from the wanted men? In such a situation, does *Tohar Haneshek* permit killing them?

Francisco de Vitoria is of the opinion that it is forbidden to deliberately kill innocents. However, killing them is permitted as a military necessity—that is, when there is no other way to vanquish the guilty.[25] Richard Wasserstrom thinks that military necessity is a concept with a central role to play in the implementation of the laws of war and offers general justification for the breach of the prohibitions that form the basis of these laws.[26] In his view, the doctrine of military necessity transforms the laws of war into a general moral precept but enables them to be circumvented.

The doctrine of military necessity is similar to Walzer's description of the emergency situation as a time when it is possible to trample the right to life even of innocents.[27] Even John Rawls, who thought that "there is never a time when we are free from all moral and political principles and restraints,"[28] recognized emergency situations as an exception to that rule. Accordingly, "Rawls, following Walzer, argues that '[civilians] can never be attacked directly except in times of extreme crisis.' Therefore, we can violate human rights—we can directly attack civilians—if we are sure that we can do some 'substantial good' by so doing, and if the enemy is so evil that it is better for all well-ordered societies that human rights be violated on this occasion."[29]

There is no doubt that terror is a cruel and dangerous enemy, and conceivably the decision to fight against it without harming the innocent means sacrificing the lives of the citizens of the fighting state. In such situations, the sense of moral urgency to avoid harm to innocents may retreat in the face of the sense of moral urgency to defend the citizens of the state. In exceptional circumstances, such a retreat may be legally and morally justified. Take, for example, the situation where senior wanted terrorists, who plan, send, and carry out horrendous terrorist attacks, hide among innocent civilians, and it is not possible to capture them except by engaging in a collective attack against the entire house and all its occupants. Must we refrain from such an attack? The question is not easy, and I tend to think it should be answered in the negative.

When the danger posed by these terrorists is unusual and imminent, the weight of the moral duty to protect the citizens of the state is increased, so as to supersede the moral duty to refrain from harming the innocent, in accordance with the requirement of proportionality—that is, the benefit from the action (saving the lives of the many civilians who would have been injured in the future by the terrorists) exceeds the damage caused by it (harming a limited number of innocent persons held by the terrorists, as well as the political damage and damage to the image of the state).

This is what distinguishes us from the terrorists: the latter's actions are designed to harm the innocent, whereas the democracy intends to strike at the guilty. Injury to the innocent, even if unavoidable, is certainly not deliberate.

The presumption that there are no absolute moral obligations, and consequently there is also no absolute duty not to kill the innocent, may assist us in removing the moral taint that has adhered to the killing of innocent persons. Every duty may be construed in at least two ways: as an absolute duty, on the one hand, or as a prima facie universal duty— one that may be breached in the event of exceptional circumstances—

on the other.[30] An absolute duty is a duty that will never clash with other duties because there are no circumstances in which it does not exist. In contrast, a prima facie universal duty may fall into conflict with other duties in certain situations.[31]

In cases where a just war is being waged, and the duty to avoid harming the innocent and the duty to protect the citizens of the state cannot be implemented simultaneously, the moral duty not to kill the innocent is more compatible, in my view, with the case of a prima facie duty, which in exceptional circumstances—such as may be created during the war against terrorism—may be breached even though we are aware that our activities will lead to the death of innocents who are located in the vicinity of the terrorists.

However, to prefer the democratic state's duty to protect its own citizens over its moral and legal duty to avoid causing harm to the innocent does not mean that the latter duty should be abandoned. The prohibition on harming the innocent remains a universal moral duty that retreats in the face of another universal moral duty that has superior status in the specific circumstances.

This approach to resolving the dilemma is close to the consequential doctrine to the effect that soldiers are entitled to kill innocent civilians if the consequence of this act is to achieve the primary goal of killing terrorists and saving the lives of many other innocent persons. However, permission to deprive innocent civilians held by terrorists of their right to life is not an all-encompassing permission; rather it is one that is subject to the principle of proportionality, which requires that harm be done to the least possible number of civilians and that the harm be essential in order to frustrate the acts of the terrorists hiding in their midst.

Terrorism challenges principles of freedom and thereby forces on the liberal state a "regime of necessity" whereby it is compelled to put aside certain guiding moral principles in favor of a moral duty to protect the lives and well-being of its citizens. The significance of the refusal to concede to this moral shunting is a de facto surrender to the brutal evil of terrorism and a life lived in constant fear of it.

Nonetheless, the deontological doctrine will find it difficult to justify the killing of innocent persons, irrespective of the purpose of such action, and will tend to see it as a repudiation of the highest moral obligations. This philosophical doctrine, at the heart of which are rights, dignity, and liberty, will adhere to the absolute prohibition against killing innocent persons. But those who criticize that reasoning would argue: "For a practical maxim I am much in favor of the slogan 'Never trade a certain evil for a possible good.' However, this does not solve the issue of the principle. If the good is certain and not just possible, is it anything more than dogmatism to assert that it would never be right to bring about this good through evil means?"[32]

A principle that may help us bridge the two doctrines—the utilitarian-consequential doctrine and the deontological-Kantian doctrine—is the principle of double effect. According to this principle, as outlined by Michael Walzer,[33] it is permissible to do an act whose consequences it is reasonably assumed will be bad (e.g., the killing of innocent civilians) under four conditions:

1. The act itself is good, or at least is not bad; that is, it serves the state's legitimate military needs.
2. The direct effect is acceptable from a moral point of view—the killing of terrorists.
3. The intention of the perpetrator of the act is good; that is, he only seeks an acceptable outcome (protection of the citizens of the state in whose name he acts). The bad outcome is not one of his objectives, and it is also not a means toward his objectives.
4. The good outcome is sufficient to compensate for causing the bad outcome, and must be justifiable in accordance with the principle of proportionality (more civilians should not be killed than is necessary from a military point of view).

According to this approach, the purpose underlying the act is important. It is possible to justify the killing of civilians who are located in the vicinity of terrorists if the intention is to achieve the good outcome of harming the terrorists.

Walzer is of the opinion that the third condition in the double effect principle requires modification. In his view, only when both good and bad outcomes are the product of a dual intention is it possible to defend the principle of double effect. In other words, on the one hand there must be an intention to achieve only the "good," and on the other hand if the person performing the act is aware of the bad outcome entailed by his act, he must limit it as much as possible.[34]

I agree that there is indeed something problematic about a situation where a person declares that he did not intend the bad outcome of his act even though he uses lethal measures whose bad outcome is known in advance. Accordingly, Walzer's view is persuasive: a person is aware of the bad of his actions and therefore he must limit it as much as possible. This approach is also compatible with the law of war. We have seen that it is a duty to give the civilian population an effective advance warning before taking military actions that may affect it. In cases where terrorists are dispersed among the civilian population and the military objective is to harm the terrorists and not the civilians, it is necessary to warn the civilians before attack and thereby enable them to take precautionary measures. The state is subject to a duty to limit harm to innocent civilians within the framework of the war against terror even if it is not possible to avoid such harm absolutely. According to the principle of double effect, harm to civilians is not the means for achieving the objective of harming the terrorists (and accordingly this principle is not compatible with the consequential doctrine), and the harm does not ensue from disregard for the right of the innocent to live (so that this principle does not contradict the Kantian doctrine). It is rather a by-product under which, by virtue of the recognition of the innocents' right to life, the state acts to limit harm to them to the greatest extent possible. It is harm from which the sense of moral guilt can be removed.

Notwithstanding that deontological-Kantian doctrines will find it difficult to justify the killing of the innocent, there are those who believe it possible to interpret Kant's theory as giving central importance not to the outcome of the act but rather to the purpose behind it, a purpose that is compatible with the Kantian categorical imperative: "Kant seems to mean that, fundamentally moral goodness is not a matter of maximizing best consequences in the world; rather, it is a matter of: 1) having the proper intention for action, namely, respect for the categorical imperative; and 2) conscientiously making serious efforts to realize this intention through action."[35]

Such an interpretation is very close to the principle of double effect described above. In both, the moral standard for action is determined in accordance with the purpose behind the action; however, Kant's theory limits the range of objectives that are legitimate from a moral point of view and confines them to categorical imperatives. Accordingly, an action will be deemed to be morally permissible only if from a universal point of view every rational person would have permitted it and acted accordingly, and in addition it embodies respect for the rational person. The right to self-defense is an inherent right that is universally recognized, and certainly every rational person would act in accordance with it in order to defend himself against those seeking to kill him. There are those who hold the opinion that Kant's categorical imperative does not contradict the theory of a just war based on the right to self-defense, for which Kant himself expressed support. According to Kant, writes Brian Orend, "one may justly kill another human being in self-defense, though one is to be praised if one is able to repel the attacker in such a way as to spare his life. The most relevant conclusion to draw from this passage is that a state, *qua* moral person, would seem to possess quite similar rights to violent response in the case of an armed attack by another state which credibly threatened to seriously injure its body politic."[36] Yet, Kant's recognition of the need to protect a person's life does not afford moral permission to harm an innocent man who does not threaten that person's life, even if harm to the innocent person is required in order to save the life of that person or anyone else. At the same time, notwithstanding that harm to the innocent is not moral even in circumstances where a person fully believes that causing harm to the innocent is required in order to save his own life, no punishment should be imposed on the perpetrator of the harm.[37]

Since history has shown that there is no war in which innocent civilians are not injured, and Kant was certainly aware of this, two points may explain why it is nonetheless possible to fight a just war according to Kant:

> 1. As Orend puts it, "[W]hile the killing of civilians is not justified (because it is a violation of their human rights), it is nevertheless excusable in times of war, given that it is simply not reasonable to expect a state and its people simply to succumb to an armed invasion."[38]
> 2. Kant would have supported the doctrine of double effect. In other words, a state is entitled to go to war and even to make use of measures that may injure innocent civilians only if the war and the measures used are for a just purpose and if the injury to the civilians is not a means to that purpose. In such circumstances, the blame for the injury to the civilians is placed on the shoulders of those who have breached the rights of the state and who by their acts have caused the injured state to implement its right and duty to defend itself against them.[39]

The battle against terrorism is a just battle which a democratic state wages with the intention of striking at terrorists and protecting innocent civilians on both sides. In circumstances where civilians are nonetheless harmed, it is necessary to examine whether the harm to them has been used by the state as a means of injuring the terrorists. According to Kantian theory, this is the moral standard for examining the injury to the innocent. It follows that even Kantian theory does not necessarily assert that the prohibition on harming these civilians is absolute.

DILEMMA III

Unlike the two dilemmas discussed above, there are incidents in which innocent civilians are taken hostage by terrorists. The dilemma arising here is whether to meet the demands of the terrorists—for example, to release imprisoned terrorists—or to refuse to surrender to them in order not to encourage future kidnappings, and instead deploy a military force to rescue the hostages. The outcome cannot be certain in either case. If the state concedes to the terrorists' demands, there is no guarantee that they will not harm the hostages nonetheless. On the other hand, deploying a military force against the terrorists entails a grave risk to the lives of the soldiers involved, as well to the lives of the civilians themselves, whom the terrorists would not hesitate to kill once they understood that the state had chosen not to meet their demands.

I have explained that from a moral point of view it is acceptable to place soldiers' lives at risk in two situations— when facing the enemy and in order to save human life. "Within the framework of the fair arrangements of a democratic state there is moral justification for military operations that entail risk and for the deployment of soldiers in circumstances in which there is a risk, where the risk the soldier takes upon himself and the risk he causes his soldiers to take upon themselves are necessary in the circumstances."[40] In a case that involves saving citizens from the hands of the terrorist enemy, the two situations merge. It is true that a state succumbing to the demands of terrorists instead of carrying out military operations to vanquish them by force does so after concluding that this is the best possible way of protecting the lives of the civilians held by them. Nonetheless, the choice to meet demands directed solely at strengthening the terrorist organization in order to enable it to continue to attack the state's citizens in the future sends a signal to all other terrorist organizations that they can make gains by engaging in similar operations. In effect, the result is that the state compromises the safety of all its citizens. Accordingly, it would seem that, in most cases, the consequential doctrine as well as the principle of double effect would lead us to conclude that the proper course of action is to reject the terrorists' demands and engage in military action to defeat them. The International Convention against the Taking of Hostages also imposes an express obligation on a signatory state to take "all measures it considers appropriate to ease the situation of the hostage, in particular, to secure his release and, after his release, to facilitate, when relevant, his departure."[41]

At the same time, one cannot deny the possibility of exceptional circumstances that would dictate a different solution. An example is the murderous attack that took place in the Israeli town of Ma'alot in May 1974, the shocking results of which earned it the name of the "Ma'alot schoolhouse massacre." A terrorist unit made up of three members of the Democratic Front for the Liberation of Palestine, headed by Naif Hawatmeh, succeeded in infiltrating Israel from Lebanon and reached the area of western Galilee. On May 15 the terrorists entered a home in Ma'alot, murdered a couple and their son, and injured their daughter. Afterward they moved toward the school, Nativ Meir, where there were a group of children and their teachers, who had been touring the area. The terrorists took the group hostage, threatening to kill them within a few hours unless Israel freed imprisoned members of their organization. Israel decided to conduct negotiations with the kidnappers, but when the latter refused a request to extend the deadline, the Israeli authorities decided to break into the building and take them by force. All the members of the terrorist unit were killed in the operation, but before dying they managed to set off explosions and shoot the hostages, causing the death of more than twenty schoolchildren and injuring many others.

In the beginning of the crisis, the supreme need to ensure the safety of the kidnappees, most of whom were children, combined with the conclusion that a military operation would create a real danger to the lives of the kidnappees and the lives of the military rescue forces, led the State of Israel to acknowledge its moral and legal obligation to negotiate with the terrorists, notwithstanding the shortcomings of this course of action. However, as the deadline neared without any indication that the kidnappers would fulfill their side of the bargain, Israel decided to exercise military force, despite the concomitant dangers. The result was disastrous, and many of the children paid with their lives. What would have happened to them had Israel submitted to the demands of the kidnappers? We will never know, since the uncertainty of "what might have been" is inherent to every dilemma. But in the light of what we know, the decisions reached by Israel—to initially try the path of negotiations and thereafter to use force—were correct under the special circumstances of this incident.

There is no doubt that ideals and fundamental moral principles clash with the need to fight effectively against an enemy eager to kill innocent citizens and willing to endanger the lives of its own innocent compatriots "on whose behalf" it has taken to arms. I have sought to show that this clash does not make the commitment to norms and moral values impossible or unreal. The democratic state's commitment to human life—any human life—is profound and entrenched, and therefore the state is obliged to ensure that its acts are the outcome of a proper balance between the moral obligations derived from this value, as expressed in the special circumstances of every case.

Conclusion

In a world where international terrorism aspires to destroy the countries of the free world by mass murder, democratic states have been forced to turn to military measures to combat terror. The immunity of civilians from harm, and the moral dilemmas this principle gives rise to, is a matter for discussion by those who abide by moral principles; terrorists themselves do not grant any immunity whatsoever but are prepared to harm or kill anyone in order to advance their national or fundamental goals.

The attempts to justify terrorism by presenting it as the weapon of the weak fighting for their freedom, who make use of it not out of choice but as the only weapon available to them, cannot stand up against the phenomenon of modern terrorism. The terrorist attacks the entity which he perceives as his enemy, not because he does not possess legitimate alternative means for promoting his goals, but because he perceives the terrorist mode of action as the most effective to advance his radical ideological vision.

The war being waged by the countries of the free world against world terrorism must be based on a coherent morality in terms of which nothing can justify terrorism. Terrorism is the deliberate harming of the innocent and is always a crime. Accordingly, we must recognize the inherent moral and legal duty of democratic liberal states to fight against the terror dispatched against them. In this war they should do everything possible to adhere to moral principles, at whose core lies respect for human life. Retreating from these principles without the legal and moral justifications that were presented in this chapter will lead to nothing less than the victory of terrorism. Attacking an appropriate target at the cost of the lives surrounding that target is generally prohibited, yet in exceptional cases, complying with the test of proportionality, it is possible to neutralize the moral flaw attached to such an action. Accordingly, in unpreventable cases where we have caused harm to innocent civilians, we must admit that we have so acted and investigate whether such harm accorded with the balancing formula or whether it was a prohibited and wrongful act for which a legal price must be paid in accordance with the rules of international law.

In times of war, there is always a danger that "the moral resources of those fighting may be eroded and at times overwhelmed."[42] In war against terrorism, since terrorists do not see themselves as subject to any moral or legal restraints, the democratic states must take special care not to be caught in a moral slide, and to keep in mind at all times that their moral backbone is the recognition of the values of human life and human dignity. In the eyes of democracy, man is the object. In the eyes of terrorists, man is merely the means. In the conflict between democracy and terrorism, only he who accords importance to the value of human life and who is willing to conduct his war while protecting human life, will triumph. According to the Israeli High Court of Justice:

> What distinguishes war conducted by a state from war conducted by its enemies—one fights in accordance with the law, and the other fights in contravention of the law. The moral strength and substantive justification for the authorities' war depend completely on compliance with the laws of the state: in waiving this strength and this justification for its war, the authorities serve the purposes of the enemy. The moral weapon is no less important than any other weapon, and perhaps even surpasses it—and there is no more effective moral weapon than the rule of law.[43]

EIGHT

Thwarting Terrorist Acts by Targeted Preventive Elimination

The moral rule is not "when one is about to kill you, preempt him and kill him first" but rather "when one is about to kill you, do everything necessary in order to thwart his intention." Accordingly, if there is no alternative but to kill him, strike first. If there is an alternative other than killing him, thwart his intention without striking first, without killing him.

—Asa Kasher, *Military Ethics*

As EXPLAINED in previous chapters, the task of delineating the boundaries between modes of fighting terrorism which are legal and moral and those which are inappropriate requires the formulation of a delicate balance between the need to meet legitimate military objectives and the democratic state's obligation to respect the basic rights and freedoms of the individual. Thus, not long after the end of the American Civil War, the U.S. Supreme Court stated in its judgment in *Ex parte Milligan:* "No doctrine involving more pernicious consequences was ever invented by the wit of man than that any of its provisions can be suspended during any of the great exigencies of government. Such a doctrine leads directly to anarchy or despotism, but the theory of necessity on which it is based is false."[1]

Bearing in mind the fundamental axioms regarding the ways in which a liberal state should fight terror, in this chapter I examine the legality and moral justification of perhaps one of the most extreme methods of preempting terrorist attacks, namely, pursuing the policy of "targeted preventive eliminations," that is, methodically and deliberately killing senior leaders of the guerilla organizations, the people who conceive and plan terrorism, as well as junior members, the persons responsible for executing such operations.

Times of emergency require the adoption of emergency measures which are completely prohibited in times of peace. At the same time, even in times of crisis, however difficult and pressing, there are extraordinary methods that are not permissible. This is the significance of the balance between the state's obligation to protect the safety of its citizens and its obligation to abide by the rule of law even in its most difficult hour.

Targeted elimination entails a verdict of death against a person without first affording him due process of law before an impartial tribunal charged with preserving his constitutional rights in a criminal trial. Acting in the name of security, the state uses its most lethal weapons against a man it suspects of posing a danger to the security of its citizens. Accordingly, even though these preventive measures are some of the most effective means of foiling the routine activities of terrorist organizations, they give rise to profound legal and moral difficulties. I would emphasize that I am referring here solely to preventive actions aimed at preventing terrorist organizations from carrying out future attacks, and not to acts of vengeance or punishment for past activities which target terrorists uninvolved in the planning or execution of future terrorist attacks. Activities that are carried out for motives that are not preventive are by definition not preemptive actions; in general they are not legal, and the remarks in this chapter are not intended to apply to them.

Our examination of the inherent difficulties of the policy of targeted elimination will focus on the Israeli experience in the light of the international laws of war. It is true that Israel is not the only country to have carried out targeted elimination against terrorists; at the same time, Israel's experience in this area is richer than that of other Western countries, and therefore it alone can provide a sufficient factual basis for engaging in a comprehensive and exhaustive discussion of this issue. Yet, despite focusing on the Israeli perspective, the following statements are equally valid to every other liberal democratic state.

The Israeli Policy of Targeted Eliminations: The Factual Background

While the State of Israel has been forced to defend itself against incessant terrorist attacks since its establishment, for many years it did so without initiating strikes aimed at eliminating wanted men. True, in the beginning of the 1990s a number of human rights associations alleged that the IDF had set up units of pseudo-Arabs whose official mission was to catch wanted terrorists and whose operation procedures de facto allowed them to kill their targets in many cases rather than take them alive. Israel vehemently denied these claims, however, and asserted that the fatalities were not preplanned but the outcome of the special circumstances of the particular operation, either because of dangers encountered by the soldiers (the wanted terrorist was killed to remove an imminent danger to the lives of the soldiers) or because of the practice employed in arresting the suspect (the intention was to merely wound the terrorist, but he was inadvertently killed). In any event, it is undisputed that Israel did not at that time pursue a declared policy of deliberate killings of suspects as part of its routine preemptive operations.[2]

In October 2000 a sharp escalation took place in the level of hostilities between Israel and the terrorist organizations operating within the territory of the Palestinian Authority, an entity that has not been recognized as an independent state and is at most a "state in the making" or an independent political authority. As a result of this escalation, Israel officially adopted a strategic military policy aimed at neutralizing terrorist organizations by targeting wanted terrorists suspected of initiating, planning, and executing terrorist activities against Israeli citizens. Under this policy, Israel eliminated Sheikh Ahmed Ismail Yassin, the founder of the Hamas organization (The Islamic Resistance Movement), and Salah Shehade, the commander of the military wing of the organization, among others.

The measures employed by the IDF to eliminate its targets are varied. The preferred method is firing missiles from attack helicopters, but other measures include booby-trapping the vehicles of wanted men, artillery fire, sniper shooting, or close-quarter shooting. To date, dozens of eliminations have been carried out in this way. Some succeeded, some failed, and some ended with the death of innocent bystanders who happened to be in the area. Others ended with the death of suspects who the authorities sought to arrest and prosecute but not to kill. After many eliminations, Israel accepted official responsibility for the policy both through notices issued by IDF spokesmen and through interviews given to the media by senior political figures or defense officials.

From the moment the policy of targeted eliminations was adopted, it became the subject of intense public, political, and legal controversy in domestic and international arenas.[3] Some argue that the policy is manifestly illegal and contrary to internal state law, the international laws of war, and the fundamental principles of human morality, since a state that as a matter of policy pursues a man to death without first engaging in due judicial process is in grave breach of the fundamental principles to which it is committed as a liberal, law-abiding state.

But others claim that although the measure is indeed exceptional in its gravity, it is essential to employ it in order to deal with the special situation in which Israel finds itself. The constant threat of terror does not enable the citizens of the state to pursue a normal way of life. Many are afraid to travel on buses, to sit in restaurants and coffeehouses or visit shopping malls—the sites preferred by terrorists for carrying out their attacks. Since October 2000 this situation has worsened, with the fundamental Palestinian terrorist organizations increasing the frequency of their suicide attacks, and the secular Palestinian terrorist organizations, which in the past refrained from using such methods, now also employing them with a vengeance. To the advocates of targeted elimination it is therefore clear that, in this reality, the state cannot fulfill its obligation to protect its citizens merely by operations aimed at locating and eliminating the suicide terrorists who have already buckled the explosive belts around their waists and departed on their missions. Rather, it must also locate and target those who have sent out these terrorists, who enlisted and trained them and planned their operations. In fact, they assert, it would be morally wrong for the state to invest its efforts solely in locating suicide bombers—who are merely junior terrorists— and not first seek and prosecute their commanders.

The Supreme Court, contrary to its otherwise consistent policy of bringing within the purview of its judicial review the legality of military measures used by the IDF to eradicate terrorism (such as applying moderate physical pressure during the interrogation of terrorists and administrative detention) initially dismissed outright a petition against the constitutionality of the policy of target eliminations. It did so after holding that the political authorities' choice of military measures to preempt murderous terrorist attacks against the citizens of the state is not a subject whose constitutionality the court sees itself as suitable to judge.[4] As noted, this reasoning is contrary to a long tradition of active judicial intervention; and even in 2002 when another petition was submitted, which was not dismissed *in limine*, the court has not been in a hurry to give judgment.[5] Accordingly, the following discussion relies on guidelines that the court has laid down in relation to other defense issues.

The Choice of Law: Rules of Self-Defense in Both International and Internal State Law

The Israeli-Palestinian conflict is, in many senses, a complex dispute. In terms of the issue at hand, the Palestinian Authority has not been recognized by international law as a sovereign state. In contrast, the Palestinian Liberation Organization, under the chairmanship of Yasser Arafat until his death in 2004, has been recognized as an international organization, holding the status of an observer at the United Nations.[6] Since the Palestinian Authority has not been recognized as having an international legal status, it is not clear whether the conflict underway and the discussions being held to resolve it are indeed being conducted according to the rules of international law. In the international arena, relations are conducted between states, and so the international customary and treaty norms concerning the prohibition on the use of force against a state are by definition applicable only to other states.

In chapter 2 we discussed the reasons for the difficulty in classifying terrorist attacks as armed attacks that vest the state under attack with the right to defend itself. I concluded that since the terrorist act has the principal characteristics of an armed attack, it should be classified as one. Consequently, two questions arise. The first arises out of the laws relating to going to war, *jus ad bellum*, namely, is the state vested with the right of self-defense only after it has been attacked, or is the state also entitled to engage in preemptive activities directed at preventing anticipated attacks? If I conclude that the laws of self-defense permit the use of force for preventive purposes, I must then ask whether a state, which is entitled to defend itself by using force against terrorist attacks planned against its citizens, is entitled to implement this right by deliberately killing the leaders and members of a terrorist organization. This question arises out of the laws of war, *jus in bello*, which regulate the conduct of armed conflicts. In chapter 2 I concluded in relation to these laws that, as in the majority of cases there is insufficient evidence to attribute the activities of nonstate terrorist organizations to a sovereign state which has sent them on their missions and therefore it is not possible to regard the disputes as international armed conflicts, it would be right to regard these attacks as amounting to armed conflicts not of an international character, and consequently to directly apply to these disputes Article 3 common to the four Geneva Conventions of 1949, which establishes minimum humanitarian norms binding on all the parties to a dispute, and indirectly—by way of analogy—all the rules of *jus in bello* which apply to the conduct of international armed conflicts.

Preemptive Action in Self-defense

As noted in chapter 2, the customary laws of self-defense have an independent existence that runs parallel to corresponding laws arising out of treaties. Customary law, which recognizes the right of the state to defend itself in every case of aggression, provides that the right to self-defense embraces the right to adopt the tactic of a defensive self-defense in the face of an anticipated act of aggression.[7]

The right to preemptive self-defense means that the state is not obliged to wait for the enemy to actually commence its attack if it is certain that it is about to be attacked by an armed force.

Israel has attempted to resolve the current conflict by peaceful means. Sadly, at the time of writing it does not appear that this approach has met with success, and shooting, bombing, and suicide attacks have not ceased. In view of the lack of willingness, or alternatively the inability, of the Palestinian Authority to prevent terrorist operations, Israel must defend itself. In terms of the requirements established by the *Caroline* case regarding the implementation of self-defense, Israel can be considered to face an immediate threat from terrorists, especially where the terrorists are willing to commit suicide. In the absence of any less harmful alternative, or any peaceful means of preventing the immediate danger, Israel is entitled to defend itself against that immediate threat by conducting anticipatory forceful attacks against terrorists.

Whether the right to anticipatory self-defense also exists under treaty law has yet to be determined. Article 51 of the UN Charter accords a state "*the inherent right* of individual or collective self-defense *if an armed attack occurs*" (emphasis added). On one side are those who argue that the language of the article is unambiguous, that it is clear that a state is prohibited from employing armed force as an anticipatory measure and that it must wait for an actual armed attack.[8] Others contend that the language of the Charter is not so unequivocal, since it does not purport to create a new right to self-defense but refers to the inherent rights of states to defend themselves, and the customary law referred to by the Charter recognizes the right of states to anticipatory self-defense. A further argument is that considering how much military capabilities have changed in recent years, Article 51 of the Charter should be interpreted to comply with the new world situation. Thus, for example, it would clearly be absurd to assert that international law requires a state to absorb a severe nuclear attack before it is permitted to defend itself. In my opinion, in view of the modern means of warfare available to states and to nonstate terrorist organizations, Article 51 must be interpreted, in light of its contents and purpose, to also enable self-defense in the face of future terrorist attacks.

It would seem that this is also the understanding of the UN General Assembly, since in a resolution concerning the definition of acts of aggression, it decided that the first use of force in breach of the Charter would constitute prima facie evidence of aggression, but that the Security Council is entitled to decide, depending on the circumstances surrounding the commission of the act, that it should not be perceived to be an act of aggression.[9] In effect this amounts to indirect recognition of the legality of the use of force as anticipatory self-defense.

In any event, I believe that this controversy is of purely theoretical importance, since the moment the terrorists' intentions begin to be put into practice by real steps preparatory to the commission of the attack— such as planning or enlisting persons to perpetrate it—it may be said that the terrorists have in fact begun to commit the attack, and therefore the state is indisputably vested with the right to defend itself.

Targeted Elimination under International Laws of War

Article 23 of the Hague Rules, annexed to the Fourth Hague Convention, prohibits a party to an armed dispute from doing the following: "To kill or wound an enemy who, having laid down his arms, or having no longer means of defense, has surrendered at discretion."[10] Article 3(1) common to the four Geneva Conventions provides:

> Persons taking no active part in the hostilities, including members of armed forces who have laid down their arms and those placed hors de combat by sickness, wounds, detention, or any other cause, shall in all circumstances be treated humanely, without any adverse distinction founded on race, colour, religion or faith, sex, birth or wealth, or any other similar criteria.
>
> To this end the following acts are and shall remain prohibited at any time and in any place whatsoever with respect to the above-mentioned persons:
> (a) violence to life and person, in particular murder of all kinds. . . .[11]

Moreover, the Second Hague Convention and the Third Geneva Convention regulate the status of lawful combatants as prisoners of war following capture by the enemy, with the result that the state holding them must grant them humane treatment and guarantee their safety.[12]

The laws regarding the protection of the civilian population during battles were discussed extensively in the first part of the previous chapter. These laws make it clear that it is the duty of the state to make every possible effort not to endanger civilians. The fact that the terrorists conceal themselves among their own people in order to shield themselves does not release the state of this duty. Nonetheless, after examining all the relevant considerations, I concluded that this duty is not absolute but depends on the special circumstances of the case. Thus "guilty civilians" are not entitled to the same protection as "innocent civilians," even though both groups are called "protected civilians." Civilians who choose of their own free will to protect terrorists with their bodies by letting terrorists live in their homes, and thereby exploit the protection afforded to those civilians, lose the protection to which they themselves are entitled. In such a situation, although the state is not entitled to kill them deliberately, if it is entitled to kill the terrorists hiding in their midst—an issue which is discussed below—and there is no reasonable way of targeting the terrorists without harming the civilians, the state is entitled to harm the human shields, because they have freely chosen to act as such.

In contrast, in a situation where the civilians act as human shields involuntarily, out of coercion, their acts are not morally flawed, and as a rule the state is not entitled to perform any action that may endanger them, save in unusual circumstances in which the price of refraining from acting likely to be paid by the citizens of the state is much heavier than the price of killing innocent civilians.

Targeted Elimination under Israeli Domestic Criminal Law

Article 300(a) of the Penal Law, which defines the elements of the offense of murder, provides that

> A person who does one of the following is guilty of murder and is
> liable to imprisonment for life and only to that penalty: . . .
> (2) with premeditation causes the death of any person.[13]

Section 301(a) provides that "(f)or the purposes of Section 300, a person shall be deemed to have killed another person with premeditation if he resolved to kill him, and killed him in cold blood without immediate provocation in circumstances in which he was able to think and realize the results of his actions and after having prepared himself to kill him or after having prepared the instrument with which he killed him."

The policy of elimination pursued by Israel satisfies these elements, since before carrying out the elimination, there is a lengthy and extensive preparatory process. First, the relevant political and defense officials consult together to determine appropriate targets for preemptive action. After a decision is reached, the army engages in planning and intelligence operations. Only after this process is complete is the elimination itself carried out.

Nonetheless, the penal laws relieve a person from criminal liability if the elements of any of the circumstances depriving an act of criminal characteristics apply. One of these qualifying circumstances is that of self-defense, which is anchored in Section 34J of the Penal Law: "A person is not criminally responsible for an act which was immediately required in order to avoid an unlawful attack which gave rise to a real risk of harm to the life, freedom, person or property of that person or another; provided that a person does not act in self-defense where his improper conduct led to the attack and he anticipated the possibility of this development." In order for the plea of self-defense to be available to the accused, he must show that the act he contends was performed in self-defense was immediately required, and that the act he wished to forestall was an unlawful attack that posed a real danger to the life, freedom, person, or property of himself or another. Underlying this defense is the concept that a person will instinctively defend himself against an anticipated attack when he senses that he is in jeopardy.

The defense will be available to a person if he acted in order to prevent an anticipated attack. If the attack has already taken place and no further danger is expected, the qualification of self-defense will no longer be available to him. Here too, where an act may be regarded as one of retaliation or punishment, it will not be deemed to be prevention of anticipated danger, and therefore it will not be an act of self-defense. Further, according to the court,

> a distinction has to be drawn between defense in the spirit of warfare and defense by way of protection: the warrior repels an attack, and the fact that he is defending himself against the aggression of his enemy is only a pretext for fighting; whereas someone protecting himself abhors war and is reluctant to fight and makes every effort to avoid it, and every act of violence performed by him in his own protection he does against his will and for lack of any other choice. The protection of the law is conferred upon a person who defends himself in the absence of any other choice, and not to a warrior using the pretext of self-defense.[14]

In order that the defense of self-defense be available to the accused, he must also prove that he did not provoke the aggression by an unlawful act, and that he could not have anticipated events in advance. This defense entails a delicate balance between society's desire to prevent acts of violence on the one hand, and to permit a person who is in jeopardy to protect himself on the other hand, even if this involves harming his attacker.

The requirement of proportionality in the response of the person defending himself against the anticipated attack is expressed by the words in the law "to avoid an unlawful attack." Force that exceeds what is requisite to avert an attack should not be used.

We can see that the domestic law requirements are not very different from those of international law, notwithstanding that the former refers to individuals and the latter to states. In domestic law, too, the use of lethal force is justified by showing that it was the least harmful measure available. Similarly, for the justification of self-defense to apply, it must be shown that there was no other way of resolving the dispute, and the act that was performed was required as an immediate unplanned response. It should be noted that even if the preemptive actions are planned actions, they are carried out as a response to an imminent threat. An army is not equivalent to an individual who has the ability to act in a spontaneous manner. An army must pursue a plan in order to be able to function. Accordingly, when we say that an immediate, spontaneous, and unplanned response is needed in order for us to describe the ensuing act as one of self-defense, we are not saying that the army is forbidden to plan its actions in advance. The analogy to an individual applies so long as the army is attempting to prevent an imminent and real threat.

Acts of Self-Defense within the Territory of a Foreign State: Standard of Proof Required in Cases of Preemptive Action

As already noted, the Palestinian terrorist organizations are operating out of the territory of the Palestinian Authority. The question that arises, therefore, is what measures Israel may legitimately take in order to thwart terrorists' activities within the domain of the Palestinian Authority.

It is accepted that in domestic cases of terrorism the state is entitled to use force against terrorists operating within its own territory. However, even this is subject to constraints. If no imminent danger is anticipated, it is forbidden to use force against the terrorists. A terrorist may not be killed for his past actions, thereby preventing him from realizing his right to a fair trial. In other words, force may not be used against a terrorist as a punitive act but only as a preemptive act. Similarly, the state is subject to a number of humanitarian requirements and minimum human rights obligations as provided in international law.

It is also possible to act in such a way, subject to the limitations described above, in the territory of a foreign state if the latter agrees to a request to this effect. Should the foreign state (out of whose territory the terrorists are operating) not agree, the preemptive strike against the terrorists might be regarded as an attack against the foreign state. Attacking terrorists within the territory of another state without the latter's permission infringes the sovereignty of that foreign state. But in a situation where, for example, terrorists are kidnapped, although such an action might in technical legal terms be regarded as infringing the sovereignty of the foreign state, from a moral point of view it would be justified. Such an action avoids bloodshed and enables the terrorists to be brought to a fair trial. Possibly, in view of the refusal or inability of the "host state" to give up the terrorists or to take steps against them, this might also be the only way of bringing the terrorists to a fair trial.

The question that arises is whether these exceptions to the right of sovereignty of a state over its own territory also enable activities that involve killing the terrorists. Some argue that killing terrorists as an act of self-defense may be regarded as lawful only if the specific people who pose the real and imminent threat are the targets of the preemptive measures, if the measures taken against the terrorists are essential and proportional to the event it is hoped to prevent, and if there is convincing evidence, beyond any reasonable doubt, that the destructive activity has been or is being planned. While I agree with the general proposition, I would dispute the standard of proof required. In my opinion, since the authority in Israel that makes the security decisions is not a judicial authority, the administrative bodies in general, and in this case in particular, must indeed reach a high level of proof, beyond the minimum balance of 51 percent. The standard must be one of clear and convincing evidence, but not evidence beyond a reasonable doubt. It is difficult to collect evidence relating to terrorist activities which is absolutely certain. Often, this difficulty persists even after the act has been committed, and it is hard to determine which organization is responsible. Sometimes responsibility is not taken for an attack, whereas at other times an organization that did not carry out the attack nonetheless assumes responsibility for it. The departmentalization of terrorist organizations can mean that the political arm is not responsible for the activities of the executive arm, and so on. However, the collection of convincing evidence is still required, despite these difficulties, in the case of preemptive action that involves killing terrorists. It is necessary to be convinced at a high level of certainty that that terrorist poses a real danger and that no other practical, less harmful measure is available to prevent him from executing his plan. It should be noted that the process of identifying him in the field must also be carried out to a standard of high certainty in order to prevent the killing of an innocent man, wrongly identified as the terrorist.

What is the position where there is no evidence of a specific threat, that is, where there exists a terrorist organization that poses a constant threat, but there is no information about its intention to implement future attacks? In such a situation, is there sufficient evidence for the defending state to argue that it is possible to attack individuals as a permitted preemptive attack, which amounts to self-defense? On the one hand, if the state were not to take any preventive measures whatsoever, it would be endangering numerous citizens. On the other hand, attacking terrorists without evidence of an imminent and specific threat might be regarded as a prohibited attack. The solution in such a situation—as proposed by the scholar Michael Schmitt—is to focus on the likelihood and plausibility of future attacks by the terrorist organization.[15] States rarely know the plans of their enemies so thoroughly as to know that there is an immediate danger, and a fortiori they can know little about the planned attacks of terrorist organizations that operate underground. Nonetheless, there may be reliable intelligence information that allows future attacks to be predicted. In circumstances where it is possible to conclude that a terrorist organization is expected to carry out an armed attack in the future, then even if no specific intelligence exists about a particular planned operation, it will be possible to preempt the activity as a defensive act.

According to the judgment of the International Court of Justice in the case of *Nicaragua v. United States*, there are minimum evidentiary preconditions that must be met in order to permit a military response against a terrorist attack. The state must cautiously examine the evidence available to it in order to assure a high level of certainty regarding the identity of those responsible for the terrorist attack and the conclusion that additional attacks are imminent. It must also expose its decision-making process to public debate, as well as the available evidence underpinning this process.[16]

This last demand, that decisions regarding preemptive actions that involve the use of force against terrorists be open to public oversight, is not realistic. It also cannot be expected that a disclosure of the intention to carry out a preemptive action will become a compulsory standard. States will not be eager to expose intelligence sources in order to provide absolute justification of the defensive action. On the other hand, a state cannot argue self-defense without any public justification whatsoever. An incorrupt, judicial, or "quasi-judicial" body must be established to examine security decisions and authorize them on the basis of the appropriate level of evidence.

When, therefore, will a state under attack be permitted to defend itself by taking action within the territory "hosting" the terrorists?

Such an action may be taken in one of the following situations:

1. Where the foreign state does not wish to extradite the terrorists.
2. Where there is no convention regarding extradition between the two states concerned.
3. Where the terrorist did not breach the law of the state in which he is present.
4. Where the extradition request will disclose to the terrorist that he is being sought and thus give him a chance to flee; in other words, where it is desired to hide from the terrorist the fact that his extradition is being sought, since otherwise he will escape capture.
5. In situations where a civil war is underway in the host state or it is subject to social chaos, and there is no strong governmental body capable of fighting and stopping those known terrorists operating from within the territory of the state.[17]

Where there are hostilities between states, it is not realistic to expect that one state will extradite terrorists to another. In such a situation, the likelihood is that no peaceful resolution of the problem will be possible, since no extradition arrangement exists or there is no way of extraditing the terrorists, save in the situation where it is hoped to conceal from the terrorist the fact that he is being sought. Despite all this, an attempt must first be made to find a peaceful way of resolving the problem, and an attempt should be made to request the host state to prevent the terrorist activities; alternatively, permission must be sought from that state to act within its territory. Only if there is no other choice may the defending state engage in permitted self-defense.

Moral Questions Involved in Preemptive Actions

Alongside the difficult legal issues, numerous moral questions arise. Even though we are considering the elimination of a terrorist who seeks the death of innocents, such a killing still involves the death of a human being.

Alongside the question whether the killing of terrorists is justified from a moral point of view lies an even more difficult moral question. It is a tactic of terrorists in general, and in the Israeli-Palestinian context in particular, to find cover among the protected civilian population in order to secure their own safety. The difficult question that arises, therefore, is whether, in certain circumstances, it is possible from a moral point of view to attack terrorists even though doing so entails endangering the population that is affording them cover. If the answer to this question is positive, what level of danger to the population is acceptable from a moral point of view?

Is the Killing of Terrorists Justified from a Moral Point of View?

As explained in the previous chapter, if the killing of terrorists will prevent the death or serious injury of many innocent people, then, at least according to the principle of moral utilitarianism, it would seem possible to kill them. The justification of any action as proper, according to this approach, is determined by whether the action will lead to the best possible result among all the possible outcomes in that situation. In other words, one must aspire to the maximum general good in each and every situation. If the good result ensuing from the performance of the act outweighs the bad ensuing from it, then it must be performed, irrespective of whether the act entails killing, torture, or the like. However, according to the concept of absolute morality, the killing of a person is prohibited in all situations. According to Kant, the moral imperative is an absolute categorical imperative which cannot be made the subject of conditions in any situation or circumstance. Thus, if the principle of the sanctity of life is a supreme principle, and the preservation of human life a supreme moral imperative, injury to human life is prohibited from a moral point of view, regardless of the situation faced or, indeed, the existence of opposing moral values.

However, I explained in chapter 7 why, in my opinion, we should reject this approach and refrain from inflexible conclusions and the categorization of moral obligations and moral injunctions as "absolute." Michael S. Moore believes that the injunction "thou shalt not kill" is a good example of a moral commandment that is not absolute in every situation. In the case of self-defense—for example, the case where the killing of one attacker will save an entire family—the person defending himself will be allowed to strike preemptively, even if the outcome is the death of the original attacker. In Moore's view, the injunction should be modified to read, "Don't kill, unless in self-defense, to protect your family, to aid in a just war lawfully declared."[18] The question whether it is permitted to kill a terrorist may be compared to the question whether it is permitted to kill an enemy soldier in time of war. The killing of soldiers in time of war is a by-product of the warfare itself and of the attempt to defeat the enemy. The killing is in the nature of "when one is about to kill you, preempt him and kill him first," that is, a defense of one's own army and one's own soldiers, and it is an inseparable part of any combat.

In other words, it is possible to understand that if the soldier standing before me does not raise his hands in surrender but rather wishes to kill me, then I am permitted morally to strike first and kill him, as a legitimate defensive act of war. Similarly, if it is likely that the terrorist will kill or seriously injure many people, it is possible for the state to defend itself and take preemptive action as it would do in a battle. Killing a person because that person will attempt to maim and kill civilians by engaging in a lethal attack in the future must be interpreted as engaging in self-defense. I am not talking about taking punitive action for past activities, but rather attempting to foil a future destructive act. Thus, the State of Israel, like a private individual, may attempt to forestall a real attempt to injure its citizens. This is even its duty as a democratic state. There is no moral need to fold one's hands and wait for the blow to fall.

Asa Kasher asserts that the killing of a person by a state body will be regarded as a justified preemptive action if it meets a number of strict moral conditions. First is the condition of certainty. The state must have firm evidence that the person concerned will almost certainly attempt to attack its citizens. Second is the condition of necessity. The possibility of a preemptive attack is conditional on its being a last-ditch measure. In other words, there is no other feasible way of stopping the person concerned in advance, or if there is a less harmful way, it involves jeopardizing the lives of one's own soldiers. Third is the requirement that an independent professional review body confirm that the first two conditions have indeed been met. Fourth is the requirement that a convincing answer be possible in the event that a soldier is asked whether the order to kill a person is or is not a manifestly illegal order. In Professor Kasher's view, if all these conditions are satisfied, there is no moral difficulty in killing for preemptive purposes.[19]

It follows that so long as the preemptive action of killing terrorists is based on self-defense in situations where no other less harmful but effective alternatives are available, such actions will be justified morally as well.

The argument that fighting terrorism is different from fighting in an ordinary battle—because there is no face-to-face combat in the former, and thus not the same degree of certainty that the enemy will attack— is only partially correct. First, today most wars are not conducted entirely on a face-to-face basis, and therefore they bear a greater resemblance to fighting terrorism than did past wars, which were fought hand to hand. Today, most battles are battles of wits, but the ethics of war have not changed. Second, terror is a fighting tactic in which the attackers refrain from direct contact with the enemy army. Finally, no one is arguing that it is possible to kill every person who is suspected of terrorist activities. A relatively high degree of certainty must be proved that the particular terrorist will cause great damage and even the deaths of innocent civilians. The decision to foil a terrorist act by killing the enemy—the terrorists—must be made after thorough consideration and after exhausting all other possible avenues of action. However, if there is no other *reasonable* way of preventing the terrorist action, then in the same way that it is possible to kill enemy soldiers who are about to attack one's army, it is possible to kill the "soldiers of terror." The emphasis placed above on the word "reasonable" is not without cause. It is necessary to consider only reasonable alternative methods, and not all the methods that are theoretically available but are unrealistic. I shall return to this point below.

The next difficult issue I wish to raise relates to the harm to the civilian population among whom the terrorist organization has found cover. Many terrorist organizations find shelter in areas populated by innocent people in order to exploit the rules in the international arena, which categorically state that the civilian population must not be involved in the armed conflict. As I explained in the previous chapter, as a rule populations whose members are not combatants should not be harmed during the course of fighting the enemy, and they should not be regarded as a target for possible military attack. However, on occasion they may be harmed as a result of being adjacent to the battleground. In such a case, there is no need to stop the fighting, but a certain amount of caution must be exercised not to injure those people who are not combatants unless the harm caused to them complies with the principle of double effect.[20]

I shall now examine the morality of preemptive actions taken in populated areas against terrorists which may also cause injury to those protected populations. The prevention of terror and the prevention of killing and injury to people is undoubtedly a legitimate act of war and constitutes a "good act," an act that saves lives or prevents injury to innocent people. The purpose of the activities carried out by the fighting bodies of the State of Israel is to strike at the terrorists—in other words, the direct planned result of the activity is legitimate and acceptable from a moral point of view. The fighting bodies of the State of Israel do not seek the deaths of innocent people. The purpose of preemptive action is solely to strike at strategic targets in order to neutralize them and thereby prevent a possible attack against Israeli citizens. Needless to say, if the purpose of these forces were to sew destruction among the civilian population, their activities would not be morally justified.

Human rights organizations usually voice a number of contentions.[21] First, it is always possible to make a mistake in identification and thereby eliminate an innocent civilian who resembles a wanted terrorist in looks, name, or other relevant characteristic. Testifying clearly to this danger is the United Kingdom's declared policy of preemptive targeted killing of suicide terrorists, known as the "shoot-to-kill-to-protect" policy, which was adopted following the July 2005 suicide attacks in London. This policy, which authorizes the police to shoot to the head of a suspected suicide terrorist (rather than to the chest or elsewhere, in order to avoid detonating any explosives the suspect may be carrying), has already led to the death of an innocent young Brazilian man who was shot in the head several times at close range after he refused a police command to surrender, just because his appearance and behavior made the police mistake him for a terrorist.[22] Second, on occasion attacks end not only with the elimination of the wanted terrorist but also with the death and injury of innocent people who have chanced by; or worse, back at the decision-making stage, the manner in which it was decided to perform the assassination and the type of explosives chosen in order to increase the probability of success created a likelihood of injuring the innocent. Third, the security forces do not do enough to eliminate the wanted terrorist alone, in cases where it is known in advance that he will be in the vicinity of other wanted men who are not themselves targets for elimination because they can be caught and prosecuted; instead it is decided to eliminate them as well. For example, during the elimination of the spiritual leader of the Hamas, Sheikh Ahmed Yassin, in March 2004, his son and bodyguard were killed with him.

In its preemptive actions, the army relies primarily on large quantities of reliable intelligence. On occasion, notwithstanding the almost certain identification of terrorists, failures occur, as they do in other war operations. However, despite the embattled situation in which the State of Israel finds itself, it must do everything possible to avoid mistakes during the decision-making process and target identification in the field. All decisions must comply with all the standards detailed above and be based on sufficiently sound evidence, so as to avoid killing innocent persons. As explained in the previous chapter, according to Walzer it is possible to justify a strike that kills innocent people on the grounds of its being a necessity of war. It is possible that the particular soldier who carried out the strike believed that innocent civilians located nearby would not be harmed as a result. The original intention of the army was not to harm the civilian population as a direct and primary target.

According to the fourth requirement of the double effect principle (see chap. 7), before every preemptive and preventive action the fighting bodies must weigh whether an action that may cause injury to the protected population will indeed prevent the occurrence of a more harmful act; in other words, whether it will prevent a worse situation than possible harm to the protected population. These considerations must be weighed each time, and this process must be carried out on the basis of intelligence about the planned terrorist activity and an assessment of the prospective location of the clash with the terrorists. On the basis of a profile of the majority of preemptive actions, one may assume that the fighting bodies indeed try to minimize harm to the protected population as much as possible. In cases where it is feared that civilians may be killed, precision weapons must be used to minimize damage. Of course, in certain cases the human shield will not assist the terrorists. In particular, the civilian population may, upon receiving due warning, decide to leave the area and avoid all danger. If the population chooses, of its own will, to stay in the battle zone, it takes a calculated risk of possible harm. But if the population is being held hostage by the terrorists, it is prevented from making this choice, and an attempt must be made to reduce as much as possible the harm to it.

As already pointed out, all alternative means must be preferred, such as capturing the terrorists and detaining them, or infiltrating the civilian population itself and pinpointing the terrorists. But not all alternative actions must be weighed positively. An operation which minimizes harm to the population within the range of fire but which may result in multiple victims among the state's armed forces is not an operation that must be launched. An attempt must be made to minimize the harm both to the enemy and to the population that surrounds and protects them, but not at any cost.

It follows that it is necessary to try to refrain from a preemptive act that causes the death of a terrorist if it is possible to capture and detain him. However, if this act will greatly endanger the state's soldiers, that specific measure need not be taken and another preemptive measure may be preferred. If it is possible to capture terrorists without significantly jeopardizing the state's soldiers, that is the proper course to take. However, even as a matter of common sense it is clear that had it been possible to capture those terrorists killed in preemptive operations, they would have been captured—if only in order to interrogate them and thereby garner vital information.

Let us consider the following example: On the night of June 22, 2002, Israel killed Salah Shehade, the head of the military arm of Hamas. Shehade was responsible for hundreds of terrorist attacks against Israel which resulted in the death and injury of hundreds of innocent civilians. Shehade was chosen as a target for elimination on the basis of clear evidence of his deep and prolonged involvement in initiating, planning, financing, and dispatching attack forces and suicide bombers in Gaza and Judea and Samaria. The targeted killing was conducted from the air by an F-16 jet launching a "smart bomb" weighing one ton at a house in which Shehade was staying that night, accompanied by his wife and son. The outcome of the operation was harsh. The goal of eliminating Shehade was achieved, but an additional Hamas activist and another fifteen civilians were also killed, among them nine children. The elimination of a mass murderer such as Shehade is a clear example of the difficult dilemma: should one attack a terrorist who is responsible for the deaths of hundreds of innocent civilians when an attack against him entails the risk of harm to innocent persons among whom he is hiding?

In the previous chapter I explained that in my opinion the answer to this question is yes in exceptional cases where the benefit ensuing from the action (saving many innocent civilians) exceeds the damage caused by it (harm to civilians in the vicinity of the terrorist). In this case, one could argue that, notwithstanding the grave outcome, Israel made its decision in accordance with the principle of double effect. The act was good per se: the direct objective—killing a senior terrorist—was acceptable from a moral point of view. The injury to the civilians was not a measure employed by the IDF in order to strike at the terrorist. On a number of occasions the IDF had canceled operations against Shehade following intelligence to the effect that he was surrounded by civilians. Aware of the terrorists' use of civilians as a human shield, Israel attempted to minimize the "bad" outcome as far as possible; the operation was authorized on the basis of intelligence that the likelihood of injury to civilians was not high. Accordingly, Israel anticipated that the benefit from the act would greatly exceed the damage entailed by it and would be justified in accordance with the principle of proportionality. The lives of many Israeli civilians would be saved, and if innocents were harmed during the course of the operation, that harm would be minor and an unavoidable price to pay in order to save the lives of many Israeli civilians. The death of fifteen civilians was not an outcome that Israel anticipated.[23]

However, I am of the opinion that the above approach fails to reflect the true state of affairs. Even if we accept the argument that dispatching a ground unit of soldiers into the Occupied Territories to attack a wanted terrorist hiding among the civilian population would have entailed significant risk to the lives of the soldiers and injury to innocent civilians caught up in the ensuing fighting, the decision-making process in Israel was not compatible with the moral and legal prohibition to protect the civilian population, according to the principle of double effect. In view of the professional experience of those who planned and authorized the operation, and considering the unique conditions on the ground (i.e., a dense neighborhood, many of whose "houses" are nothing but rickety warehouses and sheds), the bad outcome should have been expected in advance. Israel had the choice of postponing the assassination to a later date and operating in a manner that would minimize the danger to civilians. By using a one-ton bomb, Israel in fact chose to ignore all the risks and protect her own civilians by killing innocent Palestinians in a disproportional manner.

There is no doubt that the threat of terror hanging over the State of Israel is existential, and it is Israel's moral duty to respond to this threat in self-defense. But Israel's moral duty is not exhausted by the defense of its citizens. In going to war against terrorism it must choose means that are compatible with the moral standards required of a democratic state. The State of Israel should not clap itself on the back and present itself as the guardian angel of its citizens because it has strictly adhered to moral norms. It must admit that there have been occasions on which its adherence faltered, and draw the necessary lessons from them. The ability to admit mistakes and to examine the reasons for flaws in one's actions is itself, in my opinion, an expression of moral values.

Preemptive Action as Part of the Concept of Defense

The Rule of Proportionality

In conflicts between states it is necessary to exhaust all the possible "tools of peace." However, this rule does not apply to relations between a terrorist leader, who is not a head of state, and a state. Negotiations between a terrorist organization and a state cannot be conducted for a number of reasons. On the one hand, the very existence of such negotiations recognizes the legitimacy of the organization and the legitimacy of its activities—a result that the state shuns. Thus, there is no reason to conduct negotiations of this type, apart from those few cases where talks are essential for the release of hostages and persons kidnapped. But, on the other hand, since the terrorist organization does not represent a state, the weapon of economic sanctions, which is generally employed against states that breach international agreements, would have no influence. There is no effective means of ensuring that the agreement will be implemented by the terrorist organization. Further, the international courts will be of no assistance, as again the dispute is not one being waged between two states.

In addition to attempts to resolve the conflict by peaceful means, there is the requirement that if these fail, a means must be chosen which is proportional to the activity that is to be prevented. Just as in a war, where fighting must be conducted with weapons that meet certain criteria in order to minimize the resulting damage, proportionality must be ensured in activities aimed at foiling terrorist attacks. It is necessary to consider whether the preemptive attack will cause harm to more people than is expected from the commission of the terrorist act itself.

Preemptive Acts Other than Killing

In addition to the requirement of proportionality, it is necessary for the preemptive measure to cause the least possible harm. As a rule, it is necessary to try to impose economic and diplomatic sanctions to prevent terrorist attacks before acting in self-defense. If it is possible to preempt the terrorist act by taking other actions that are less harmful, and that entail minimum risk to the forces of the defending state, these must be taken. For example, destroying terrorist infrastructure by bombing a terrorist training camp is justified as a legal act of self-defense according to the UN Charter. However, while such an act may perhaps prevent attacks in the immediate future, it may prove futile in the long term, since despite the destruction of the infrastructure the terrorists themselves still pose a real threat and can quickly recover by establishing new training sites. In particular, such a measure is unsatisfactory in the case of suicide terrorists, where only an attack against them or their commanders will prevent them from implementing their designs. An additional possible measure is kidnapping. The kidnapping of terrorists who are not the leaders of a state is permitted according to international law, since no protective norm exists in respect of them.

An additional mode of fighting terrorism adopts the approach of imposing responsibility on the state out of which the terrorists operate—the "host state." However, on occasion this declarative step is of no avail, even if worldwide pressure is placed on the host state, since the latter is unable to meet its international commitments.

Consider the circumstances in which the United States bombed Libya. In 1986 warnings were sounded about Libya's intention of engaging in terrorist action against American citizens. Despite the warnings, it was not possible to prevent the attacks. In 1986 a bomb exploded in a discotheque in Berlin, killing at least one American civilian and two American soldiers and injuring another fifty. In response, it was decided to bomb Libya. It follows that this operation was not preemptive but rather retaliatory, and its primary if not its sole purpose was punitive. The purpose of Israel's preemptive actions, on the contrary, is to prevent future acts of terrorism and not to avenge past terrorist acts. But the United States explained the bombing of Libya as an act of self-defense, which was designed to end the threat of terror and the use of force on the part of Qaddafi and the terrorist organizations of Libya. Accordingly, argued the United States, the attack was aimed at destroying Libya's capacity to carry out future terrorist attacks. Moreover, it argued that the American attack was proportional because it was directed against isolated military facilities from which various terrorist missions were routinely sent out, and also because the United States had tried to avoid harming civilians and confine the ensuing damage. If the U.S. attack was indeed defensive and intended to obstruct future acts of terrorism, it could be justified as a permitted preemptive act. However, if the attack was motivated solely by the desire to punish, then it cannot be described as a preemptive act and must not be justified as such.

When are Preemptive Acts that Cause Death Permitted?

The law and national policy of the United States prohibit assassinations. The U.S. Army Field Manual 27–10 on the Law of Land Warfare provides that political assassination is a war crime, and therefore anyone breaching this prohibition, in time of war, is liable to be tried for his acts. The justification that the act was carried out for self-defense is unacceptable. However, in a situation that is not one of manifest war, such as the United States' attempt to foil the activities of Al Qaeda, one of the most notorious terrorist organizations in the world, it is not clear what law applies. Executive Order 12333 provides that no person employed by or acting on behalf of the U.S. government shall engage in, or conspire to engage in, assassination.[24] The policy prohibiting assassinations was initiated in 1977, during President Ford's term in office, in consequence of CIA involvement in the assassination of a number of foreign leaders. The order, however, does not define what would be considered an assassination. It has been argued that because the order was issued following the assassination of a number of foreign government officials, and because Al Qaeda leaders are not heads of state or the political representatives of any state, the prohibition on assassinations does not apply to them.[25]

Assassination is defined as illegal homicide for a political purpose. All existing definitions of the term "assassination" contain the word "murder" or words with a similar meaning. The majority of the definitions also include the requirement that the homicide be for some political purpose.[26] Accordingly, if the homicide is directed against a political state figure, with the purpose of achieving a political goal, it will be regarded as an assassination. It follows that preempting a terrorist action by killing the terrorists does not amount to a prohibited assassination or killing, according to and in the light of the definitions of the term "assassination."

Thus, killing in the course of war will be deemed to be an assassination if two cumulative conditions are met: first, that the aim of the action is to kill the particular person; and second, that the killing is undertaken through the use of treacherous fighting tactics. If one of these conditions is not met, there is no assassination. With regard to the first requirement, reference is to an attack against a single person or individuals, enemy personnel, or personnel belonging to the other side, depending on which interpretation of the term is preferred. Assassination, under this definition, is never a legitimate pursuit in wartime. There was concern that if each side feared such a ploy, the parties' ensuing paranoia would make it impossible to engage in negotiations and end the war. Another reason is humanitarian: no strike should be conducted against a person who is not about to fight and who is therefore unaware of the threat hanging over him, or who is not a combatant and is therefore protected by international law.

Every assassination is prohibited under the law. However, not every homicide is an assassination. Even a homicide that is not the result of wartime necessity will not be deemed an assassination or a hit if the element of treacherous conduct is missing. A breach of the requirement that the action be proportional will also not inevitably cause the action to be regarded as an assassination. Thus, the killing of an individual on the grounds of self-defense will not be regarded as an assassination.[27]

During President Clinton's terms the approach followed was that, both in times of war and in times of peace, when individuals or groups, such as bin Laden, posed an immediate danger, killing them—with the purpose of eliminating the threat—would not be regarded as a prohibited assassination.[28] It should be noted that in Executive Order 12333 the right was reserved to both Congress and the president to amend or modify the order as needed. This shows that from the beginning it was not intended that the prohibition be general and all-embracing. The order will not apply in cases that are defined as acts of self-defense. The failure of Congress to amend the order may be interpreted as conferring the sole power of amendment on the president. Thus, people who endanger the public and the American nation continue to be killed. For example, when the United States attacked Libya and Qaddafi's own headquarters, the action was justified as one of self-defense; since the action was a defensive military action and not a political one, the order was not applicable to the situation. The United States recognizes acts as performed in self-defense if they are against persistent threats, including persistent terrorist threats.[29] Congress has attempted to enact a law that would prohibit assassinations, but to date has failed to do so.[30]

In recent years, however, Congress has made several attempts to override Executive Order 12333, claiming that it excessively limits armed actions needed by the United States in order to adequately deal with potential threats against the nation.[31] Shortly after the terrorist attack of September 11, 2001, the two Houses of Congress passed a joint resolution, Authorization for Use of Military Force, which empowered the president "to use all necessary and appropriate force against those . . . persons he determines planned, authorized, committed, or aided the terrorist attacks that occurred on September 11, 2001 . . . in order to prevent any future acts of international terrorism against the United States by such nations, organizations or persons."[32] Relying on this authorization, U.S. Armed Forces were sent to Afghanistan with a mission to subdue Al Qaeda and quell the Taliban regime that was known to support it. As part of the attempt to kill the Taliban and Al Qaeda leadership, U.S. forces attacked convoys, destroyed caves, and bombed homes associated with the wanted leaders. At the same time, the government asserted that it would pursue suspected terrorists in other countries as well. In November 2002 an American pilotless Predator aircraft launched a Hellfire missile at a car traveling through the desert outside Sanaa, Yemen, an attack carried out with the consent of the Yemeni government. The six passengers in the car—all suspected members of Al Qaeda—were killed, including an American citizen and an Al Qaeda leader who was believed to have been substantially involved in the October 2000 attack on the American carrier USS *Cole* off the coast of Yemen that killed seventeen U.S. navy members.[33]

Targeted eliminations also took place during the armed conflict in

Iraq in 2003, when the United States attempted to target senior Iraqi leadership officials in an effort to hasten the fall of Saddam Hussein's regime.[34]

There are four ways of evading the prohibition on assassinations, all of which rely on a number of loopholes in Order 12333. The first is by declaring open war. However, even in time of war, civilians who do not take part in the war should not be killed. Further, while it is possible to kill military leaders as part of a war, it is doubtful whether it is legal to kill civilian leaders who are also military leaders. If a state of war is not declared, use may be made of Article 51 of the UN Charter. According to one view there are three degrees of self-defense: first, self-defense against a hostile or aggressive act; second, a defensive action against an expected imminent attack; and finally, self-defense against a persistent threat. The two additional openings provided by Order 12333 are a restrictive interpretation of the order so as to include the least possible number of situations, and the possibility of amendment or modification of the order, a possibility retained in the order itself, as already explained above. Accordingly, even if the three previous loopholes had not existed, it would still be possible to circumvent the order by either the president or Congress amending or modifying the order, as indeed happened with the passing of the joint resolution.

One argument that has been raised in relation to the contest between the United States and Al Qaeda leaders is that the only completely effective preemptive act, certain to prevent the massacre of innocent persons protected by international law, is to kill bin Laden and his people. Further, it has been added that killing him would deter other terrorists from attacking civilians. I do not agree with this dogmatic statement. A preemptive act that causes death may only be carried out if any other less harmful preemptive act either does not exist or is inconceivable in light of the great danger it poses to the forces of the defending state. Preemptive acts that cause death and are adopted solely in order to deter other terrorists should also be dismissed. Consideration of such an option is not appropriate. Possibly in the field such an act would have deterrent effect; however, this is not a factor that may be legitimately weighed when deciding which type of preemptive act is appropriate.

Before dismissing, morally and legally, an attempt to thwart acts of terrorism by killing terrorists, it should be remembered that such measures can and do save many lives.

Conclusion

We have seen that according to both customary international law and treaty law, notwithstanding the differences between them, a state is authorized to engage in acts of self-defense if a number of conditions have been met. Further, we have seen that the preemptive acts that the State of Israel carries out can fall within the category of self-defense.

The right to life is also not absolute. Article 2 of the European Convention on Human Rights asserts the right to life as prima facie an absolute right. However, Article 2 should not be read as conferring an absolute right that may not be impaired under any circumstance or condition. There are situations, exceptional and even highly exceptional, in which it is permissible to impair the right to life. These situations include acts of self-defense. At the same time, it should be recalled that generally and even usually people should not be harmed without due process of law. Proof must be adduced as to why the life of someone who ought to stand trial should be taken. In the exceptional cases, there is a duty to exercise caution and make the appropriate arrangements to ensure that we are indeed facing exceptional circumstances in which we have no other choice but to take the life of a certain person. As pointed out, it is still necessary to meet a reasonable level of proof. There is still a requirement of clear and convincing evidence. Great caution must be taken when deciding to utilize the tool of preemptive action against terrorism by taking the lives of terrorists. There is a danger of sliding down a slippery slope. A regime may arise which may use this tool as a routine and daily measure, with disastrous consequences. Such a regime may swiftly move from the systematic killing of terrorists to the systematic killing of political opponents within the boundaries of the state.

Precautions should be taken against falling into a situation where use is made of this tool in order to prevent a person from undergoing a fair trial and having the opportunity to defend himself. An effective judicial or quasi-judicial body must be established which shall, first, examine whether the preemptive action exceeds what is permissible, and second, prevent the defensive-fighting measure from being improperly used against people who could be put on trial, or who do not fall within the category of terrorists.

Even if the preventive action that involves killing terrorists is legitimate, an examination must be conducted as to whether this action is indeed proportional and whether no other measure can be taken which is less harmful—such as the detention or trial of a person—but will also prevent the undesirable outcome. It should be pointed out that the question of timing, that is, the date on which the bomb or suicide bomber is due to explode, is not relevant to the level of urgency of the preventive action. Moreover, even if all the conditions for a preemptive action that causes killing are met, it is still necessary to conduct a thorough examination in order to ensure that the intelligence information regarding the planned terrorist attack is accurate and that no mistake has been made regarding identification of persons in the field. This is necessary in order to minimize harm to innocent persons.

In conclusion, the State of Israel acts lawfully so long as it follows a policy in which the preemptive action that involves killing is carried out as a last-ditch measure. If it is possible to stop the attacker in another way, such as by stopping him at a military roadblock, the less harmful measure must be taken, and it is forbidden to kill that terrorist. At the same time, it should be recalled that even if there is a less harmful measure, if that measure jeopardizes the lives and safety of our soldiers, there is no legal or moral obligation to follow that course of action. Nonetheless, care and precautions should be taken to ensure that killing not become the routine and exclusive course of action. Care should be taken to avoid the slippery slope, which leads to the improper exploitation of this legitimate preventive fighting measure. I am not talking about the execution of people in order to prevent them from having a fair trial. The objective is to prevent terrorist attacks and protect the lives of the citizens and residents of the State of Israel. So long as the Palestinian Authority, from whose territory the terrorists set out, does nothing to prevent their activities, Israel has the responsibility and the duty to foil these attacks. Almost nothing can be done against suicide bombers once they have set out on their mission. They must be prevented before the fuse is lit. On occasion there is no choice but to take preemptive action which involves killing in order to prevent the attack from taking place and causing even more bloodshed, death, and destruction.

Conclusion

LESSONS OF THE PAST AND
CHALLENGES FOR THE FUTURE

FOR MANY YEARS the Western world had stood back, gazing in aston-
ishment at how the long-standing phenomenon of terrorism was evolv-
ing and successfully adapting to contemporary times. True, states had
not completely disregarded this process, and certain measures were
taken against terrorist organizations and against states sponsoring terrorism; however, none deluded itself into believing that these measures
would be sufficient to eradicate terrorism. The prevailing perception
was that terrorism was a local phenomenon, fed by the soil in which it
was developing. The Western world shut its eyes to the fact that terrorism was an infectious plague, similar to the phenomenon of piracy in
the nineteenth century, and failed to understand that if it did not stamp
it out in one place, that would send a signal to extremist elements in
other places around the world, ultimately leaving no country untouched.

The terrorist attack of September 11, 2001, was a watershed in the
history of this flawed concept. The decisive rhetoric of President Bush's
warning to all world leaders, "Either you are with us, or you are with
the terrorists,"[1] is perhaps the best example of that conceptual change.

In previous chapters I conducted a comparative analysis of how the
United States, Great Britain, and Israel—the three democratic states on
the front line today in the war against terrorism—coped with the principal legal and moral aspects of the war against terror, both before September 11 and in its aftermath. My goal was to examine whether these
countries had succeeded in dealing with the range of modern terrorist
threats directed against them by creating an array of constitutional bal-

ances between national interests in state and public security and the fundamental rights and freedoms of the individual. The overall conclusion that, in my view, emerges from this comparative analysis is unequivocal: for the United States, the horrific attack of September 11, 2001, which took place on its soil and killed close to three thousand people, completely and comprehensively changed the rules of the game—both in terms of its foreign policy toward states sponsoring terrorism and in terms of its internal security policy. Although its response was less extreme at the beginning, Great Britain, having had long and bitter experience with Irish terrorism, declared a state of public emergency following the attack of September 11 and decided that it ought to pursue the same path as its American ally to reduce the risk that its own citizens would fall victim to similar attacks. This approach has become more forceful following the direct attacks in London in July 2005, when Britain decided to pursue the enactment of even more severe counterterrorism measures, such as the power to revoke the citizenship of British nationals who encourage terrorism, and the creation of a new offense of indirect incitement to commit terrorist acts.

Israel, unlike the United States and Great Britain, did not regard the attack of September 11 as grounds for engaging in hasty and far-reaching changes in its defense policy. As the president of the Supreme Court of Israel, Aharon Barak, writes in the foreword to this book, this is because the State of Israel has been under a continuous state of emergency since its establishment, in May 1948, and its citizens have always been subject to threats and murderous attacks from religious and nationalist Palestinian terrorist organizations. While the United States felt the true horrific force of the terrorist enemy only on September 11, 2001, Israel had internalized this threat many years earlier, and the dilemmas entailed in finding ways of dealing with terrorism that would satisfy not only security needs but also the fundamental democratic values of the state have become a matter of routine forced on Israel by the prevailing tragic situation.

The attack of September 11 abruptly and painfully tore apart the illusions in which the United States, Great Britain, and other countries of the free world had unconsciously wrapped themselves, and made clear to them what Israel had known for many years: that they could not evade conducting a third world war—a war against modern terrorism, in particular Islamic fundamentalism but also Islamic nationalism—and that this war, unlike its predecessors, could last many years, perhaps even for generations to come.[2]

The understanding of this situation led the United States and Great

Britain to modify their attitude toward international terrorism. One of the primary features of this shift in approach was reflected in constitutional reforms that drastically tilted the array of constitutional balances from individual freedoms toward national security, such as the enactment of the Patriot Act in the United States and the Anti-terrorism, Crime and Security Act in Great Britain. Unlike in Israel, the creation of normative rules for dealing with the war against terrorism in the United States and Great Britain is now only in its first stages. The courts in these countries have not yet managed to clearly and comprehensively delineate the boundaries of what is permissible and what forbidden in the management of the war, and history proves that traditionally they avoid formulating far-reaching rules as long as the emergency is at its height.[3] The strategic character of the war against terrorism now being waged by the United States and Great Britain is, therefore, found in the approach taken by the executive authority—the assumption that when facing such a cruel enemy, which violates every rule and consensus, it is sometimes better to err on the side of excessive use of extraordinary measures than to discover too late that too few measures were employed.

In contrast, in Israel, perhaps because of its establishment as a democratic state surrounded by states governed by traditionally dictatorial or centrally controlled regimes, and because of the incessant need to deal with security emergencies, the High Court of Justice understood the importance of stubbornly preserving fundamental democratic principles in times of war, and over the years—while the fighting was ongoing—handed down a number of rulings concerning security issues that considerably restricted the force that the executive branch could apply. The willingness of the High Court of Justice to delineate the boundaries of the permissible and the forbidden in times of emergency in order to ensure that the democratic character of the State of Israel would be preserved has led to a situation in which Palestinians—civilians and terrorists alike—do not hesitate to petition the High Court to review the legality of the measures that the security forces wish to employ against them. These petitions include applications for injunctions against the demolition of the homes of terrorists' families, appeals against the legality of interrogation methods used against security detainees, and attacks on the decisions of the executive branch to deprive suspected terrorists of their physical liberty by an administrative process. In dealing with these issues, the justices of the High Court held:

> It is our duty to safeguard the legality of the regime even with difficult decisions. Even when the cannons roar and the muses are silent the

law exists in practice and determines what is permissible and what forbidden, what is legal and what is illegal. And where the law exists, there is also a court which determines what is permissible and what forbidden, what is legal and what is illegal. Some of the public will be pleased with our decision; another part will oppose it. Conceivably, neither will peruse our reasoning. But we shall perform our task, this is our work and this is our duty as judges . . . we are one of the branches of government, and it is our function to oversee that the other branches act within the framework of the law in order to ensure the rule of law in government. The branches of government hold a high place, but the law is higher than all of us.[4]

The armies of the United States and Great Britain, like other Western fighting armies, are not subject to similar thorough judicial review in times of crisis.

In chapter 3, for example, where I examined the investigative policies of the security forces regarding terrorists suspected of possessing information concerning future terrorist attacks, I showed that, notwithstanding the unusual difficulty involved in persuading these suspects to talk, until September 11 the United States exercised interrogational methods that relied on sophistication and ingenuity and not on force. However, the aftermath of the attack saw a sharp trend toward increasing the severity of interrogation measures, climaxing with the brutal treatment of Iraqi prisoners held by the Americans in Abu Ghraib prison. In Great Britain, although the judgment in *Republic of Ireland v. United Kingdom* (1978) was followed by a consistent trend toward strengthening the rights of persons suspected of involvement in terrorist acts, it was possible to distinguish signs of diminishing rights after September 11. The primary example may be found in the judgment of the court of appeal delivered in August 2004 which held that "evidence obtained by other governments through torture can be used to indefinitely detain terrorist suspects in Britain," before it was reversed by the House of Lords in December 2005.

In Israel, on the other hand, the long-standing General Security Services practice of using extraordinary interrogational methods ended with the precedent set by the Supreme Court in September 1999. That ruling prohibited the use of unusual pressure during interrogations; the only opening it left was to grant an interrogator a retroactive defense against criminal liability for his acts if he managed to prove that he had performed those acts in exceptional circumstances, that the security need was pressing, and that he had no alternative less grave means for persuading the suspect to talk.

Likewise, in chapter 5, which examined the attitude of the three democracies to the issue of preventive administrative detention, it was shown that the three countries permit foreign nationals to be detained under less stringent procedures than those applicable to the detention of their own nationals. In Israel and in Great Britain these procedures are anchored in statute, and consequently every person may appeal to a neutral judicial tribunal against the legality of his detention. In contrast, in the United States the executive branch has deprived foreign nationals and American citizens suspected of being "enemy combatants"—the criteria for being assigned such a status are vague and uncertain—of their physical liberty without relying on express statutory provisions and has simply relied on a broadly formulated resolution of Congress read together with the powers of the president as the commander in chief of the army. Indeed, the rulings of the U.S. Supreme Court have significantly restrained the excessive powers which the executive branch has attempted to take for itself in the name of the war against terror; however, they have not created an adequate balance between security needs and the physical freedom of the individual.

It should be made clear that the State of Israel and its courts have not met all the challenges posed by the war against terrorism. Two prominent examples are use of "neighbor practice" when arresting wanted suspects (discussed in chapter 7), until this was prohibited by the court, and the policy of targeted eliminations (discussed in chapter 8). As regards targeted eliminations, there is no dispute about its operational effectiveness, and it is certainly possible to find legal and moral justifications for the practice. Nonetheless, today this measure is used liberally and routinely, and there is an argument for making the threshold conditions for its application considerably more stringent. As explained, this issue has been pending for a number of years before the High Court of Justice, which has hesitated in making its opinion heard. At the same time it is noteworthy that, notwithstanding the broad use Israel makes of the policy of targeted elimination, it has never been directed against terrorists possessing Israeli nationality, whereas the United States has used the same policy in Yemen to eliminate a number of suspected terrorists, one of whom held American nationality.

A democracy that struggles with terrorism faces a state of emergency. It is entitled, and indeed under a duty, to protect the safety of its citizens. For this purpose, it is entitled to make use of measures, and occasionally force, which restrict the constitutional freedoms of its citizens and sometimes lead to a serious impairment of the fundamental rights of the terrorists, of individuals suspected of terrorism, and occasionally also of people among whom the terrorists conceal themselves. These restrictions are the fruit of necessity—of a situation of incessant struggle against terrorism which has transformed our democracy into a "defensive democracy" and at times into a "militant democracy." Yet, we are obligated to enforce stringent precautions to ensure that such defensive and militant measures do not denude our government of its democratic character, that is, that our defensive and militant democracy does not become an "uncontrolled democracy" that arbitrarily tramples on the fundamental freedoms of the individual under the cover of the war against terrorism.[5]

As we have seen, the judicial authority performs a critical role in protecting the values of a democratic regime in times of emergency. When the judiciary does not carry out sufficiently active judicial review, there is an increased danger of the constitutional scales tilting excessively toward security needs at the expense of the fundamental rights of the individual. In the United States, this danger is particularly noticeable, in light of the far-reaching constitutional and executive initiatives that followed the events of September 11. Consequently, in my opinion, the fact that in recent years, more than in the past, there have been increased calls advocating restrictions of the powers of judicial review of the courts and granting greater powers to the executive—on the grounds that only this will allow an effective war against the terrorist enemy—is cause for great concern. Generally speaking, these radical proposals may be divided into two categories, where the first concerns the nature of the constitutional framework within whose boundaries the balance is conducted, and the second—which is derived from the first—concerns the manner of drawing the balance within the boundary of the given constitutional framework. I shall deal with these two issues in order.

The Constitutional Framework in Times of Crisis

At first glance, many would be surprised at the need to deal with this issue. Is it not obvious that the constitutional framework—the array of traditional basic values that guide the nation in times of peace—will continue to guide it also in its most difficult hours? Is it conceivable that a democratic state would pursue a certain constitutional framework only in good periods, whereas in times of crisis it would turn its back on them and adopt—with the same moral determination—a completely different constitutional framework? This would mean, in practice, the division of the democratic regime into two: one for periods of contentment and happiness, the other for periods of despair and suffering, with the nature of the second differing unrecognizably from the first.

Is this division so unfeasible as appears at first glance? We should not forget that this is the basis of international law. In 1625 Hugo Grotius, the father of international law, wrote his book *The Law of War and Peace* (*De jure belli ac pacis*), whose very title indicates that it is possible to derogate from many of the international laws of peace in times of war and replace them with other legal norms.[6] On the domestic level, there are those who hold that it would be proper to act in a similar manner, by confining the "regular" constitutional framework to times of peace only and creating an emergency constitutional regime that would take effect in times of crisis. Within this emergency framework the executory powers of the government authorities will be expanded, with a corresponding narrowing of the scope of judicial review over the manner of their implementation.

Bruce Ackerman, for example, is of the opinion that the idea that only one constitution ought to regulate the entirety of democratic life is faulty, because one constitution is incapable of guaranteeing the proper level of protection to civil liberties in the face of contemporary security threats—in particular terrorist threats. Every time terrorist organizations succeed in carrying out a murderous attack, never a mind an attack on an unusual scale, the feeling sweeping through the general public is that the security mechanisms are subject to overly restrictive constitutional restrictions which prevent them from making use of effective measures which might have prevented the attack that took place; therefore they must be removed, creating a new normative balance between civil liberties and the public interest in national security. A government that relies on the support of the majority, and that possesses an interest in acquiring the greatest possible power in order to expand the scope of its activities, may act in accordance with these feelings, even in cases where they are not backed by valid objective needs, and cause irreversible harm to the fundamental rights of an individual. Accordingly, Ackerman is of the opinion that only a fundamental change of the existing constitutional structure, a change designed to establish a constitutional legal doctrine that presents a clear distinction between the powers of the democratic regime in times of emergency and its powers in times of peace, will guarantee the limitation of the violation of the rights of the individual to times of emergency only, and prevent unnecessary and long-range restrictions on individual freedoms in times of peace.[7]

Underlying the theory of the "emergency constitution" proposed by

Ackerman one may find the concept that the democratic model may be divided—one model in times of peace, and another in times of crisis, where "the democratic emergency model" is required in order to enable government agencies to deal effectively with crisis situations, in a manner that will reassure the fearful public and prevent the continuation of the violation of constitutional human rights even after the end of the emergency. I do not agree with this concept, which I believe completely overturns the fundamental pillars of the democratic-liberal paradigm.

In his important work *The End of History*, published in the 1990s, Francis Fukuyama argued that the ideological war between democratic theory and its opponents had ended, and that the former had won an unquestionable victory.[8] Since Western liberalism had succeeded in surviving the many moral blemishes that human kind had created for itself during the course of the twentieth century, headed by the transformation of Germany from a country with a long democratic tradition to a brutal Nazi dictatorship, the world recognized that the liberal democracy would be the dominant type of regime in the future. The terrorist attack of September 11, 2001, was put an end to this erroneous idea. Western states understood that the conceptual dispute was still far from resolved, and that the fight of the democratic states against fundamentalist and nationalist terrorists was not only a fight to reassure the public and ensure its peace and security but also a fight of liberal ideology for its continued conceptual supremacy.

It follows from Ackerman's thesis that he believes that the correct legal doctrine for dealing with emergency situations in the life of a democracy, in particular emergency situations created by terrorist attacks, may be found in the framework of an "emergency constitution," which affords the government legal and moral authorization to implement counterterrorism measures that lack any constitutional and moral validity in a "peace constitution." Ackerman considers insufficient a "regular" constitution that enables the constitutive declaration of an emergency, a declaration that would vest government authorities with the power to implement the balancing formula between security interests and individual freedoms differently from its implementation in times of peace, so that the relative weight given to the differing interests may vary, in accordance with the circumstances of the emergency, and matters prohibited in times of peace may be permitted in times of crisis. Instead, he is interested in changing the formula itself. He offers us a different regime (one that is also democratic and constitutional, in his understanding) for a limited period of time. A regime following which everything will revert to its former state.

Is it reasonable to believe that a "peace democracy" will not remember the acts of an "emergency democracy"? I can only concur with the comments of the president of the Supreme Court of Israel, Aharon Barak:

> It is a myth to think that it is possible to maintain a sharp distinction between the status of human rights during a period of war and the status of human rights during a period of peace. It is self-deception to believe that we can limit our judicial ruling so that they will be valid only during wartime, and that we can decide that things will change in peace time. The line between war and peace is thin—what one person calls peace, another calls war. In any case, it is impossible to maintain this distinction long-term. We should assume that whatever we decide when terror is threatening our security will linger many years after the terror is over. . . . A wrong decision in a time of war and terrorism plots a point that will cause the judicial graph to deviate after the crisis passes.[9]

Fundamental democratic principles—the rule of law, the separation of powers, the independence of the judicial authority, and recognition of principles of social morality and justice at the core of which lie human rights—are not luxuries of peacetime which make the democracy in which we live a better one; rather, without them the democracy does not exist. A democracy that permits itself to deviate from respect for these values—even for a limited period of time—is not a bad democracy, but from a substantive point of view it is not a democracy at all. Accordingly, the manner in which democratic states deal with emergency situations in general, and security emergencies in particular, must fall within the boundaries of the existing constitutional framework.

Drawing the Balance between National Security and Individual Rights within the Existing Constitutional Framework

In the light of my above conclusion, I shall now turn to an examination of the weight that should properly be accorded to each of the competing values in view of the emergency situation forced on the state by threats of terrorist guerilla organizations. It is the weight given to the special emergency circumstances which determines the scope of protection properly accorded to each of the clashing values.

A democratic state is required to conduct its struggle against terrorism by creating a suitable constitutional balance between two clashing values.[10] On the one hand is the public interest in the security of the state and the security of its citizens. Fundamental human rights—however important and essential—are not absolute, and the need to preserve them does not justify undermining national security in every situation. On the contrary, a democracy that does not defend itself, that consciously decides "to self-destruct in order to prove its existence,"[11] fails to comply with its obligation to maintain a sound civilian infrastructure for its citizens, an essential precondition for the citizens' ability to realize their basic rights. On the other hand, national security, too, is not a supreme value, and the need to ensure it does not grant the government an unlimited license to violate the constitutional rights of the individual.

This complex normative balance raises difficult moral and legal dilemmas, in that we come to draw the balance knowing in advance that its outcome will not make our struggle easier. Any proper balance between security and freedom will impose certain restrictions both on security and on freedom. Moderation of the response and willingness to compromise are the price of democracy. Accordingly, I reject proposals such as that made by Oren Gross, who offers us the "Extra-Legal Measures model," under which public officials are entitled to adopt measures that are contrary to constitutional norms, principles, and rules in those circumstances where they believe that such an extreme response is essential, as a last resort, for the purpose of defending the nation and the public against extremely grave dangers and threats, provided that these unconstitutional responses are open to the scrutiny of the public. In such a case, suggests Gross, the lawless actions of the public official will require him to face public accountability, in the sense that the public will be required to choose between the public legal trial of the lawless official (in cases where he acted in the absence of essential security needs), or, alternatively, it will retroactively grant moral and social authorization to the extralegal measures he adopted (in cases where his acts were in response to compelling security needs). This model, which asserts the public individual responsibility of the public official, does not, so Gross believes, weaken the state's loyalty to the rule of law but actually strengthens it, since it is designed to preserve long-term compliance with constitutional values. It expresses the political and moral responsibility of the government toward its citizens. After all, using this model, the democracy may avoid normalizing the exception, referring to the unlawful measures as such—as measures that were required in view of the unusual nature of the threat—while remaining unequivocally aware of the serious significance of the decision to act outside the boundaries of the law, without trying to garb it with the cloak of a lawful act through the broad interpretation of existing laws. Were we to act thus, we would risk creating legal precedents that would permeate the regular legal system and pollute it.[12]

Notwithstanding the real dangers pointed out by Oren Gross, I believe that his model raises even greater constitutional and moral difficulties and dangers in that he does not propose drawing a balance between the competing values but rather proposes deviating altogether from the balancing formula in unusual emergency situations. The preference for security interests over human rights must always be carried out within the boundaries of the law—within the framework of the constitutional balancing formula. Which precedent is more dangerous: one that permits an unusual violation of one of the basis rights within the framework of the constitutional balancing formula, or one that permits a departure from constitutional fetters in certain emergency situations? The constitutional balancing formula draws a balance between the terrorist threat and the rights that ought properly to be protected, and it determines the scope of the protection that ought to be supplied to those rights in the circumstances. Accordingly, every departure from the boundaries of the law is categorically unjustified. An unconstitutional violation of the constitutional liberties of the individual, even if he is suspected of involvement in terrorist activities, impairs the rule of law and the steadfastness of democracy in precisely the same way as according excessive weight to individual rights at the expense of the security interest infringes that interest.

The war against religious and national terrorism is apparently going to become the war of the twenty-first century. A war in which, contrary to the past, a sovereign country no longer faces an enemy that resembles it, but rather a conglomeration of radical guerilla organizations that do not hesitate to breach even the minimal rules for conducting armed conflict, with the aim of hurting the "enemy" in the most painful way and challenging the pillars of its regime in the most vexatious way. The democratic state is forced to conduct this war in a manner that compromises with norms that are foreign to the liberal ethos that it holds dear. A person can no longer board an airplane without exposing his person and private property to a series of invasive checks. On occasion there is no choice but to make the life of the civilian population more harsh if terrorists hide among them. On occasion it is necessary to engage in preventive administrative detentions of persons suspected of terrorism, and on occasion there is also no choice but to kill a terrorist without trial, by targeted elimination, in order to thwart future attacks. The liberal state, which places the individual at the center of its attention and seeks to vest him with the freedom to shape his life as he sees fit, finds itself forced to impose fetters on the individual's most basic rights in order to enable it to guarantee its own existence, for that person's sake.

This new war, which is perhaps the most difficult in Western history, will only come to an end when a decisive and absolute victory is achieved. Cease-fires are not an option at all, and neither is the unconditional surrender of the attackers. Complete neutralization of the terrorist enemy is required, and the blocking of any opening for its future rehabilitation—a goal that can only be achieved through the capture and incarceration of the enemy or his destruction. This is why it appears that the struggle against terrorism is still in its infancy. True, most countries of the world have now understood the level of danger, and thus there exists a common global interest in the elimination of terrorism. However, these countries have not yet succeeded in finding a way to overcome disputes over the nature of the acts that amount to "terrorism" and the nature of the rules of war that may be applied against it.

Until international unity can be achieved, the war against terrorism will continue to be conducted almost entirely on the domestic state level. The justifiable fear of future terrorist attacks may sometimes lead to the advocacy of revolutionary initiatives, such as the establishment of a constitutional emergency government, that manifestly contradict the core elements of a democratic regime, out of a sense that only this will allow terrorism to be suppressed. The erosion in the sense of personal security of its citizens may also lead the leaders of the state—elected public officials—to support measures that thwart, prevent, and punish terrorism yet cause irreversible harm to the rights of the individual.[13] Thus, even though no further terrorist attack has taken place on American soil since September 11, the American government not only does not believe that the time has come to bring back the traditional balance between security interests and the individual right to privacy—a balance grossly violated by many of the provisions of the Patriot Act—but actually initiated the enactment of supplementary legislation in the form of the act to extend and modify authorities needed to combat terrorism, which is likely to cause even deeper erosion of the individual's right to privacy.

The democratic state's war against terror is a just war; its purpose is to drive back those who seek to destroy the liberal rule of law. When the state itself undermines the foundations of its own democratic regime in the name of its war against terror, what just cause can it assert in pursuance of its fight against those who seek to achieve the very same result?

Notes

Foreword

1. William J. Brennan, "The Quest to Develop a Jurisprudence of Civil Liberties in Times of Security Crises" 18 *Isr. Yearbook Hum. Rts.* 11 (1988).

Introduction

1. See, e.g., *R. (Daly) v. Secretary of State for the Home Department*, [2001] UKHL 26, [2001] 2 A.C. 532, 548, per Lord Johan Steyn.

2. John Hooper et al., "Fearful Europe Steps Up Security: Unease: Vulnerable Countries Act Quickly to Bring in New Powers" *Guardian* (London) (July 28, 2005), 7.

3. David Leppard & Robert Winnett, "Blair's Extremism Proposals Attacked as the Hunt Continues for Terror's New Breed" *Sunday Times* (London) (Aug. 7, 2005) 12; Ben Russell, "New Anti-Terror Laws Will Target 'Indirect Incitement'" *Independent* (London) (July 16, 2005), 6. The offense of indirect incitement to commit acts of terror—in contrast to direct incitement, which is already outlawed—is the most controversial part of the proposed legislation. The proposed ban on indirect incitement is intended to prevent both community leaders, such as radical preachers, and private persons from condoning or glorifying terrorism if the intention is to incite people to take part in future attacks. However, in light of the vague nature of this offense, it is unclear to which statements it applies and which remarks are permissible.

4. Steven Kimelmen, "Protecting Privilege" *Nat. L.J.* (Dec. 3, 2001) A21.

5. For a survey of the background of the terrorists who committed the London atrocities, see David Leppard and Jonathan Calvert, "The Web of Terror" *Sunday Times* (London) (July 17, 2005) 11.

6. Samuel P. Huntington, *The Clash of Civilizations and the Remaking of World Order* (New York: Touchstone Books, 1996).

7. Readers seeking further extensive discussions of the issues raised in this book

are invited to consider my earlier articles: "The Laws of War Waged between Democratic States and Terrorist Organizations: Real or Illusive?" 15 *Fla. J. Int'l L.* 389 (2003); "Legal Aspects of Tackling Terrorism: The Balance between the Right of a Democracy to Defend Itself and the Protection of Human Rights" 6 *UCLA J. Int'l L. & For. Aff.* 89 (2001); "Democracy's Struggle against Terrorism: The Powers of Military Commanders to Decide upon the Demolition of Houses, the Imposition of Curfews, Blockades, Encirclements and the Declaration of an Area as a Closed Military Area" 30 *Ga. J. Int'l & Comp. L.* 165 (2002); "Human Rights, Terrorism and the Problem of Administrative Detention in Israel: Does a Democracy Have the Right to Hold Terrorists as Bargaining Chips?" 18 *Ariz. J. Int'l & Comp. L.* 721 (2001); "The Struggle of a Democracy against Terrorism—Protection of Human Rights: The Right to Privacy versus the National Interest—the Proper Balance" 37 *Cornell Int'l L.J.* 27 (2004); "Use of Civilians as a Human Shield: What Legal and Moral Restrictions Pertain to a War Waged by a Democratic State against Terrorism?" 16 *Emory Int'l L. Rev.* 445 (2002); "Thwarting Terrorist Acts by Attacking the Perpetrators or Their Commanders as an Act of Self-Defense: Human Rights versus the State's Duty to Protect Its Citizens" 15 *Temp. Int'l & Comp. L.J.* 195 (2001).

8. William J. Brennan, "The Quest to Develop a Jurisprudence of Civil Liberties in Times of Security Crises" 18 *Isr. Yearbook Hum. Rts.* 11 (1988).

ONE **What Is Terrorism?**

1. Paul Wilkinson, *Political Terrorism* (London: Macmillan, 1974) 12–13.

2. Thomas P. Thornton, "Terror as a Weapon of Political Agitation," in *Internal War: Problems and Approaches* (H. Eckstein ed., New York: Free Press of Glencoe, 1964) 72.

3. Wilkinson, *Political Terrorism*, 36–44.

4. Professor Richard R. Baxter argued, for example, that "we have cause to regret that a legal concept of 'terrorism' was ever inflicted upon us. The term is imprecise; it is ambiguous; and above all, it serves no operative legal purpose." Baxter, "A Skeptical Look at the Concept of Terrorism" 7 *Akron L. Rev.* 380 (1974). See also Geoffrey Levitt, "Is 'Terrorism' Worth Defining?" 13 *Ohio N.U. L. Rev.* 97 (1986).

5. The late Israeli jurist Haim Cohn, formerly attorney general and a justice of the Supreme Court, was of the opinion that "every crime is different, it may even be said that it is worse to kill a man out of envy or greed than out of idealistic motives." Lili Galilee, "Execution by a State Is Deliberate Murder" [in Hebrew] *Ha'aretz* (Dec. 30, 1983).

6. Dalya Schori, "In His Private Life He Is Humane, When We Speak of Israelis, He Is Not" [in Hebrew] *Ha'aretz* (June 15, 2003).

7. The indiscriminate nature of the terrorist act is also reflected in its name, which is derived from the Latin verb *terrere*, which means to cause trembling, fear, and dread. This word was first adopted to describe the collective mental condition of fear and dread prevailing during the Reign of Terror instituted by the French Revolutionary Committee of Public Safety led by Robespierre in France in the years 1793–94. See Walter Laqueur, *Terrorism* (London: Weidenfeld & Nicolson, 1977) 6.

8. General Assembly Resolution 49/60, Measures to Eliminate International Terrorism (1994).

9. Security Council Resolution 1566 (2004).

10. Terrorism Act, 2000, c. 1.

11. Uniting and Strengthening America by Providing Appropriate Tools Required to Intercept and Obstruct Terrorism (USA PATRIOT) Act of 2001, Pub. L. No. 107-56, 115 Stat. 272. Sec. 802 (amending 18 U.S.C. 2331).

12. The Prevention of Terrorism Ordinance, 5708-1948, O.G. 24, 1948, Supp. A, p. 73.

13. Prohibition on Financing Terrorism Law [in Hebrew], 5765-2005, S.H. 1973, 76.

14. Louis Rene Beres, "The Meaning of Terrorism—Jurisprudential and Definitional Clarifications" 28 *Vand. J. Transnat. L.* 239, 241–42 (1995).

15. Rome Statute of the International Criminal Court, July 17, 1998, U.N. Doc. A/CONF. 183/9.

16. Ibid., Art. 5(1). It should be pointed out that the jurisdiction of the court embraces not only the direct perpetrators of the completed act but also persons assisting, aiding, and soliciting the commission of an offense. See ibid., Art. 25(3).

17. Ibid., Art. 5(2).

18. Antonio Cassese, "Terrorism Is Also Disrupting Some Crucial Legal Categories of International Law" 12 *Euro. J. Int'l L.* 993, 994 (2001). Available at http://www.ejil.org/journal/Vol12/No5/120993.pdf (accessed Oct. 4, 2004); William Bradford, "Barbarians at the Gates: A Post–September 11th Proposal to Rationalize the Laws of War" 73 *Miss. L.J.* 639, 669–87 (2004).

19. Nehemiah Robinson, *The Genocide Convention: A Commentary* (New York: Institute of Jewish Affairs, 1960) 58–62.

20. As noted, the question whether cyberterrorism meets the requirements of this provision raises certain difficulties.

21. Yacob Habkuk & Shaciv Salah, *Terror in the Name of Islam* [in Hebrew] (Tel Aviv: Ministry of Defense Press, 1999) 21–27; Mashkit Borgin & David Tal, *Islamic Terrorism and Israel* [in Hebrew] (A. Korz ed., Tel Aviv: Papirus, 1993) 121–22.

22. Moshe Shemesh, "PLO: 1964–1993—from Armed Struggle to Destroy the State of Israel to a Peace Treaty with It," in *The Palestinian National Movement—from Enmity to Acceptance?* [in Hebrew] (M. Maoz & B. Z. Kader eds., Tel Aviv: Ministry of Defense Press, 1996) 299; Menahem Klein, *PLO and the Intifada: From Elation to Despair* [in Hebrew] (Tel Aviv: Moshe Dayan Center for Middle Eastern and African Studies, 1991) 18–21.

23. Charter of the International Military Tribunal, Annexed to London Agreement for the Prosecution and Punishment of the Major War Criminals of the European Axis (Aug. 8, 1945), 82 U.N.T.S. 284.

24. Rome Statute, cited n. 15, Art. 30.

25. Alberto R. Coll, "The Legal and Moral Adequacy of Military Responses to Terrorism" 81 *Am. Soc'y Int'l L. Proc.* 297, 298 (1987).

TWO **The Laws of War Waged between Democratic States and Terrorist Organizations**

1. Elazar Weinrib, *Religion and State: Philosophical Aspects* [in Hebrew] (Tel Aviv: United Kibbutz, 2000) 155–72.

2. Asa Kasher, *Military Ethics* [in Hebrew] (3rd ed., Tel Aviv: Ministry of Defense Press, 1998) 38–39.

3. F.H. 7048/97 *Anon. v. Minister of Defense* [in Hebrew], 54(1) P.D. 721, 741.

4. Yoram Dinstein, *The Laws of War* [in Hebrew] (Tel Aviv: Shocken, 1983) 46.

5. Hague Convention for the Pacific Settlement of International Disputes (Hague I) (July 29, 1899, Oct. 18, 1907).

6. General Pact for the Renunciation of War (Kellogg-Briand Pact of Paris), 1928.

7. Dinstein, *Laws of War*, 51.

8. Art. 1 of the Charter of the United Nations (June 26, 1945).

9. Art. 53 of the Vienna Convention on the Law of Treaties (1969); Case Concerning Military and Paramilitary Activities in and against Nicaragua (*Nicaragua v. United States of America*), 1986 I.C.J. 14, 100–101, 153, 199 (hereafter, *Nicaragua* case).

10. The use of force according to Chapter VII of the UN Charter is not relevant to our discussion and therefore will only be considered to the extent that it concerns the use of force in terms of the exception of self-defense.

11. *Nicaragua* case, at 93–96.

12. Art. 38 of the Statute of the International Court of Justice, 1945; *North Sea Continental Shelf Cases*, 1969 I.C.J. 3, 44.

13. Robert F. Teplitz, "Taking Assassination Attempts Seriously: Did the United States Violate International Law in Forcefully Responding to the Iraqi Plot to Kill George Bush?" 28 *Cornell Int'l L.J.* 569, 575–76 (1995).

14. Alberto R. Coll, "The Legal and Moral Adequacy of Military Responses to Terrorism" 81 *Am. Soc'y Int'l L. Proc.* 287, 301 (1987).

15. Dinstein, *Laws of War*, 68–70.

16. See generally Richard N. Gardner, "Agora: Future Implication of the Iraq Conflict: Neither Bush nor the 'Jurisprudes'" 97 *Am. J. Int'l. L.* 585 (2003).

17. *Nicaragua* case, at 94.

18. See the language of Art. 1(1) and 39 of the UN Charter.

19. Dinstein, *Laws of War*, 19–22.

20. See, e.g., Security Council Resolution 573 (1985).

21. Security Council Resolution 1368 (2001).

22. James Terry, "Countering State-Sponsored Terrorism: A Law-Policy Analysis" 36 *Naval L. Rev.* 159, 170 (1986).

23. Teplitz, "Taking Assassination Attempts," 580.

24. Mark B. Baker, "Terrorism and the Inherent Right of Self-Defense (A Call to Amend Article 51 of the United Nations Charter)" 10 *Hous. J. Int'l L.* 25 (1987).

25. Abraham D. Sofaer, "Terrorism, the Law, and the National Defense" 126 *Military L. Rev.* 95, 101 (1989).

26. Teplitz, "Taking Assassination Attempts," 614.

27. General Assembly Resolution 3314 (1975).

28. Jami Melissa Jackson, "The Legality of Assassination of Independent Terrorist Leaders: An Examination of National and International Implications" 24 *N.C. J. Int'l L. & Com. Reg.* 669, 683 (1999).

29. *Nicaragua* case, at 103.

30. Security Council Resolution 1373 (2001).

31. See Asa Kasher & Amos Yadlin, "Military Ethics of Fighting Terror: An Israeli Perspective" 4(1) *Journal of Military Ethics* 3 (2005).

> We take the defense of citizens from terror to be not only a prime duty of a democratic state but also, under present circumstances, as *the* prime duty, in

the sense that a state that faces the danger of terror has to do more in order to fulfil that duty than it has to do with respect to other prime duties related to danger to life and well-being of its citizens. It has to do more since the danger posed by terror is new and is of a special nature. Since it is a new danger, the state has to create new systems of defense or adapt available ones to the new duty of defense. Since it is a danger of a special nature, such a process of creation and adaptation tackles many difficulties of a variety of types. Until the state is able to provide its citizens with an effective defense against that danger, they are left exposed to it more than they are exposed to familiar types of danger, such as those of a military attack waged by a hostile state.

32. Lassa Oppenheim, *International Law* (H. Lauterpacht ed., vol. 2, 7th ed., London: Longman, 1955) Art. 54.

33. Richard Bernstein, "Biggest U.S. Terrorist Trial Begins As Arguments Clash" *New York Times* (Jan. 31, 1995) A1.

34. Spencer J. Crona & Neal A. Richardson, "Justice for War Criminals of Invisible Armies: A New Legal and Military Approach to Terrorism" 21 *Okla. City U. L. Rev.* 349, 359 (1996).

35. Efraim Inbar, *The War* [in Hebrew] (Tel Aviv: Open University Press, 1998) 9.

36. Gregory M. Travalio, "Terrorism, International Law, and the Use of Military Force" 18 *Wis Int'l L.J.* 145, 160–61 (2000).

37. H.C. 2056/04 *Beit Surik Village Council v. Government of Israel*, 58(5) P.D. 807; 43 *ILM* 1099 (2004).

38. Ibid., paras. 26–31.

39. Legal Consequences of the Construction of a Wall in the Occupied Palestinian Territory, Advisory Opinion, I.C.J. (July 9, 2004), 43 *ILM* 1009 (2004), paras. 138–39. For an analysis of the opinion of the International Court of Justice compared to the ruling of the Israeli Supreme Court, see Emanuel Gross, "Combating Terrorism: Does Self-Defence Include the Security Barrier?—The Answer Depends on Who You Ask," 38 *Cornell Int'l L.J.* 569 (2005).

40. Dinstein, *Laws of War*, 75.

41. Oscar Schachter, "The Extra-Territorial Use of Force against Terrorist Bases" 11 *Hous. J. Int'l L.* 309, 312 (1989).

42. Coll, "Legal and Moral Adequacy," 307.

43. Frederic L. Kirgis's response. Available at http://www.asil.org/insights/insight77.htm (accessed May 10, 2004).

44. Jordan J. Paust, "Responding Lawfully to International Terrorism" 8 *Whittier L. Rev.* 711, 716–17 (1986).

45. Travalio, "Terrorism, International Law," 166–68.

46. Roslyn Higgins, *Problems and Process: International Law and How We Use It* (Oxford: Clarendon Press, 1994) 240.

47. Emanuel Gross, "Human Rights in Administrative Proceedings: A Quest for Appropriate Evidentiary Standards," 31 *Cal. West. Inl'l L.J.* 215 (2001).

48. Jules Lobel, "Colloquy: The Use of Force to Respond to Terrorist Attacks: The Bombing of Sudan and Afghanistan" 24 *Yale J. Int'l L.* 537, 547 (1999).

49. Michael N. Schmitt, "State-Sponsored Assassination in International and Domestic Law" 17 *Yale J. Int'l L.* 609, 648–49 (1992).

50. Travalio, "Terrorism, International Law," 171–73.

51. Security Council Resolution 1333 (2000); Security Council Resolution 1267 (1999).

52. Dinstein, *Laws of War*, 84.

53. Art. 4 of the Geneva Convention Relative to the Treatment of Prisoners of War (Geneva III) (Aug. 12, 1949), 75 U.N.T.S. 135.

54. Article 27 of the Fourth Geneva Convention, which establishes the basic provision of international humanitarian law in wartime, states, "Protected persons are entitled, in all circumstances, to respect for their persons, their honor, their family rights, their religious convictions and practices, and their manners and customs. They shall at all times be humanely treated, and shall be protected especially against all acts of violence or threats thereof and against insults and public curiosity. . . . However, the Parties to the conflict may take such measures of control and security in regard to protected persons as may be necessary as a result of the war." See Art. 27 of the Geneva Convention Relative to the Protection of Civilian Persons in Time of War (Geneva IV) (Aug. 12, 1949), 75 U.N.T.S. 287; *The Geneva Conventions of 12 August, 1949: Commentary* (J. S. Pictet ed., vol. 4, Geneva, 1958) 199.

55. Yoram Dinstein, *The Conduct of Hostilities under the Law of International Armed Conflict* (Cambridge: Cambridge University Press, 2004) 29; Rosa Ehrenreich Brooks, "War Everywhere: Rights, National Security Law, and the Law of Armed Conflict in the Age of Terror" 153 *U. Pa. L. Rev.* 675, 731 (2004).

56. White House Fact Sheet, Status of Detainees at Guantánamo, Office of the Press Sec'y (Feb. 7, 2002). Available at http://www.whitehouse.gov/news/releases/2002/02/20020207-13.html (accessed Sept. 20, 2004). For elaboration on the status of the Guantánamo detainees, see chap. 5.

57. Dinstein, *Laws of War*, 97.

58. Art. 43(3) of Protocol Additional to the Geneva Conventions of 12 August 1949, and Relating to the Protection of Victims of International Armed Conflicts (Protocol I) (June 8, 1977), 1125 U.N.T.S. 3.

59. Regulation 1, Annexed to the Hague Convention Respecting the Laws and Customs of War on Land (Hague IV) (Oct. 18, 1907).

60. Crona & Richardson, "Justice for War Criminals," 366.

61. Dov Waxman, "Terrorism: The War of the Future" 23 *Fletcher F. World Aff.* 201, 202–3 (1999).

62. For a different opinion, in support of the view that the Fourth Geneva Convention applies to all enemy nationals, including unlawful combatants, not protected by the other conventions, see Derek Jinks, "The Declining Significance of POW Status" 45 *Harv. Int'l L.J.* 367, 381–86 (2004).

63. *Ex parte Quirin et al.*, 317 U.S. 1, 30–31 (1942).

64. Harold Hongju Koh, "The Spirit of the Laws" 43 *Harv. Int'l L.J.* 23 (2002).

65. *Nicaragua* case, at 65.

66. Draft Articles on Responsibility of States for Internationally Wrongful Acts, Art. 8. Available at http://www.un.org/law/ilc/texts/State_responsibility/responsibility_articles(e).pdf. (accessed Mar. 19, 2004).

67. Derek Jinks, "September 11 and the Laws of War" 28 *Yale J. Int'l L.* 1, 23 (2003).

68. Ibid., 38–39.

69. Ibid., 47.

70. H.C. 2056/04, cited n. 37, paras. 44–85.

71. Inbar, *The War*, 72–75.

72. Address before a Joint Session of the Congress on the United States Response to the Terrorist Attacks of September 11, 37 *Weekly Comp. Pres.* DOC. 1347 (Sept. 20, 2001). Recently, the Bush administration has replaced the term "war" with the term "struggle," which has a broader meaning. See Eric Schmitt & Thom Shanker, "Washington Recasts Terror War as Struggle" *International Herald Tribune* (July 27, 2005), A8.

73. Waxman, *Terrorism*, 207.

74. Yossi Deskel, "Way of the Mind, Not the Might" [in Hebrew] *Ha'aretz* (Nov. 7, 2001) 2B.

75. Jeffrey D. Simon, *Misperceiving the Terrorist Threat* (Santa Monica, CA: Rand, 1987) 11.

76. Address before a Joint Session of the Congress (cited n. 72).

77. M. Cherif Bassiouni, *International Terrorism: Multilateral Conventions, 1937–2001* (Ardsley, NY: Transnational Publishers, 2001) 53.

78. Convention on the Marking of Plastic Explosives for the Purpose of Detection (Mar. 1, 1991); Convention on the Safety of United Nations and Associated Personnel, U.N. Doc. A/49/742 (1994); Convention for the Suppression of Terrorism Bombings, U.N. Doc. A/Res/52/164 (1998); International Convention for the Suppression of Financing of Terrorism, G.A. Res. 109, U.N. GAOR 6th Comm, 76th mtg., Agenda Item 160, U.N. Doc. A/54/109 (1999). There are also other proposals, e.g., Draft Convention on the Suppression of Acts of Nuclear Terrorism, U.N Doc. A/C.6/53/L.4 (1998); Draft Comprehensive Convention on International Terrorism, Working Document Submitted by India, U.N. Doc. A/C.6/55/1 (Aug. 28, 2000).

79. Bassiouni, *International Terrorism*, 67.

80. H.C. 168/91 *Marcus v. Minister of Defense et al.* [in Hebrew], 45(1) P.D. 467, 470.

THREE **Interrogation of Terrorists**

1. Art. 3 of the European Convention for the Protection of Human Rights and Fundamental Freedoms (Nov. 4, 1950), 213 U.N.T.S. 221; Art. 5 of the United Nations Universal Declaration of Human Rights, G.A. Res. 217A, U.N. GAOR, pt. 1, at 71, U.N. Doc. A/810 (1948); Art. 7 of the International Covenant on Civil and Political Rights (Dec. 19, 1966), 999 U.N.T.S. 3 (entered into force Mar. 23, 1976).

2. Art. 1(1) of the Convention against Torture and Other Cruel, Inhuman or Degrading Treatment or Punishment (Dec. 10, 1984), 1465 U.N.T.S. 85.

3. Human Rights Watch, *Torture and Ill-Treatment—Israel's Interrogation of Palestinians from the Occupied Territories*, 77–78 (1994).

4. *The Republic of Ireland v. The United Kingdom*, App. No. 5310/71, 2 Eur. Hum. Rts. Rep. 25 (1978) (hereafter, *Ireland* case).

5. Ibid., at 80.

6. Ibid., at 145.

7. Ibid.

8. Ibid., at 108–9.

9. Ibid., at 109.

10. Ibid., at 125, 127.

11. Daniel Statman, "The Question of Absolute Morality regarding the Prohibition on Torture" [in Hebrew] 4 *Law & Gov't* 161, 163 (1997).

12. Leon Shelef, "The Least Possible Evil and the Best Possible Good—on the Landau Report, Terrorism and Torture" [in Hebrew] 1 *Plilim* 185, 199–200 (1990).

13. Statman, "Question of Absolute Morality," 166–68.

14. Ibid.

15. Statman proceeds from this starting point, and even from the assumption that almost no one disputes this view.

16. David B. Kopel & Joseph Olson, "Preventing a Reign of Terror: Civil Liberties Implications of Terrorism Legislation" 21 *Okla. City U. L. Rev.* 247, 282 (1996).

17. Statman suggests the following test: if the authorization of the torture does not ensue from a preconception regarding the particular Islamic terrorist organization, then that form of interrogation will be authorized. Otherwise, it will not be authorized. See Statman, "Question of Absolute Morality," 179.

18. Mordechai Kremnitzer & Re'em Segev, "Exercising Force in GSS Interrogations—the Lesser Evil?" [in Hebrew] 4 *Law & Gov't* 667, 714 (1998).

19. Statman, "Question of Absolute Morality," 174.

20. Ibid., 185, 191.

21. Michael S. Moore, "Torture and the Balance of Evils" 23 *Israel L. Rev.* 280, 315 (1989).

22. Ibid., 296.

23. Ibid., 291–93.

24. Report of the Commission of Inquiry into the Methods of Investigation of the General Security Service regarding Hostile Terrorist Activity [in Hebrew] (Jerusalem, 1987) (hereafter, Landau Report) 1–3.

25. Section 34K of the Penal Law, 5737-1977: "A person will not bear criminal liability for committing any act immediately necessary for the purpose of saving the life, liberty, body or property, of either himself or his fellow person, from substantial danger of serious harm, imminent from the particular state of things, at the requisite timing, and absent alternative means for avoiding the harm."

26. Kremnitzer & Segev, "Exercising Force," 694.

27. Ibid., 722.

28. Landau Report, 35, 49–52.

29. S. Z. Feller, "Not Actual 'Necessity' but Possible 'Justification'; Not 'Moderate' Pressure, but Either 'Unlimited' or 'None at All'" 23 *Israel L. Rev.* 201, 207 (1989).

30. Section 34M of the Penal Law:
A person shall be exempt from criminal liability for an act performed in one of the following cases:
(1) He was obliged or authorized, by law, to perform it;
(2) He performed it by virtue of an order of a competent authority which he was obliged by law to obey, save if the order was manifestly unlawful;
(3) The act as a matter of law required consent, where the act was required immediately in order to save human life or his person, or to prevent serious damage to his health, and if in the circumstances of the case it was not possible for him to obtain the consent;

(4) He performed it on a person with lawful consent, during a medical act or treatment, the purpose of which was his good or the good of another;
He performed it during a sporting activity or sporting game, which is not prohibited by law and which is not contrary to the public good, and in accordance with the rules practiced therein.

31. John Smith & Brian Hogan, *Criminal Law* (8th ed., London: Butterworths, 1996) 251–59.

32. Aharon Barak, *Interpretation in Law* [in Hebrew] (vol. 3: Constitutional Interpretation, Jerusalem: Nevo, 1994) 386–88.

33. Feller, "Not Actual 'Necessity,'" 212.

34. Sanford H. Kadish, "Torture, the State and the Individual" 23 *Israel L. Rev.* 345, 354 (1989).

35. Ibid.

36. Ibid., 355.

37. Ibid., 355–56.

38. Alan M. Dershowitz, "Is It Necessary to Apply 'Physical Pressure' to Terrorists—and to Lie about It?" 23 *Israel L. Rev.* 192, 197 (1989).

39. H.C. 5100/94 *The Public Committee against Torture in Israel et al. v. Government of Israel et al.* [in Hebrew], 53(4) P.D. 817, 841–42 (hereafter, GSS interrogation case), emphasis added. It should be noted that in that judgment it was not decided conclusively whether the defense that should be available to the interrogator is the defense of necessity or the defense of justification, and whether such a defense is actually valid.

40. Ibid., judgment of Justice Yaakov Kedmi.

41. Ibid., at 835.

42. In the GSS interrogation case, it was held for the first time that the methods described below are illegal.

43. For an extensive description of the range of investigative means used by GSS interrogators against persons suspected of involvement in terrorist activities, see *Torture as Routine: The Methods of Interrogation of the GSS*, B'Tselem—The Israeli Information Center for Human Rights in the Occupied Territories (Jerusalem, Feb. 1998); Human Rights Watch, *Torture and Ill-Treatment*, 111–46.

44. *Torture as Routine*, 14.

45. Ibid., 23.

46. Ibid., 17–18. For an additional description of the various methods used, see Human Rights Watch, *Torture and Ill-Treatment*, 27–29.

47. GSS interrogation case, at 836.

48. Ibid., at 836–40.

49. *Ireland* case, at 59.

50. Ibid., at 60–61.

51. Ibid., at 66, 70–71.

52. Ibid., at 79–80.

53. Ibid., at 133.

54. Ibid., at 138.

55. Ibid., at 143–44.

56. It should be pointed out that the European Commission on Human Rights was also of the opinion that the five techniques listed above amounted to torture.

See Evelyn Mary Aswad, "Torture by Means of Rape" 84 *Geo. L.J.* 1913, 1927 (1996).

57. *Ireland* case, at 107.

58. *Position Paper: Legislation Permitting Physical and Mental Pressure in GSS Interrogations,* B'Tselem—The Israeli Information Center for Human Rights in the Occupied Territories (Jerusalem, Jan. 2000) 50–51.

59. David R. Lowry, "Draconian Powers: The New British Approach to Pretrial Detention of Suspected Terrorists" 8–9 *Columbia Hum. Rts. L. Rev.* 185, 204–5 (1976–77).

60. *Position paper,* 70, 50.

61. *A and Others v. Secretary of State for the Home Department,* [2004] EWCA CIV 1123, [2004] All ER (D) 62 (Aug.) (approved judgment).

62. *A and Others v. Secretary of State for the Home Department and Conjoined cases* [2005], UKHL 71.

63. For elaboration, see chap. 5 above.

64. Stephen Grey & Ian Cobain, "Suspect's Tale of Travel and Torture: Alleged Bomb Plotter Claims 2? Years of Interrogation under US and UK Supervision in 'Ghost Prisons' Abroad" *Guardian* (London) (Aug. 2, 2005), 6.

65. Seth F. Kreimer, "Too Close to the Rack and the Screw: Constitutional Constraints on Torture in the War on Terror" 6 *U. Pa. J. Const. L.* 278, 310–17 (2003).

66. See the judgment in *Ingraham v. Wright,* 430 U.S. 651 (1977), as well as the position of Alan Dershowitz regarding the absence of a constitutional obstacle to torturing a terrorist who refuses to reveal what is known to him because he does not want to undermine his colleagues' murderous plans in a situation where there is no other way to prevent the attack from being foiled. Dershowitz, *Why Terrorism Works: Understanding the Threat, Responding to the Challenge* (New Haven: Yale University Press, 2002) 131–63.

67. *Position paper,* 51–52, 55.

68. John T. Elliff, "The Attorney General's Guidelines for FBI Investigations" 69 *Cornell L. Rev.* 785, 786 (1984).

69. Melissa A. O'Loughlin, "Terrorism: The Problem and the Solution—the Comprehensive Terrorism Prevention Act of 1995" 22 *J. Legis.* 103, 104 (1996).

70. Elliff, "Attorney General's Guidelines," 786, 791.

71. Kopel & Olson, "Preventing a Reign of Terror," 320.

72. Elliff, "Attorney General's Guidelines," 797–803; A. G. Theoharis, "FBI Surveillance: Past and Present" 69 *Cornell L. Rev.* 883, 889 (1984).

73. Neil A. Lewis & Eric Schmitt, "Lawyers Decided Bans on Torture Didn't Bind Bush" *New York Times* (June 8, 2004); Adam Liptak, "Legal Scholars Criticize Memos on Torture" *New York Times* (June 25, 2004).

74. White House Fact Sheet, Status of Detainees at Guantánamo, Office of the Press Sec'y (Feb. 7, 2002). Available at http://www.whitehouse.gov/news/releases/2002/02/20020207-13.html (accessed Sept. 20, 2004). For elaboration, see chap. 5.

75. Kate Zernike, "Defining Torture: Russian Roulette, Yes. Mind-Altering Drugs, Maybe." *New York Times* (June 27, 2004).

76. Detainee Treatment Act of 2005, 109 Pub. L. No. 109-148, 119 Stat. 2680; Elisabeth Bumiller, "How Bush Tries Shaping New Laws to His Liking: White House Letter" *International Herald Tribune* (Jan. 16, 2006) 2.

77. For a similar opinion, see also Jackson Diehl, "How Torture Came Down from the Top" *Washington Post* (Aug. 27, 2004).

78. Art. 4 of the Covenant on Civil and Political Rights (cited n. 1), United Nations Human Rights Committee (General Comment No. 29 Regarding Art. 4 to the International Covenant on Civil and Political Rights) (Aug. 31, 2001), para. 7.

79. Protocol Additional to the Geneva Conventions of 12 August 1949, and Relating to the Protection of Victims of International Armed Conflicts (Protocol I) (June 8, 1977), 1125 U.N.T.S. 3; Geneva Convention for the Amelioration of the Condition of the Wounded and Sick in Armed Forces in the Field (Geneva I) (Aug. 12, 1949), 75 U.N.T.S. 31; Geneva Convention for the Amelioration of the Condition of the Wounded, Sick and Shipwrecked Members of the Armed Forces at Sea (Geneva II) (Aug. 12, 1949), 75 U.N.T.S. 85.

80. Geneva Convention Relative to the Treatment of Prisoners of War (Geneva III) (Aug. 12, 1949), 75 U.N.T.S. 135; Geneva Convention Relative to the Protection of Civilian Persons in Time of War (Geneva IV) (Aug. 12, 1949), 75 U.N.T.S. 287.

81. International Criminal Tribunal for the Former Yugoslavia, Trial Chamber, *Prosecutor v. Furundzija* (1998), Case IT-95-17/1, 121 ILR 213, 254–57, 260–61; *Case of Al-Adsani v. The United Kingdom*, App. No. 35763/97, paras. 60–61 (Nov. 21, 2001). Available at http://hudoc.echr.coe.int/Hudoc2doc2/HEJUD/200308/al-adsani .batj.doc (accessed Mar. 24, 2004).

82. Aharon Barak, "The Rule of Law and the Supremacy of the Constitution" [in Hebrew] 5 *Law & Gov't* 375, 381 (2000).

83. For the importance of conducting such a discussion, see Oren Gross, "Are Torture Warrants Warranted? Pragmatic Absolutism and Official Disobedience" 88 *Minn. L. Rev.* 1481, 1553–54 (2004).

FOUR **Administrative Powers of Military Commanders in the Struggle against Terrorism**

1. H.C. 428/86 *Barzilai v. Government of Israel* [in Hebrew], 40(3) P.D. 505, 621, 622.

2. H.C. 5100/94 *Public Committee against Torture in Israel v. Government of Israel* [in Hebrew], 53(4) P.D. 817, 845.

3. Dexter Filkins, "Tough New Tactics by U.S. Tighten Grip on Iraq Towns" *New York Times* (Dec. 7, 2003).

4. Defense (Emergency) Regulations, 1945, O.G. 1442, Supp. 2, p. 855.

5. H.C. 4697/91 *Salam et al. v. Commander of I.D.F. Forces in the West Bank* [in Hebrew], 46(5) P.D. 467, 473.

6. Regulation 43, Annexed to the Hague Convention Respecting the Laws and Customs of War on Land (Hague IV) (Oct. 18, 1907). Even though Israel redeployed its forces and effectively left Gaza in August 2005, the local law remains in force.

7. Justice Cheshin in H.C. 4772/91 *Hizran v. Commander of I.D.F. Forces in Judea and Samaria* [in Hebrew], 46(2) P.D. 150, 156.

8. Sec. 3: "There shall be no violation of the property of a person"; Sec. 10: "This Basic Law shall not affect the validity of any law in force prior to the commencement of the Basic Law"; Sec. 8: "There shall be no violation of rights under this Basic Law except by a law befitting the values of the State of Israel, enacted for a proper purpose, and to an extent no greater than is required." Basic Law: Human Dignity and Liberty [in Hebrew], S.H. 1391, 1992, 150.

9. H.C. 798/89 *Shukri v. Minister of Defense* [in Hebrew] (not yet published).

10. H.C. 2006/97 *Janimat et al. v. Commander of the Central Command* [in Hebrew], 51(2) P.D. 651.

11. Ibid.

12. Editorial, "The Houses Were Destroyed, the Hatred Was Enhanced" [in Hebrew] *Ha'aretz* (Feb. 17, 2005). On February 2005 a military committee appointed by the commander in chief of the IDF to examine the influence of house demolitions determined that the practice had not only failed to achieve its goal to deter potential terrorists but also intensified the hatred and animosity among the Palestinian public. Owing to the committee's findings, the minister of defense ordered the IDF to stop this practice, unless unusual circumstances require otherwise in the future. See ibid.

13. Quoted in Smadar Peri, "My Son, the Suicide Attacker" [in Hebrew] *Yedioth Aharonot* (Oct. 10, 2002).

14. Justice Matza, in H.C. 6026/94 *Nazal et al. v. Commander of I.D.F. Forces in Judea and Samaria* [in Hebrew], 48(5) P.D. 338, 347–48.

15. H.C. 6696/02 *Amar et al. v. Commander of I.D.F. Forces in Judea and Samaria* [in Hebrew], 56(6) P.D. 110, 115. See comments of President Barak to the effect that the

> non-application of the right to be heard in the case of a military operation is derived from the balance between the right of the individual to be heard in respect of the injury to his person or to his property, on one hand, and the essential public need to carry out the military operation—a need behind which, *inter alia*, lies concern for the safety and lives of the soldiers—on the other. Accordingly, if there is a serious fear that granting a right to be heard may endanger the lives of the soldiers and frustrate the operation itself, the right to be heard is deferred to essential fighting needs. However, where the danger (to the soldiers) and the possibility (of not carrying out the operation) do not exist, the right to be heard reverts to its place, and it would be right to implement it even in cases of military activities. Consequently, if in the circumstances of a specific case there is no real fear for the lives of the soldiers or the success of the operation, the right to be heard must be implemented. Moreover, even in a case where the right to be heard should not be implemented in full, everything should be done to implement it in part, for example, in a hearing before the military commander in the area prior to him damaging the property. Finally, the more the force of the right to be heard lessens in cases of essential military need, the greater the need to ensure that the military commander possesses verified and well-founded data that circumstances indeed exist which justify, from his point of view, the use of the operational measure.

16. It should be pointed out that this position relies on a very problematic legal basis, since the Fourth Geneva Convention does not make the application of its provisions contingent upon recognition of property rights, but rather applies to every case of full or partial occupation of the territory of a signatory party. See Art. 2 of the Geneva Convention Relative to the Protection of Civilian Persons in Time of War (Geneva IV) (Aug. 12, 1949), 75 U.N.T.S. 287.

17. H.C. 7015/02 *Ajuri et al. v. Commander of I.D.F. Forces in Judea and Samaria et al.* [in Hebrew], 56(6) P.D. 352, 363–64.

18. Art. 64 of the Fourth Geneva Convention.

19. Cheryl V. Reicin, "Preventive Detention, Curfews, Demolitions of Houses, and Deportations: An Analysis of Measures Employed by Israel in the Administered Territories," 8 *Cardozo L. Rev.* 515, 521 (1987).

20. Deuteronomy 24:16.

21. Yoram Dinstein, "The International Law of Belligerent Occupation and Human Rights," 8 *Isr. Y. B. Hum. Rts.* 104, 141 (1978): "The article does not make it clear when the population can be held jointly responsible for individual acts, nor does it answer the question whether vicarious individual responsibility of one person for the acts of another (usually his relative) is admissible. Article 33 of the Convention solves this dual problem by banning collective penalties generally as well as all punishment of a person for an offence which he has not personally committed."

22. Regarding this concept, see the compilation of the official interpretation of the Fourth Geneva Convention, published by the International Committee of the Red Cross:

[T]he occupying forces may . . . undertake the total or partial destruction of certain private or public property in the occupied territory when imperative military requirements so demand. Furthermore, it will be for the occupying power to judge the importance of such military requirements. It is therefore to be feared that bad faith in the application of the reservation may render the proposed safeguard valueless, for unscrupulous recourse to the clause concerning military necessity would allow the occupant power to circumvent the prohibition set forth in the convention. The occupying power must therefore try to interpret the clause in a reasonable manner: Whenever it is felt essential to resort to destruction, the occupant authorities must try to keep a sense of proportion in comparing the military advantage to be gained with the damage done.

The Geneva Conventions of 12 August, 1949: Commentary (J.S. Pictet ed., vol. 4, Geneva, 1958) 302.

23. H.C. 2722/92 *Alamrin v. Commander of I.D.F. Forces in Gaza Strip* [in Hebrew], 46(3) P.D. 693, 699–700.

24. Dan Simon, "The Demolition of Homes in Israeli Occupied Territories," 19 *Yale. J. Int'l L.* 1, 69 (1994).

25. H.C. 1730/96 *Sabich v. Commander of I.D.F. Forces in Judea and Samaria* [in Hebrew], 50(1) P.D. 353, 364; emphasis added.

26. In those cases in which private property was seized in order to facilitate an urgent military need, the military must pay compensation for the damage to property. See, e.g., the case discussed in H.C. 4112/90 *Association for Civil Rights in Israel v. Commander of Southern Command* [in Hebrew], 44(4) P.D. 626.

27. Sec. 8 of Basic Law: Human Dignity and Liberty [in Hebrew]; H.C. 6893/05 *MK Yitzhak Levy et al. v. Government of Israel* [in Hebrew], 59(2) P.D. 876, para. 14.

28. H.C. 393/82 *Cooperative Society v. O.C. Judea and Samaria Areas* [in Hebrew], 37(4) P.D. 785, 810.

29. See the comments of Justice Elon in the *Association for Civil Rights in Israel* case, at 631: "But since the right to be heard is a basic right in the Israeli legal system, it is both appropriate and correct that it be implemented in any case where an Israeli authority functions, even if the law in that place, whether domestic or pub-

lic international, does not require such application. The silence of domestic and international public law on this matter is not a negative arrangement."

30. H.C. 361/82 *Hamri v. Commander of Judea and Samaria* [in Hebrew], 36(3) P.D. 439, 442.

31. Emanuel Gross, "Human Rights in Administrative Proceedings: A Quest for Appropriate Evidentiary Standards" 31 *Cal. West. Int'l L.J.* 215 (2001).

32. H.C. 4764/04 *Physicians for Human Rights et al. v. Commander of I.D.F Forces in Gaza Strip* [in Hebrew], 58(5) P.D. 385; H.C. 3451/02 *Almandi et al. v. Minister of Defense et al.* [in Hebrew], 56(3) P.D. 30.

33. This is true even though the Supreme Court stressed the need to allow the residents during a curfew to come before the court and state their objections regarding the legality of the curfew. See, e.g., H.C. 1358/91 *Arshid et al. v. Minister of the Police* [in Hebrew], 45(2) P.D. 747.

34. H.C. 7277/94 *Anon. v. Military Governor in Gaza Strip* [in Hebrew] (not yet published).

35. Justice Zamir in H.C. 1759/94 *Srozberg et al. v. Minister of Defense* [in Hebrew], 55(1) P.D. 625, 628.

36. International Covenant on Economic, Social and Cultural Rights (Dec. 16, 1966), 999 U.N.T.S. 171 (entered into force Jan. 3, 1976).

FIVE **Administrative Detentions and the Use of Terrorists as Bargaining Counters**

1. F.Cr H. 7048/97 *Anon. v. Minister of Defense* [in Hebrew], 54(1) P.D. 721 (hereafter, F.H. *Anon.*).

2. Ibid., at 744.

3. Federalist No. 84 (Alexander Hamilton), *The Federalist Papers* (New York: New American Library, 1961) 512.

4. The Emergency Powers (Arrest) Law [in Hebrew], 5739-1979, S.H. 930, p. 76 (hereafter, Administrative Detention Law).

5. See the Order Regarding Administrative Detention (Temporary Provisions) (Judea and Samaria) (No. 1229), 5748-1988, as well as the Order Regarding Administrative Detention (Temporary Provisions) (Gaza Strip) (No. 941), 5748-1988.

6. H.C. 1635/90 *Zharzhevski v. Prime Minister et al.* [in Hebrew], 48(1) P.D. 749, 855–57.

7. According to Sec. 4 of the Administrative Detention Law, if the order is not confirmed by the court within forty-eight hours, the detainee must be released.

8. H.C. 4400/98 *Baraham v. Legal Judge* [in Hebrew], 52(5) P.D. 337, 342–43.

9. A.A.D. 1/88 *Agbariyya v. State of Israel* [in Hebrew], 42(1) P.D. 840, 844–45.

10. A.A.D. 2/86 *Anon. v. Minister of Defense* [in Hebrew], 41(2) P.D. 508, 514–16.

11. Emanuel Gross, "Criminal Code in Time of Emergency" [in Hebrew] 3 *Law & Gov't* 263, 267–68 (1995).

12. H.C. 5591/02 *Yassin et al. v. Kziot Prison Facility* [in Hebrew], 57(1) P.D. 403.

13. *Brogan et al. v. United Kingdom*, 11 Eur. H.R. Rep. 117 (1988).

14. See, e.g., Lord Shacldeton, Report of the Operation of the Prevention of Terrorism (Temporary Provisions) Acts 1974 and 1976 (1978), summary available at http://www.bopcris.ac.uk/bop1974/ref4807.html (accessed Apr. 4, 2004).

15. See, e.g., *R. v. McIlkenny* [1992] 2 All E.R. 417, C.A; *R. v. Maguire* [1992] 1 Q.B. 936, C.A.

16. Terrorism Act, 2000, c. 11, sec. 41, schedule 8.

17. Anti-terrorism, Crime and Security Act, 2001, c. 24.

18. See the explanatory notes to the act which were prepared by the government departments. Available at http://www.hmso.gov.uk/acts/en/2001en24.htm (accessed Apr. 4, 2004).

19. *A and Others v. Secretary of State for the Home Department*, [2002] EWCA Civ 1502.

20. *A and Others v. Secretary of State for the Home Department*, [2004] UKHL 56.

21. Prevention of Terrorism Act, 2005, c. 2.

22. David Cole, *Enemy Aliens: Double Standards and Constitutional Freedoms in the War on Terrorism* (New York: New Press, 2003) 116–28.

23. *Korematsu v. United States*, 323 U.S. 214 (1944).

24. C. Edwin Baker, "Limitations on Basic Human Rights—a View from the United States," in *The Limitation of Human Rights in Comparative Constitutional Law* (A. de Mestral et al. eds., Cowansville, 1986) 75, 97 (quoting the U.S. Commission on Wartime Relocation and Internment of Civilians).

25. *Center for National Security Studies et al. v. U.S. Department of Justice*, 331 F.3d 918 (App. D.C., 2003).

26. Ibid.

27. The report published by the Justice Department's inspector general stated that many of the detentions relied on general suspicions, such as anonymous tips delivered to the FBI by members of the public who thought their Arab neighbors might be keeping odd schedules. Likewise, the report revealed that when FBI agents arrived at a particular place when searching for persons suspected of involvement in the September 11 attacks, they would detain all the aliens found in the location, without distinguishing between the actual suspects and others incidentally there, in an effort to ensure that no terrorist was inadvertently set free. See Office of the Inspector General, U.S. Department of Justice, "The September 11 Detainees: A Review of the Treatment of Aliens Held on Immigration Charges in Connection with the Investigation of the September 11 Attacks" (June 2003), 15–17. Available at http://www.usdoj.gov/oig/special/0306/full.pdf (accessed Sept. 20, 2004).

28. Ibid., 69–71; Danny Hakim, "2 Arabs Convicted and 2 Cleared of Terrorist Plot against the U.S." *New York Times* (June 4, 2003).

29. Pub. L. No. 107-40, 115 Stat. 224 (2001).

30. Military Order—Detention, Treatment and Trial of Certain Non-Citizens in the War against Terrorism, 66 Fed. Reg. 57, 833 (Nov. 16, 2001).

31. Department of Defense—Military Commission Order No. 1 (Mar. 21, 2002).

32. White House Fact Sheet, Status of Detainees at Guantánamo, Office of the Press Sec'y (Feb. 7, 2002). Available at http://www.whitehouse.gov/news/releases/2002/02/20020207-13.html (accessed Sept. 20, 2004).

33. Ibid. See also Anthony Lewis, "Civil Liberties in a Time of Terror" 2003 *Wis. L. Rev.* 257, 260–61.

34. For elaboration, see chap. 2, pp. 47–54.

35. Neil A. Lewis, "2 Prosecutors Faulted Trials for Detainees" *New York Times* (Aug. 1, 2005) A1.

36. *Salim Ahmed Hamdan v. Donald H. Rumsfeld*, 344 F. Supp. 2d 152, 2004 U.S.

Dist. (D.D.C., 2004); *Salim Ahmed Hamdan v. Donald H. Rumsfeld, United States Secretary of Defense, et al.*, No. 04-5393, 2005 U.S. App.

37. *Ex parte Quirin*, 317 U.S. 1, 37–38 (1942).

38. It should be pointed out that the Non-Detention Act of 1972 provides that "[n]o citizen shall be imprisoned or otherwise detained by the United States except pursuant to an act of Congress" (18 U.S.C. sec. 4001(a)) and therefore the question is, first, whether the act applies only to the civilian arrest of a citizen or also when he is arrested under the laws of war; and second, whether it is possible to regard Congress's decision of 2001 to grant the president powers to fight terrorism as an empowering law. For the various views, see *Jose Padilla v. Donald Rumsfeld*, 352 F.3d 695 (2003); Brief for the Petitioner in the matter of *Donald H. Rumsfeld, Secretary of Defense v. Jose Padilla*, at 32–49 (Docket No. 03-1027).

39. The government has emphasized that it exercises great caution in these situations, and that when it is suspected that an American citizen is an "enemy combatant," in accordance with the legal standard established in the *Quirin* case, a multistage process commences that involves a number of independent bodies. An initial examination is conducted by the Justice Department relying on the information available at the time, to decide whether a person meets the above standard. Thereafter, the director of the CIA also conducts a comprehensive examination of the intelligence evidence concerning the particular person and provides a recommendation to the Ministry of Justice. The secretary of defense then conducts his own individual assessment relying on the intelligence known to his department at the time. The assessment of the secretary of defense, as well as the intelligence gathered by the CIA and the Department of Defense, and additional information held by the FBI and other sources, is transmitted to the attorney general, who must give his opinion whether it is possible from a legal point of view, and right on a policy level, to take the person into custody as an enemy combatant. All the existing evidentiary material, together with the recommendations of the various bodies and the attorney general, are provided to the president. Attorneys at the White House examine the material and counsel to the president transmits the material and his recommendation to the president in writing. The president considers the materials given to him. If he concludes that the person is indeed an enemy combatant, he signs an order requiring the secretary of defense to take the person into his custody. See *Rumsfeld v. Padilla*, Brief for the Petitioner, at 6–7.

40. *Rasul et al. v. Bush, President of the United States, et al.*, 124 S.Ct. 2686 (2004).

41. *Rumsfeld, Secretary of Defense v. Padilla et al.*, 124 S.Ct. 2711 (2004); *Hamdi et al. v. Rumsfeld, Secretary of Defense, et al.* 124 S.Ct. 2633 (2004).

42. *Hamdi et al. v. Rumsfeld, Secretary of Defense, et al.*, at 25.

43. Ibid., at 26–27.

44. Todd S. Purdum, "In Classic Check and Balance, Court Shows Bush It Also Has Wartime Powers" *New York Times* (June 29, 2004).

45. *Hamdi et al. v. Rumsfeld, Secretary of Defense, et al.*, at 23.

46. Stephen J. Schulhofer, "Checks and Balances in Wartime: American, British and Israeli Experiences" 102 *Mich. L. Rev.* 1906, 1913–14 (2004).

47. The American government has clarified that it does not intend to try American citizens before these military tribunals but only before the federal court. Nonetheless, this clarification is based primarily on political considerations and not

on compliance with binding legal standards. See Editorial, "Reaffirming the Rule of Law" *New York Times* (June 29, 2004).

48. *Hamdi et al. v. Rumsfeld, Secretary of Defense, et al.*, at 12–14; *Rasul et al. v. Bush, President of the United States, et al.*, at 17.

49. *Hamdi et al. v. Rumsfeld, Secretary of Defense, et al.*, at 32; *Rasul et al. v. Bush, President of the United States, et al.*, at 17.

50. U.S. Const. amend. XIV; Bernard Schwartz, *Constitutional Law* (2nd ed., New York: Macmillan, 1979) 11–17.

51. Although in the *Rasul v. Bush* decision the Supreme Court held that federal courts have jurisdiction to consider challenges to the legality of the detention of foreign nationals incarcerated at Guantánamo Bay, it did not determine whether those detainees have any judicially enforceable rights to violate, thus leaving the judicial arena open to irreconcilable opinions of lower courts. For example, on January 19, 2005, Judge Richard J. Leon of the U.S. district court concluded that no viable legal theory existed by which it could intervene in the military's handling of detentions at Guantánamo. Two weeks later, Judge Joyce Hens Green of the same court reached the opposite conclusion. In her opinion, in light of the Supreme Court's decision in *Rasul v. Bush*, it was clear that Guantánamo Bay must be considered the equivalent of a U.S. territory, in which fundamental constitutional rights apply. Accordingly, the detainees at Guantánamo Bay have the fundamental right not to be deprived of liberty without due process of law, under the Fifth Amendment to the Constitution. As a result, the court determined that the procedures implemented by the Combatant Status Review Tribunal (CSRT)—a military tribunal created by the government shortly after the issuance of the Supreme Court's decision to review the status of each detainee at Guantánamo Bay as an "enemy combatant"—did not comply with the necessary constitutional requirements and violated the petitioners' rights to due process of law under the Fifth Amendment. Inter alia, the CSRT procedures failed to provide the detainees with access to the material evidence on which the tribunal affirmed their "enemy combatant" status; it failed to permit the assistance of counsel to compensate for the government's refusal to disclose classified information directly to the detainees; it relied on statements allegedly obtained through torture or otherwise alleged to have been provided by some detainees involuntarily; and the definition of "enemy combatant" in the CSRT order is vague and potentially overly broad. See *Ridouane Khalid v. George Walker Bush et al.*, Civil Case No. 1:04-1142 (RJL) (decided Jan. 19, 2005); *In re Guantánamo Detainee Cases*, Civil Case No. 02–CV-0299 (CKK) (decided Jan. 31, 2005).

52. *Johnson v. Eisentrager*, 339 U.S. 763 (1950).

53. F.H. *Anon.*, at 738–39.

54. Ibid., at 743.

55. A.A.D. 10/94 *Anon. v. Minister of Defense* [in Hebrew], 53(1) P.D. 97, 107.

56. Ibid., at 108.

57. Ibid., at 106.

58. Ibid., at 112.

59. Justice Dorner gave a dissenting opinion in the initial judgment on appeal, and concurred with the majority opinion in the Further Hearing, whereas President Barak explained that after he perused and rethought the matter, he reached the conclusion that he had been mistaken in his first judgment.

60. F.H. *Anon.*, at 749.

61. Art. 1. of the International Convention against the Taking of Hostages (Dec. 17, 1979) 18 *ILM* 1456: "Any person who seized or detains and threatens to kill, to injure or to continue to detain another person (hereinafter referred to as the 'hostage') in order to compel a third party, namely, a state, an international inter-governmental organization, a natural or juridical person, or a group of persons, to do or abstain from doing any act as an explicit or implicit condition for the release of the hostage commits the offence of taking of hostages ('hostage-taking') within the meaning of this Convention."

62. F.H. *Anon.*, at 744–45.

63. Imprisonment of Illegal Combatants Law [in Hebrew], 5762-2002, S.H. 1834, p. 192.

64. Ibid., Art. 1.

65. *Secretary of State for the Home Department v. M*, All E.R. 367 (C.A.) [2004].

SIX **The Right to Privacy in Times of Terrorism**

1. "The right to be let alone," in the words of Warren & Brandeis, adopting the expression coined by Judge T. Cooley. See Samuel D. Warren and Louis D. Brandeis, "The Right to Privacy" 4 *Harv. L. Rev.* 193 (1890).

2. Alan F. Westin, *Privacy and Freedom* (5th ed., New York: Atheneum, 1968) 13.

3. M. C. Slough, *Privacy, Freedom and Responsibility* (Springfield, 1969) 3.

4. Arthur R. Miller, *The Assault on Privacy* (Ann Arbor: University of Michigan Press, 1971) 25.

5. Charles Fried, "Privacy (a Moral Analysis)," in *Philosophical Dimensions of Privacy: An Anthology* (Ferdinand D. Schoeman ed., Cambridge: Cambridge University Press, 1984) 210.

6. Deckle Mclean, *Privacy and Its Invasion* (Westport, CT: Praeger, 1995) 49 (quoting Robert Ellis Smith's definition).

7. Hyman Gross, "Privacy and Autonomy," in *Privacy* (R. J. Pennock & J. W. Chapman eds., New York: Atherton Press, 1971) 169.

8. Ruth Gavison, "Privacy and the Limits of Law" 89 *Yale L.J.* 421, 423 (1980); Sissela Bok, *Secrets: On the Ethics of Concealment and Revelation* (New York: Pantheon Books, 1982) 11.

9. See generally Fried, *Philosophical Dimensions*; Sidney M. Jourard, "Some Psychological Aspects of Privacy" 31 *Law & Contemp. Probs.* 307 (1966).

10. David Leppard et al., "Cornered" *Sunday Times* (London) (July 31, 2005) 13.

11. Apart from eavesdropping on telephone conversations, it is possible to tap their identifying details, i.e., to record the telephone numbers dialed from a particular telephone number (by means of a device known as a pen register), the telephone numbers calling in (by means of a trap-and-trace device), and the time and duration of the call. Clifford S. Fishman & Anne T. McKenna, *Wiretapping and Eavesdropping* (2nd ed., vol. 1, Deerfield, IL: Clark Callaghan, 1995) 5:11 at 5-15, 5-16.

12. The Carnivore program underwent three rhetorical cycles. The FBI began developing it in 1997 under the name Omnivore, but in 1999 the name was changed to Carnivore. However, because both names had an immediate negative connotation, in 2001 the program was given a neutral technical name, Digital Collection

System 1000 (DCS-1000). But since Carnivore was the name that took hold in the public mind, I shall refer to the program by that name.

13. Steven Salvador Flores, "Gun Detector Technology and the Special Needs Exception" 25 *Rutgers Computer & Tech. L.J.* 135, 139 (1999).

14. Clifford S. Fishman, "Electronic Tracking Devices and the Fourth Amendment: Knotts, Karo and the Questions Still Unanswered" 34 *Cath. U. L. Rev.* 277, 281–82 (1985).

15. Matthew Mickle Werdegar, "Lost? The Government Knows Where You Are: Cellular Telephone Call Location Technology and the Expectation of Privacy" 10 *Stan. L. & Pol.* 103, 105–6 (1998).

16. John D. Woodward, "Biometric Scanning, Law and Policy: Identifying the Concerns—Drafting the Biometric Blueprint" 59 *U. Pitt. L. Rev.* 97, 99–101 (1997).

17. The best-known initiative to establish a super data bank was that taken by the U.S. Department of Defense to create the TIA (Total Information Awareness). A certain repugnance for this name caused it to be changed to Terrorism Information Awareness. See http://www.darpa.mil/body/tia/TIA%20ES.pdf (accessed Apr. 28, 2004).

18. Donna Smith, "Passenger Profiling: A Greater Terror than Terrorism Itself" 32 *J. Marshall L. Rev.* 167, 168–72 (1998).

19. See, e.g., "Government Agency Releases Documents on 'No Fly' List," Press Release, American Civil Liberties Union, http://www.aclu.org/SafeandFree/SafeandFree.cfm?ID=13193&c=206 (accessed Apr. 28, 2004); H.C. 4950/90 *Tikvah Franz et al. v. Minister of Defense et al.* [in Hebrew], 47(3) P.D. 36.

20. Tamar Rotem, "First the Shock of the Explosion, Afterward the Fear That They Will Think That I Am a Terrorist" [in Hebrew] *Ha'aretz* (Sept. 29, 2002).

21. International Covenant on Civil and Political Rights (Dec. 19, 1966), 999 U.N.T.S. 3 (entered into force Mar. 23, 1976).

22. Sec. 7 of Basic Law: Human Dignity and Liberty [in Hebrew], S.H. 1391, 1992, 150, provides that:

(a) All persons have the right to privacy and to intimacy.

(b) There shall be no entry into the private premises of a person who has not consented thereto.

(c) No search shall be conducted on the private premises of a person, nor in his body or personal effects.

(d) There shall be no violation of the confidentiality of conversation, or of the writings or records of a person.

23. H.C. 2481/93 *Dayan v. Superintendent of the Jerusalem District* [in Hebrew], 48(2) P.D. 456, at 470.

24. H.C. 3815/90 *Gilat v. Minister of Police* [in Hebrew], 45(3) P.D. 414, 423.

25. Sec. 8 of Basic Law: Human Dignity and Liberty [in Hebrew].

26. Aharon Barak, *Interpretation in Law* [in Hebrew] (vol. 3: Constitutional Interpretation, Jerusalem: Nevo, 1994) 536.

27. Aharon Barak, "Comments at the Opening of the Legal Year 2002" [in Hebrew] 16 *Law & Army* 1, 2–5 (2002).

28. Sec. 25 of the Criminal Procedure (Arrest and Searches) Ordinance (New Version) [in Hebrew] 5729-1969, N.V. 12, 1969 284.

29. Sec. 23, ibid.

30. Sec. 22, ibid.; Sec. 1 of the Criminal Procedure (Powers of Enforcement—Searches of the Body of the Suspect) Law [in Hebrew] 5756-1996, S.H. 1573 136 (hereafter, Criminal Procedure Law).

31. Sec. 9 and 10 of the General Security Service Law [in Hebrew] 5762-2002, S.H. 1832, 179 (hereafter, the GSS Law).

32. Sec. 9 of the Air Navigation (Safety of Civil Aviation) Law [in Hebrew], 5757-1977, S.H. 854, 126 (hereafter, the Civil Aviation Law).

33. Sec. 3 of the Powers of Search (Emergency) Temporary Provision) Law [in Hebrew], 5729-1969, S.H. 571, 226.

34. H.C. 297/82 *Berger v. Minister of the Interior* [in Hebrew], 37(3) P.D. 29, 34.

35. H.C. 721/94 *El Al Israel Airlines Ltd. v. Danielovitz* [in Hebrew], 48(5) P.D. 749, 759–60.

36. In response to the series of terrorist attacks in the London public transportation system in July 2005, the mayor of New York ordered the police to start conducting random bag searches in the transit networks of the city. However, the searches are not being conducted according to the profiling system, but according to a certain rate that is not subject to the officers' discretion—i.e., one out of every five (or more) passengers is to be searched.

Although such a policy can reassure the public and provide a sense of personal safety, it is likely to be ineffective. Furthermore, it disproportionately infringes the right to privacy of people who do not possess any of the characteristics of a potential terrorist. See Sewell Chan & Kareem Fahim, "Legal Issues Being Raised on Searches in Subways" *New York Times* (July 24, 2005) 25; Paul Sperry, "It's the Age of Terror: What Would You Do?" *New York Times* (July 28, 2005) A25.

37. Ellen Baker, "Flying While Arab—Racial Profiling and Air Travel Security" 67 *J. Air L. & Com.* 1375, 1378, 1398 (2002).

38. Sec. 26 of the Criminal Procedure Law; Misc. App. (Jerusalem) [in Hebrew] 1153/02 *State of Israel v. Abergil* (as yet unpublished), paras. 26–28.

39. H.C. *Franz* (cited n. 18), at 43–44.

40. The Secret Monitoring Law [in Hebrew], 5739-1979, S.H. 938, 118.

41. Protection of Privacy Law [in Hebrew], 5741-1981, S.H. 1011, 128.

42. Jay Stanley & Barry Steinhardt, "Bigger Monster, Weaker Chains: The Growth of an American Surveillance Society" (American Civil Liberties Union) 3, http://www.aclu.org/privacy/privacy.cfm?id=11573&c=39 (accessed Apr. 28, 2004).

43. For the purpose of this section "information" does not apply to the *content* of a conversation within the meaning of the Secret Monitoring Law, in contrast to identifying details concerning the conversation.

44. Telecommunications Law [in Hebrew], 5742-1982, S.H. 1060, 218.

45. Sec. 9(a) of the Freedom of Information Law [in Hebrew], 1998, S.H. 1667, 226.

46. *Detroit Free Press et al. v. Ashcroft et al.*, 195 F. Supp 2d 937.

47. *Griswold v. Connecticut*, 381 U.S. 479, 482 (1965).

48. *Katz v. United States*, 389 U.S. 347 (1967); *Olmstead v. United States*, 277 U.S. 438, 464 (1928).

49. *Katz v. United States*, at 351.

50. Ibid., at 361.

51. *Dow Chemicals Co. v. United States*, 476 U.S. 227, 238 (1986).

52. *United States v. Knotts*, 460 U.S. 276, 285 (1983); *United States v. Karo*, 468 U.S. 705, 715 (1984).

53. *Kyllo v. United States*, 533 U.S. 27 (2001).

54. *Davis v. Mississippi*, 394 U.S. 721, 727 (1969).

55. *United States v. Dionisio*, 410 U.S. 1, 14 (1973).

56. *Skinner v. Ry. Labor Executives' Assoc.*, 489 U.S. 602 (1989).

57. *Terry v. Ohio*, 392 U.S. 1 (1968); *United States v. Bell*, 464 F.2d 667, 673 (2nd Cir. 1972).

58. *United States v. Davis*, 482 F.2d 893, 908 (9th Cir. 1973).

59. Ibid., at 910; *Camara v. Municipal Court*, 387 U.S. 523, 532, 536 (1967).

60. *United States v. 124,570$ United States Currency*, 873 F.2d 1240, 1242–43 (9th Cir. 1989).

61. *United States v. Davis*, at 910.

62. *Veronica School District 47J v. Acton*, 515 U.S. 646, 652–53 (1995).

63. *Camara v. Municipal Court*, at 534–35.

64. Title III of the Omnibus Crime Control and Safe Streets Act of 1968, 18 U.S.C. sec. 2510; Electronic Communications Privacy Act of 1986, Pub. L. No. 99-508, 100 Stat. 1848.

65. Title III, at sec. 2518.

66. Foreign Intelligence Surveillance Act of 1978, 50 U.S.C. s. 1801; 18 U.S.C. s. 3121.

67. Pub. L. No. 104-132, 110 Stat. sec. 1214 (1996).

68. Uniting and Strengthening America by Providing Appropriate Tools Required to Intercept and Obstruct Terrorism (USA PATRIOT) Act of 2001 (hereafter, Patriot Act), Pub. L. No. 107-56, 115 Stat. 272.

69. See the guidelines of the Department of Justice regarding implementation of the powers under the law. Available at http://www.epic.org/privacy/terrorism/DOJ_guidance.pdf (accessed Apr. 28, 2004).

70. Patriot Act, at 213 (amending 18 U.S.C. 3103a).

71. 50 U.S.C. 1862.

72. Patriot Act, at 215 (amending 50 U.S.C. 1816).

73. Ibid., at 216 (amending 18 U.S.C. 3121(c)).

74. Eric Lichtblau, "Senate Makes Permanent Nearly All Provisions of Patriot Act, with a Few Restrictions" *New York Times* (July 30, 2005) A11.

75. Human Rights Act, 1998, c. 42.

76. Data Protection Act, 1998, c. 29.

77. Regulation of Investigatory Powers Act, 2000, c. 23.

78. Police and Criminal Evidence Act, 1984, c. 60.

79. Terrorism Act, 2000, c. 11. The act came into force in February 2001.

80. Anti-terrorism, Crime and Security Act, 2001, c. 24.

81. Francis Fukuyama, "The End of History?" in *Conflict after the Cold War: Arguments on Causes of War and Peace* (R. K. Betts ed., Boston: Allyn and Bacon, 1994) 5–18.

82. Shmuel N. Eisenstadt, *Democracy and Its Meanderings: Paradoxes in the Modern Democracy* [in Hebrew] (Tel Aviv: Ministry of Defense Press, 2002) 109.

83. H.C. 320/80 *Kawasma v. Minister of Defense* [in Hebrew], 35(3) P.D. 113, 120.

84. Aharon Barak, "Democracy, Terror and the Courts," lecture delivered at the

international conference Democracy vs. Terror: Where Are the Limits (Haifa University, Dec. 16, 2002).

SEVEN Use of Civilians as Human Shields

1. Art. 3(1) common to the four Geneva Conventions of 1949 for the Protection of War Victims (Aug. 12, 1949), 75 U.N.T.S. 3.

2. Protocol Additional to the Geneva Conventions of 12 August 1949, and Relating to the Protection of Victims of International Armed Conflicts (Protocol I) (June 8, 1977), 1125 U.N.T.S. 3.

3. Lassa Oppenheim, *International Law* (H. Lauterpacht ed., 7th ed., 1952) 420.

4. Ibid. See also Art. 57(2)(c) to Protocol I, which adopts this approach.

5. Geneva Convention Relative to the Protection of Civilian Persons in Time of War (Geneva IV) (Aug. 12, 1949), 75 U.N.T.S. 287.

6. Immanuel Kant, "Groundwork of the Metaphysic of Morals" in *Ethical Philosophy* (J. Ellington trans., Indianapolis: Hackett, 1993) 20, 36.

7. Richard Mervyn Hare, *Moral Thinking: Its Levels, Method and Point* (Oxford: Clarendon Press, 1981) 26–27. Hare distinguishes between the intuitive level and the critical level in relation to moral dilemmas. The intuitive level characterizes those who believe that a clash between two moral obligations is insoluble, whereas on the critical level, the situation is regarded as one that can be resolved. According to this view, "If you have conflicting duties, one of them isn't your duty."

8. Immanuel Kant, *Fundamental Principles of the Metaphysics of Ethics* (M. Shefi trans., Jerusalem: Magnes, 1973) 108–9.

9. Daniel Statman, "The Question of Absolute Morality Regarding the Prohibition on Torture" [in Hebrew] 4 *Law & Gov't* 161, 168 (1997).

10. John Stuart Mill, *Utilitarianism* (2nd ed., Jerusalem: Magnes, 1972) 16.

11. Herbert L. A. Hart, *Laws and Morality* [in Hebrew] (Jerusalem, 1981) 25–37.

12. Michael Walzer, *Just and Unjust Wars* [in Hebrew] (Tel Aviv: Am Oved, 1984) 270.

13. Ibid., at 165.

14. George I. Mavrodes, "Conventions and the Morality of War" 4 *Philosophy & Public Affairs* 117 (1975).

15. Asa Kasher, *Military Ethics* [in Hebrew] (Tel Aviv: Ministry of Defense Press, 1996) 47.

16. Daniel Statman, "Jus in Bello and the Intifada," in *Philosophical Perspectives on the Israeli-Palestinian Conflict* (T. Kapitan ed., New York, 1997) 133, 144.

17. See part 2 of the report of Human Rights Watch "Off Target: The Conduct of the War and Civilian Casualties in Iraq," http://www.hrw.org/reports/2003/usa1203/4.htm#_Toc57442235 (accessed Apr. 25, 2004).

18. Jeffrie G. Murphy, "The Killing of the Innocent," in *War, Morality and the Military Profession* (M. M. Wakin ed., Boulder, CO: Westview Press, 1979) 344, 346–47, 353.

19. Elizabeth Anscombe, "War and Murder," in *War, Morality and the Military Profession*, 285, 288.

20. Walzer, *Just and Unjust Wars*, 186.

21. Meir Pail, "A Moral Regime within Warfare" [in Hebrew], in *Tohar Hanesheq* (Seminar Issues of Israel's Security, Yad Tebenkin, 1991) 9.

22. Gideon Levy, "The Cruel Neighbour Routine" [in Hebrew] *Ha'aretz* (Aug. 18, 2002).

23. H.C. 3799/02 *Adalla—The Legal Center for Arab Minority Rights in Israel et al. v. Commander of the Central Command et al.* (as yet unpublished), Brief for the Petitioners. Available at http://www.btselem.org.il/hebrew/Legal_Documents/HC3799_02_Petition.doc (accessed Oct. 4, 2004).

24. Operational Directive—Prior Warning. Available at http://www.btselem.org/english/Legal_Documents/Advanced_Warning_Procedure.doc (accessed Oct. 4, 2004). See also H.C. 3799/02, *Adalla*, Brief for Respondents. Available at http://www.btselem.org.il/hebrew/Legal_Documents/HC3799_02_State_Response_to_Motion_for_Contempt.doc (accessed Oct. 4, 2004).

25. Francisco de Vitoria, *De Jure Belli*, quoted in Ronit A. Peleg and Iirit M. Tamir, "The Red Cross and the Moral Questions Raised by War" 26 *International Problems: Society and State* 6, 8 (1987).

26. Richard A. Wasserstrom, "The Responsibility of the Individual for War Crimes," in *Philosophy, Morality and International Affairs* (New York: Oxford University Press, 1974) 47, 62.

27. Walzer, *Just and Unjust Wars*, 294.

28. John Rawls, "Fifty Years after Hiroshima," in *Collected Papers* (S. Freeman ed., Cambridge, MA: Harvard University Press, 1999) 569, 572.

29. Darrell Cole, "09.11.01: Death before Dishonor or Dishonor before Death? Christian Just War, Terrorism, and Supreme Emergency" 16 *Notre Dame J. L. Ethics & Pub Pol'y* 81, 91 (2002).

30. William David Ross, *The Right and the Good* (Oxford: Oxford University Press, 1930) 18.

31. Malham M. Wakin, *Integrity First: Reflections of a Military Philosopher* (Lanham, MD: Lexington Books, 2000) 24.

32. Murphy, "Killing of the Innocent," 357.

33. Walzer, *Just and Unjust Wars*, 183.

34. Ibid., 185–86.

35. Brian Orend, "Kant on International Law and Armed Conflict" 11 *Can. J. L. & Juris.* 329, 333 (1998).

36. Ibid., 361.

37. Kant, *Metaphysics of Ethics*, 20, 26–28.

38. Orend, "Kant on International Law," 372.

39. Thomas E. Hill Jr., "Making Exceptions without Abandoning the Principle: Or How a Kantian Might Think about Terrorism" in *Violence, Terrorism and Justice* (R. G. Frey & C. W. Morris eds., Cambridge: Cambridge University Press, 1991) 196, 220–24.

40. Kasher, *Military Ethics*, 215.

41. Art. 3(1) of the International Convention against the Taking of Hostages (Dec. 17, 1979) 18 *ILM* 1456.

42. Jonathan Glover, *Humanity—a Moral History of the Twentieth Century* (London: Pimlico, 2001) 113.

43. H.C. 320/80 *Kawasma v. Minister of Defense* [in Hebrew], 35(3) P.D. 113, 132.

EIGHT **Thwarting Terrorist Acts by Targeted Preventive Elimination**

1. *Ex parte Milligan*, 71 U.S. (4 Wall.) 2, 120–21 (1866).

2. See the report of the organization B'Ttselem—The Israeli Information Center for Human Rights in the Occupied Territories, "Activities of the Special Units in the Territories" (May 1992).

3. Molly Moore, "Israel's Lethal Weapon of Choice" *Washington Post* (June 29, 2003).

4. H.C. 5872/01 *MK Muhammed Barake v. Prime Minister of Israel* [in Hebrew], 56(3) P.D. 1.

5. H.C. 769/02 *Public Committee against Torture in Israel et al. v. Government of Israel et al.* [in Hebrew] (judgment not yet given).

6. G.A. Res. 3237, U.N. GAOR, 29th Sess., Supp. No. 31, at 4, U.N. Doc. A/9631 (1974).

7. Yoram Dinstein, *The Laws of War* [in Hebrew] (Tel Aviv: Shocken, 1983) 68–70.

8. Yoram Dinstein, *War, Aggression and Self-Defense* (3rd ed., Cambridge, 2001) 166.

9. United Nations General Assembly, Resolution 3314 (XXIX) Art. 2.

10. Regulation 23, Annexed to the Hague Convention Respecting the Laws and Customs of War on Land (Hague IV) (Oct. 18, 1907).

11. Art. 3(1) common to the four Geneva Conventions of 1949 for the Protection of War Victims (Aug. 12, 1949), 75 U.N.T.S. 3.

12. Hague Convention Respecting the Laws and Customs of War on Land (Hague II) (July 29, 1899); Geneva Convention Relative to the Treatment of Prisoners of War (Geneva III) (Aug. 12, 1949), 75 U.N.T.S. 135.

13. Penal Law, 5737-1977, S.H. 864, p. 226.

14. Cr.App. 319/71 *Ahmed et al. v. State of Israel* [in Hebrew], 26(1) P.D. 309, 316.

15. Michael N. Schmitt, "State-Sponsored Assassination in International and Domestic Law" *Yale J. Int'l L.* 609, 649 (1992).

16. Jules Lobel, "Colloquy: The Use of Force to Respond to Terrorist Attacks: The Bombing of Sudan and Afghanistan" 24 *Yale J. Int'l L.* 537, 547 (1999).

17. Alberto R. Coll, "The Legal and Moral Adequacy of Military Responses to Terrorism" 81 *Am. Soc'y Int'l L. Proc.* 287, 305 (1987).

18. Michael S. Moore, "Torture and the Balance of Evils" 23 *Israel L. Rev.* 280, 315 (1989).

19. Asa Kasher, "The Morality of Preemptive Warfare" [in Hebrew] *Ma'ariv* (Jan. 12, 2001).

20. For elaboration on the principle of double effect, see chap. 7.

21. H.C. 769/02 *Public Committee against Torture in Israel et al. v. Government of Israel et al.*, Brief for the Petitioners.

22. John Twomey & Cyril Dixon, "Police: We Will Shoot to Kill Again" *Express* (London) (July 25, 2005) 1.

23. Amos Harel, "The GSS Assessed: There Is a Low Likelihood of Injuring Civilians in the House in Which Shehade Is Hiding" [in Hebrew] *Ha'aretz* (July 24, 2002).

24. Executive Order 12333, 46 Fed Reg. 59,941, 59,947 (1981).

25. Jami Melissa Jackson, "The Legality of Assassination of Independent Ter-

rorist Leaders: An Examination of National and International Implications" 24 *N.C. J. Int'l L. & Com. Reg.* 669, 674 (1999).

26. Abraham D. Sofaer, "The Sixth Annual Waldemar A. Solf Lecture in International Law: Terrorism, the Law, and the National Defense" 126 *Military L. Rev.* 89, 117 (1989).

27. Schmitt, "State-Sponsored Assassination," 639–41, 645.

28. Paul Richter, "White House Justifies Option of Lethal Force" *Los Angeles Times* (Oct. 29, 1998) A1.

29. Jackson, "Legality of Assassination," 675–78.

30. Boyd M. Johnson III, "Executive Order 12,333: The Permissibility of an American Assassination of a Foreign Leader" 25 *Cornell Int'l L.J.* 401, 409–12 (1992).

31. Nathan Canestaro, "American Law and Policy on Assassinations of Foreign Leaders: The Practicality of Maintaining the Status Quo" 26 *B.C. Int'l & Comp. L. Rev.* 1, 2 (2003).

32. Pub. L. No. 107-40, 115 Stat. 224 (2001).

33. David Johnston & David E. Sanger, "Threats and Responses: Hunt for Suspects—Fatal Strike in Yemen Was Based on Rules Set Out by Bush" *New York Times* (Nov. 6, 2002).

34. See part 2 of the report of Human Rights Watch, "Off Target: The Conduct of the War and Civilian Casualties in Iraq," http://www.hrw.org/reports/2003/usa1203/4.htm#_Toc57442235 (accessed Apr. 25, 2004).

Conclusion

1. Address before a Joint Session of the Congress on the United States Response to the Terrorist Attacks of September 11, 37 *Weekly Comp. Pres.* DOC. 1347 (Sept. 20, 2001).

2. Amir Oren, "Until This Generation Ends" [in Hebrew] *Ha'aretz* (Sept. 9, 2004).

3. David Cole, "Symposium: Judging Judicial Review: Marbury in the Modern Era: Judging the Next Emergency: Judicial Review and Individual Rights in Times of Crisis" 101 *Mich. L. Rev.* 2565 (2003). See also Lee Epstein et al., "The Supreme Court during Crisis: How War Affects Only Non-War Cases" 80 *N.Y.U.L. Rev.* 1, 109 (2005), which suggests that judicial decisions made in wartime are more likely to curtail constitutional rights than those made in peacetime. However, the authors also conclude that, paradoxically, times of crisis appear to affect only cases that are unrelated to the ongoing conflict.

4. F.H.C. 2161/96 *Sharif v. C.O. Homefront Command* [in Hebrew], 50(4) P.D. 485, 491.

5. Aharon Barak, *The Judge in a Democracy* [in Hebrew] (Jerusalem: Nevo, 2004), 410.

6. Yoram Dinstein, *The Laws of War* [in Hebrew] (Tel Aviv: Shocken, 1983) 13.

7. See Bruce Ackerman, "The Emergency Constitution" 113 *Yale L.J.* 1029 (2004); and Ackerman, "This Is Not a War" 113 *Yale L.J.* 1871 (2004). For criticism of Ackerman's thesis, see David Cole, "The Priority of Morality: The Emergency Constitution's Blind Spot" 113 *Yale L.J.* 1753 (2004); Laurence H. Tribe & Patrick O. Gudridge, "The Anti-Emergency Constitution" 113 *Yale L.J.* 1801 (2004).

8. Francis Fukuyama, "The End of History?" in *Conflict after the Cold War: Argu-*

ments on Causes of War and Peace (R. K. Betts ed., Boston: Allyn and Bacon, 1994) 5–18.

9. Aharon Barak, "Democracy, Terror and the Courts," lecture delivered at the international conference Democracy vs. Terror: Where Are the Limits (Haifa University, Dec. 16, 2002).

10. Emanuel Gross, "Legal Aspects of Tackling Terrorism: The Balance between the Right of a Democracy to Defend Itself and the Protection of Human Rights" 6 *UCLA J. Int'l L. & For. Aff.* 89 (2001).

11. Comment of Aharon Barak, president of the Supreme Court of Israel, E.App. 2/84 *Neiman v. Chairman of Central Elections Committee of Eleventh Knesset* [in Hebrew], 39(2) P.D. 225, 315.

12. Oren Gross, "Chaos and Rules: Should Responses to Violent Crises Always Be Constitutional?" 112 *Yale L.J.* 1011 (2003); and at 1130–33. For an additional view whereby in order to avoid broad interpretations of the existing law in times of emergency and refrain from creating legal precedents that might infiltrate the legal system in times of peace, unusual emergencies may allow public officials to employ powers outside the boundaries of the law, if the use of these powers is essential in order to cope with the emergency, see Mark Tushnet "Defending Korematsu?: Reflections on Civil Liberties in Wartime" 2003 *Wis. L. Rev.* 273, 298–307.

13. David Pannick, "Human Rights in an Age of Terrorism" 36 *Israel. L. Rev.* 1 (2002).

Index